Issues in Science Teaching

Issues in Science Teaching covers a wide range of important issues which will interest teachers at all phases in the education system. How should science education progress? What are the needs of the next generation of prospective scientists? How can we develop and support a scientifically literate society?

The issues discussed include:

- the nature and purposes of science education in a multicultural society, including the idea of science for all
- the role and purposes of investigational work in science education
- assessment, curriculum progression and pupil attitudes to their science experience
- supporting basic skills development in literacy, numeracy and ICT, through science teaching
- supporting cross-curricular work through science teaching
- taking account of individual differences, including ability, special needs, learning style and the case for inclusion.

The chapters are strongly based on current research and are intended to stimulate and broaden debate among student teachers, newly qualified teachers, science co-ordinators, classroom teachers, aspiring or practising heads of science and teacher educators. Written by practising science educators and teachers, this book offers new and interesting ways of developing science education at all levels.

John Sears is Head of Secondary ITE at University College Worcester. **Pete Sorensen** is Senior Lecturer in Science Education at Canterbury Christ Church University College.

Issues in Subject Teaching series
Edited by Susan Capel, Jon Davison,
James Arthur and John Moss

Issues in Science Teaching

Edited by
John Sears and Pete Sorensen

London and New York

First published 2000
by RoutledgeFalmer
2 Park Square, Milton Park, Abingdon OX14 4RN

Simultaneously published in the USA and Canada
by RoutledgeFalmer
270 Madison Avenue, New York, NY 10016

RoutledgeFalmer is an imprint of the Taylor & Francis Group

Transferred to Digital Printing 2005

Typeset in Goudy by Taylor & Francis Books Ltd
Printed and bound in Great Britain by Antony Rowe Ltd, Chippenham, Wiltshire

British Library Cataloguing in Publication Data
A catalogue record for this book is available from the British Library

Library of Congress Cataloging-in-Publication Data
Issues in science teaching / edited by John Sears and Pete Sorensen.
p. cm.
Includes bibliographical references and index.
1. Science–Study and teaching. I. Sears, John, 1949– II. Sorensen, Pete,
1958–
Q181 .I77 2000
507'.1–dc21   00–059205

ISBN 0–415–23484–0 (hbk)
ISBN 0–415–23485–9 (pbk)

Contents

Illustrations

Contributors

Vanessa Barker is Lecturer in Science Education in the Science and Technology Group at the Institute of Education, University of London. Her research interests include exploring how teachers teach difficult ideas in science, developing post-16 science, particularly chemistry and the influence of the mentor in training science teachers. Prior to joining the Institute she taught in four different schools and colleges in London and Hull, including posts as Head of Chemistry in a boys' grammar school and Science Co-ordinator in a former sixth form college. She has also worked as a senior examiner for EdExcel A level chemistry for many years and contributes lectures to revision conferences.

Pat Bricheno worked as an analytical chemist for six years and taught chemistry in secondary schools for fifteen years, before moving to the University of Greenwich in 1995 where she is currently studying changing attitudes to science education. She continues to teach chemistry in FE, and also works as a research assistant at the University of Hertfordshire focusing on Gender and Primary Teaching.

Jasmin Chapman is a product of a Plymouth secondary modern, and led the science PGCE course at Marjon's, Plymouth, for four years and has five years full-time and three years part-time teaching experience acquired in challenging comprehensive schools. She most recently shared a Second in Science post with Paul Hamer, with whom she co-founded The Learners' Co-operative Ltd. They are currently concentrating on the expansion of the company between teaching posts. Jasmin is also currently providing individual tuition for excluded 9–16 year-olds through a foster care association. She has two grown-up children at university.

Sandra Duggan is a research fellow at Durham University with considerable experience in research in various fields. She has co-authored a book on investigative work in science, written teaching materials and has published widely in science education and in medical research. Sandra has been involved in research in primary and secondary schools and has recently completed an intervention study in Intermediate GNVQ Science in FE colleges. Currently, she is exploring the relationship between the role of evidence in science education and its role in applied science in industry and in the public understanding of science.

Anne Goldsworthy taught for thirteen years in a variety of primary schools where she especially enjoyed teaching science, before going into advisory work. She is now an independent consultant for primary science providing INSET to schools throughout the UK and abroad. She is chair of the Primary Science Committee of the Association for Science Education and was a senior researcher for the AKSIS (ASE–King's College Science Investigations in Schools) Project. She also works with many other organisations, such as the QCA and BBC and has written many articles and books including 'Making Sense of Primary Science'.

Richard Gott was a secondary science teacher and is now professor of science education in Durham University. His interests lie in investigative work in science and, in particular, in the development of an understanding of scientific evidence. He has published extensively and is the author of a number of innovative school texts such as Active Science and more recently Science Investigations. Richard leads a team of researchers. His current research includes a project developing and trialling a multimedia CD-ROM to support teaching about evidence in investigative work and a case study of the public understanding of scientific evidence in a local controversial issue.

Paul Hamer has ten years' full-time and six years' part-time teaching experience acquired in a variety of English secondary schools. He most recently shared the post of Second in Science at Torquay Community College with Jasmin Chapman. Paul and Jasmin are the co-founders of The Learners' Co-operative Ltd. They are currently concentrating on the expansion of the company between teaching posts. The purpose of the limited company is further developing and disseminating teaching strategies such as the application of multiple intelligences and cognitive mapping techniques, designed to bridge the gap between learning theory and classroom practice.

Pauline Hoyle is currently an assistant director of education for the London Borough of Newham, responsible for curriculum support and professional development within the LEA. She was previously a science inspector and adviser in two LEAs and has national and international experience of planning, delivering and evaluating in-service training. She has researched and written extensively about language development through and in the science curriculum, and teaching bilingual learners in science, and the development of equal opportunities in the science curriculum.

Ruth Jarman is a Lecturer in Education in the Graduate School of Education at the Queen's University Belfast. She co-ordinates the science course on the PGCE programme and is also involved in Masters courses within the Continuing Professional Development programme. Her research interests include the school science curriculum and out-of-school learning in science. Primary–secondary curricular continuity is a particular concern. She has recently completed a survey, funded by the Department of Education, Northern Ireland, of Science at Key Stage 4. Current projects include investigating the use of newspapers in the science classroom and opportunities for science learning in youth organisations.

Jane Johnston is a Senior Lecturer in Education at Bishop Grosseteste College in Lincoln, where she is involved in initial teacher and in-service education. She taught in primary schools, in the Midlands, with children up to the age of eleven before working in Higher Education, firstly in primary science education at the Nottingham Trent University and then at Bishop Grosseteste College. She has particular expertise in early years and science education. Her research interests are in the areas of early years science, curricular change and the development of attitudes. These interests are brought together in many of her publications.

Graham Lenton has taught science in a variety of schools throughout Britain and science education in several universities in this country and overseas. He was a tutor at Oxford University Department of Educational Studies for five years and until recently he was responsible for the secondary science PGCE course at Oxford Brookes University where he was a Senior Lecturer. His research interests are concerned with conceptual understanding and numeracy in science, and the development of the science curriculum in developing countries.

Patricia Murphy is Reader in Education at the School of Education the Open University. She has been involved in science and technology education and gender issues since the late 1970s. She has researched and published widely on gender and assessment, and learning and teaching generally and specifically in the areas of science and technology. She is currently researching into effective practice in primary science for the Nuffield Curriculum Centre and evaluating the Young Foresight initiative.

Pat O'Brien is an independent educational consultant who concentrates upon developing support materials for schools and leading training days both nationally and in schools. He was Science Inspector Adviser for Berkshire and is an OFSTED inspector in primary, secondary and special education. He has carried out extensive work in Educational Management, Target-Setting, the use of data to inform good lesson design and curriculum development particularly with reference to differentiation, language and numeracy and the use of ICT to support science. While in Berkshire he headed a two-year research project into the scientifically able pupil. He has contributed a number of articles to journals and science issues books and a co-editor for the Key Stage 3 Science Course *Challenge Science* and Nelson Thornes' *Science Web*. Prior to becoming an inspector he was an advisory teacher in Kent, a head of department, an examiner and moderator for GCSE and taught in a range of schools for fifteen years.

Sheila Peterson has developed a strong commitment to inclusive education through her work with students and their educational needs. Sheila has worked in both special schools and mainstream settings, graduating from separate provision to a unit within a mainstream school. She is currently working with students awaiting the implementation of an inclusion project in a secondary school in Kent.

Phil Poole is currently a Principal Lecturer at Canterbury Christ Church University College where he manages a learning resources unit called TITLE (Technology in Teaching and Learning). The Unit works with staff and departments across the institution to develop their use of ICT in teaching and learning activities. Over the last twenty years Philip has worked in science, design and technology and, more recently, ICT. As a Head of Science he contributed to the Nuffield Co-ordinated Science scheme. As a Lecturer at Christ Church he has produced a number of pupils' and teachers' publications related to the use of ICT. As part of a secondment to NCET he undertook an evaluation programme which led to the publication of *Managing IT: A Guide for Senior Managers*. Philip is currently working on web-based resources to support ICT capability for training and practising teachers. His two latest publications attempt to provide an overview of the new standards for ICT in subject teaching.

Michael Reiss is Reader in Education and Bioethics at Homerton College, Cambridge, a Priest in the Church of England and an accredited psychodynamic counsellor. From January 2001 he will be the Professor of Science Education at the Institute of Education, University of London. After a Ph.D. and Post-Doc. in evolutionary biology and animal behaviour, he trained as a school teacher and taught in schools before returning to higher education in 1988. He is the author of a number of books, the latest of which is *Understanding Science Lessons: Five Years of Science Teaching* (Open University Press, 2000) and edits the Cambridge University Press Advanced Biology Series. He is the inaugural editor of the journal *Sex Education*, chairs EuropaBio's External Advisory Group on Ethics and sits on the UK Advisory Committee on Novel Foods and Processes. For further information see www.reiss.tc.

Judith Roden is a Principal Lecturer in the Department of Childhood Studies and Primary Education at Canterbury Christ Church University College. She has spent more than twenty-five years involved in science education and has extensive successful experience of teaching in schools at various levels and within ITT and CPD. In addition to her role as team leader for primary science within the university, she is currently particularly interested in supporting school-based curriculum development projects and in promoting an investigative approach to science in the primary classroom.

John Sears has recently become Head of Secondary ITE at University College Worcester. He taught science for nineteen years in mixed comprehensives before moving into higher education at Nottingham University and Christ Church College, Canterbury. He is a textbook author and is interested in curriculum development and children's attitudes to science.

Pete Sorensen is a Senior Lecturer in Science Education at Canterbury Christ Church University College. Prior to this he taught in schools in Oxfordshire and Ghana for eighteen years, with periods as a lecturer in Science Education at the University of Cape Coast and as Secretary of the Oxfordshire Teaching Associations. He is currently researching Initial Teacher education.

Bert Sorsby has published articles on children's learning in science and is currently programme director for primary teacher training and education at the University of Hull. He has lectured in science, science education and history of science at various universities in the UK, as well as working in the national museum as education officer for science. He is a member of the British Society for the History of Science and is currently working with international partners to produce in-service courses in history of science and technology for teachers across Europe. Other current research interests include argumentation studies in relation to science.

Brenda Stevens taught mathematics in Oxfordshire before she joined the advisory service in the county. She is now a Principal Lecturer at Oxford Brookes University and teaches mathematics education on undergraduate and post-graduate courses. Her research interests are mental imagery in mathematics, numeracy across the curriculum and special needs in mathematics.

Caroline Stone is Science Adviser for the London Borough of Newham. Prior to taking up this post she was a Head of Science in the London Borough of Islington, having previously been a head of biology in the London Borough of Redbridge.

Laura Sukhnandan was a Senior Research Officer at the National Foundation for Educational Research when she completed her chapter for this book. The chapter is based on a literature review, 'Streaming, Setting and Grouping by Ability', which was funded by the Local Government Association and undertaken at the NFER. Laura is currently working as a Senior Research Officer within the Equal Opportunities Division of the DfEE.

The late **Sheila Turner** was Reader in Education and Head of Science and Technology Group at the Institute of Education, University of London. Sheila died on November 4th, 2000 after a long battle against cancer. Earlier this year she received the Institute of Biology Charter Award 2000 for outstanding contributions to Biology and Biology Education. Her research interests were in biological education, nutrition and health education, in particular about diet and health; and multicultural and antiracist issues in science education. An obituary appeared on the Institute of Education, University of London Press Office website at http://www.ioe.ac.uk/media/r001115.htm.

Tony Turner is Senior Lecturer in Education at the Institute of Education, University of London, attached to the Science and Technology Group. His teaching interests are chemistry and science at secondary level. He has taught in UK schools and been involved in curriculum development in the West Indies and the UK. He was involved in new initiatives in teacher education and in setting up the Institute's school partnership arrangements for PGCE secondary courses. Research interests currently include inquiry into issues of equity in the selection and recruitment of graduates into science teaching. He is co-author of *Learning to Teach in the Secondary School*. Other publications include co-author-ship of *Learning to Teach Science in the Secondary School* and *Starting to Teach in the Secondary School, a Companion for the NQT*. He is co-editor of the Learning to Teach in the Secondary School series.

Rod Watson is a Senior Lecturer in the School of Education, King's College London. He worked for thirteen years as a school teacher and used investigative approaches in his own teaching. He has directed three major research and curriculum development projects: 'The Open-ended Work in Science (OPENS) Project', the 'National Environmental Database (NED) Project' and the 'ASE-King's Science Investigations in Schools Project'. He has also led a programme of research exploring understandings of chemical concepts from infant school up to university level. He is an experienced teacher educator working both in the UK and internationally.

Judy Williams is a committed teacher with twenty-three years experience and an addiction for Special Educational Needs. She has worked in the mainstream primary and secondary sector in England and in Africa. Her more recent experi-ence of working in a special school for pupils with severe physical disabilities lead rapidly to the creation of her current post supporting mainstream schools in their move to include all children. Within her role as a science adviser, she identifies the training needs of staff in primary and secondary schools and devises and delivers appropriate training opportunities, including the develop-ment of literacy in science. She also supports science departments in their development of the curriculum, teaching and learning styles and resource management.

Valerie Wood-Robinson has been Head of Biology in two schools and Head of Science in another. She has interspersed her teaching with work on curricu-lum development projects, including the Leeds National Curriculum Science Project based at CLIS and has written or co-authored several textbooks. She has recently retired from the post of Science Adviser for Sunderland, but continues with occasional advisory and Ofsted inspections. Valerie was a senior researcher for the AKSIS (ASE–King's College Science Investigations in Schools) Project. She has been an active member of ASE for over thirty years, serving on local and regional committees.

Introduction to the series

This book, *Issues in Science Teaching*, is one of a series of books entitled *Issues in Subject Teaching*. The series has been designed to engage with a wide range of issues related to subject teaching. Types of issues vary among subjects, but may include, for example: issues that impact on Initial Teacher Education in the subject; issues addressed in the classroom through the teaching of the subject; issues to do with the content of the subject and its definition; issues to do with subject pedagogy; issues to do with the relationship between the subject and broader educational aims and objectives in society, and the philosophy and sociology of education; and issues to do with the development of the subject and its future in the twenty-first century.

Each book consequently presents key debates that subject teachers will need to understand, reflect on and engage in as part of their professional development. Chapters have been designed to highlight major questions, to consider the evidence from research and practice and to arrive at possible answers. Some subject books or chapters offer at least one solution or a view of the ways forward, whereas others provide alternative views and leave readers to identify their own solution or view of the ways forward. The editors expect readers of the series to want to pursue the issues raised, and so chapters include suggestions for further reading, and questions for further debate. The chapters and questions could be used as stimuli for debate in subject seminars or department meetings, or as topics for assignments or classroom research. The books are targeted at all those with a professional interest in the subject, and in particular: student teachers learning to teach the subject in the primary or secondary school; newly qualified teachers; teachers with a subject co-ordination or leadership role, and those preparing for such responsibility; mentors, tutors, trainers and advisers of the groups mentioned above.

Each book in the series has a cross-phase dimension. This is because the editors believe it is important for teachers in the primary and secondary phases to look at subject teaching holistically, particularly in order to provide for continuity and progression, but also to increase their understanding of how children learn. The balance of chapters that have a cross-phase relevance, chapters that focus on issues which are of particular concern to primary teachers and chapters that focus on issues which secondary teachers are more likely to need to address, varies according to the issues relevant to different subjects. However, no matter where the emphasis is, authors have drawn out the relevance of their topic to the whole of each book's intended audience.

Because of the range of the series, both in terms of the issues covered and its cross-phase concern, each book is an edited collection. Editors have commissioned new writing from experts on particular issues who, collectively, will represent many different perspectives on subject teaching. Readers should not expect a book in this series to cover a full range of issues relevant to the subject, or to offer a completely unified view of subject teaching, or that every issue will be dealt with discretely, or that all aspects of an issue will be covered. Part of what each book in this series offers to readers is the opportunity to explore the inter-relationships between positions in debates and, indeed, among the debates themselves, by identifying the overlapping concerns and competing arguments that are woven through the text.

The editors are aware that many initiatives in subject teaching currently originate from the centre, and that teachers have decreasing control of subject content, pedagogy and assessment strategies. The editors strongly believe that for teaching to remain properly a vocation and a profession, teachers must be invited to be part of a creative and critical dialogue about subject teaching, and encouraged to reflect, criticise, problem-solve and innovate. This series is intended to provide teachers with a stimulus for democratic involvement in the development of subject teaching.

Susan Capel
Jon Davison
James Arthur
John Moss
May 1999

Introduction

John Sears and Pete Sorensen

The aim of this book is to explore some of the key issues in science education in the new century. The book has been written to examine current concerns and debates at primary and secondary level in school science teaching. It will support practising teachers of science, student teachers and teacher educators, by providing, an introduction to values, attitudes and beliefs in science education, and the outcomes of research, in relation to matters of pedagogy. Authors have written in areas of their interest and expertise in order to inform and challenge the audience. They have summarised key arguments and indicated the evidence that is available to support different views. In some cases different authors have taken contrasting positions in relation to the same issue, whilst in others authors have written from complementary standpoints. We hope that these approaches will encourage an evidence-based debate by teachers in schools and colleges, and promote teacher-led action research.

Each chapter has addressed key questions, which are indicated in their introduction. Following the arguments presented in the main body of the text, most chapters have a series of questions aimed at stimulating discussion and further enquiry. Further readings are supplied to support such endeavours. In addition, there is a detailed bibliography at the end of the book.

Many of the issues are interlinked, and there is no simple way to sequence chapters to take account of all possible connections. The book is not designed to be read in order, but we have made an attempt to place related chapters together. Similarly, in a book of this nature, it is not possible to cover all the issues which are engaging teachers' attention, nor can any one issue be covered in great depth. Instead, we have tried to produce a book which will allow readers access to the debates and give them starting points for detailed study should they so wish.

The text starts with an overview by Tony Turner of the National Curriculum, which raises key issues in relation to content, purpose and development. These are issues which are picked up and explored further in later chapters. We then move onto the question of the nature of science and science education, with complementary approaches taken by Michael Reiss and Bert Sorsby in Chapters 2 and 3. The former examines science from a cultural perspective and looks at the need to develop curricula and pedagogies which cater for diversity. The latter looks at the development of the nature of science and its importance in producing scientifically literate citizens.

Chapters 4, 5 and 6 deal with pupils' entitlement to science as a component of their lifelong learning and rehearses the arguments by focusing on different key stages. Judith Roden argues forcefully for the parity of science and other core subjects at primary level, while John Sears reviews the case for balanced science especially in compulsory secondary schooling. Vanessa Barker explores the notion of what lifelong learning in science could actually mean and the implications of this for the new post-16 courses.

The importance of investigative work is then analysed from two contrasting perspectives in Chapters 7 and 8. Sandra Duggan and Richard Gott look at the need to develop a more relevant, investigative approach, with a greater emphasis on understanding the ideas that underpin scientific evidence. Rod Watson, Anne Goldsworthy and Valerie Wood-Robinson report on the work of the ASE and Kings College Science Investigations in Schools (AKSIS) project and argue for an extension of the range of investigations used in science teaching.

Chapters 9, 10 and 11 look at curriculum areas which can be developed through science teaching. Graham Lenton and Brenda Stevens examine key areas of numeracy in science and the importance of developing clear practices to support pupils. Pauline Hoyle and Caroline Stone present the case that you cannot be a good scientist without good literacy skills and review the ways in which pupils' literacy can be enhanced through science teaching. Finally, in this section, Sheila Turner makes the case for the importance of health education and the contribution that science teachers can make in this area.

No book on issues in science teaching would be complete without tackling the thorny issue of assessment. Pat O'Brien, in Chapter 12, takes a positive and upbeat approach to the use of 'hard data' for target setting in order to improve standards. In Chapter 13, in contrast, Pete Sorensen argues for the neglected role of formative assessment as being more effective in improving learning.

Chapters 14 and 15 are concerned with issues which, although discussed through specific contexts, raise questions of general importance. Ruth Jarman looks at continuity between KS2 and 3, but the debate she raises is fundamental to the notions of progression and continuity at any age. Pat Bricheno, Jane Johnston and John Sears explore pupils' attitudes to their science education and the world of science in general. The evidence presented raises questions of pedagogy and social class, and relates back to transitions and gender.

The final chapters of the book are centred around the notion of 'difference'. In Chapter 16, Jasmin Chapman, Paul Hamer and John Sears set the scene with the thesis that learning style is more important than ability in devising teaching approaches to take account of differences. Patricia Murphy extends the challenge with a detailed account of how gender differences affect pupil attitudes and learning, and teacher expectation. Laura Sukhnandan, in Chapter 18, summarises the evidence relating to grouping methods as an approach to differentiation. Her conclusion challenges much current thinking from politicians and educators. Following these broad considerations, Pat O'Brien examines how to develop a curriculum to allow individual challenge for more able pupils. This continues the debate on what is meant by ability and how teachers should respond. In Chapter 20, Sheila Peterson, Judy Williams and Pete Sorensen extend the issue of differentiation by arguing for the inclusion of all pupils in mainstream schools irrespective of their disabilities. The book finishes with a chapter where Phil Poole shows the potential for the use of ICT in supporting teachers and developing pupils' learning. He shows how this exciting and rapidly changing area offers potential to both change and enhance the nature of the learning experience.

This book should be seen as a resource and stimulus to further work, rather than a completed project with all the answers. We found reading and editing the chapters extremely interesting and we hope that you, the reader, will equally enjoy using the book. Our thanks go to all the authors who have worked so hard to contribute challenging and stimulating material.

1 The science curriculum

What is it for?

Tony Turner

Introduction

The introduction to the National Curriculum (DES 1988a) and subsequent Acts has caused significant changes in teaching and learning and in the management of schools. These changes include a compulsory core curriculum for pupils aged 5–16, comprising English, mathematics and science. All schools have had to improve their performance; in secondary school this is measured by the number of pupils achieving five A–C grades in the GCSE and, at the end of Key Stage 3, the number achieving Level 5 in the Standard Assessment Tasks. Other judgements are also made, but it is to the academic standards that OFSTED and parents pay prime attention.

One consequence of the focus on academic performance has been the narrowing effect on teaching through pressure to teach to examinations (Millar and Osborne 1998). The publication of league tables based on public examination results, combined with OFSTED Inspection Reports, has led to improved performance in public examinations but accompanied by a growing competitive ethos between schools. Following publication of league tables, there has emerged a policy of threatening underperforming schools with closure. Unsurprisingly, some teachers are angered by this policy, and a few politicians are dismayed (Carvel 1999). Nevertheless, many underperforming schools have been 'turned round' by their staff after a poor OFSTED Report.

Science and the school curriculum

The present school curriculum is similar to the grammar school curriculum of the post-Second World War period, possibly the very curriculum which present-day legislators themselves successfully experienced as pupils. Both curricula are based around academic subjects, designed for an able minority. Although the content of many subjects has changed, teaching methods developed a little in response to new understandings about ways pupils learn and new technologies become available to support teachers and pupils, the main thrust of teaching remains the introduction of pupils to the knowledge and concepts of academic subjects.

As one historian of education has noted, the 1988 National Curriculum bears a remarkable resemblance to that established in 1904 (Aldrich 1988). Both curricula are subject based with many subject names identical; one difference is that music is now part of the curriculum. Differences in the presentation of subjects have, of course, appeared as well as changes in content. A less sexist approach to the education of boys and girls prevails today. The subject model of the school curriculum that has dominated much of the twentieth century has continued into the twenty-first century despite the absence of an adequate rationale for the choice of this curriculum model (O'Hear and White 1991; QCA 1999a). This situation is not unexpected given the continuing commitment of government ministers and their advisers to traditional subjects and traditional ways of teaching. The academic bias of the school curriculum has been cited by the OECD as a contributing factor to the UK's poor record in providing an appropriately educated workforce (Atkinson and Elliott 2000)

It is not surprising, then, that the present secondary school science curriculum is similar to the former GCE O-level syllabuses for biology, chemistry and physics. The science curriculum focuses on its constituent subjects as academic disciplines and is less concerned with the application of science, the relation of science to technology or how science and society interact. The 1995 science curriculum was a course in fundamental science knowledge, largely neglecting, for example, the issues, challenges and excitement of contemporary science or the way scientists work and validate their findings.

In the 1999 version of the science curriculum, *Science 2000* (DfEE 1999c), important changes have been made, broadening the role of scientific investigations and introducing aspects of the nature of science and the ways in which scientists work. These changes have been incorporated into Science Inquiry (the new Sc1). This, the fourth version of the Science Curriculum since 1988, essentially retains the structure of the 1995 version (DfE 1995a), which comprised a Programme of Study (PoS) for each Key Stage, itself made up of four strands and preceded by an introductory statement.

In the 1995 curriculum, the introductory statement identified five overarching themes for the PoS. The same five headings were employed for each Key Stage, although the content of each statement changed and developed in depth through KS1 to KS4. These introductory statements became known unofficially as 'Sc0'. In *Science 2000*, some of these themes have been transferred to Scientific Inquiry, while others have been moved out of the main PoS; for example, Health and Safety and Communication, both of which now appear towards the end of the document as additional skills and knowledge to be incorporated through Sc1–Sc4. In summary, the former 'Sc0' has gone from all Key Stages and replaced by a brief statement at the beginning of each Key Stage. In addition, the science curriculum as a whole is introduced by a statement explaining the importance of science to the education of young people. This statement may be read as a justification for the place of science in the school curriculum. This justification includes:

- satisfying pupils' curiosity about the world;
- stimulating pupils' curiosity and providing outlets for it;
- developing creative thinking;

- understanding how scientific ideas and knowledge contribute to changes in society and improvement in the quality of life;
- the cultural significance of science now, in the past, and in the future.

Such aspirations are difficult to fault. However, at first reading of the science curriculum document, both the choice of content and its arrangement (of three subject areas together with an investigative dimension) are not justified by the writers in terms of those aspirations. The structure and content appears as self-evidently appropriate to achieve the aims.

There are further concerns when the assessment dimension of the science curriculum is considered. The Attainment Targets, containing Level Statements, relate to the four strands of the PoS and are designed to describe the performance of pupils and hence identify and monitor progression. The Level Statements for Scientific Inquiry now include aspects of the history of science and the nature of scientific evidence. However there is scant reference to either of these topics in the Attainment Targets for Sc2–Sc4, the biology, chemistry and physics content; the link between inquiry and content is weak. This weakness will encourage teachers to continue to focus on inquiry as a unique element of assessment, separate from and discontinuous with the content. The assessment of the science curriculum remains focused on a body of subject knowledge encapsulated by Sc2–Sc4 of the PoS at Key Stages 3 and 4. This body of knowledge is, furthermore, largely devoid of the important aspirational statements used to justify the science curriculum noted earlier.

The revised science curriculum claims to place greater emphasis on contemporary science and the application of science (QCA 1999d: 5). However, the Attainment Targets scarcely refer to these ideas. The Level Statements are used to judge pupil performance from the evidence of pupils' work; teachers are not, therefore, encouraged to include contemporary science or its applications in their teaching. It appears that the new science curriculum is no better placed than its forbears to encourage and enthuse pupils and teachers. The science curriculum appears to ignore its asserted purposes, but maybe that is not surprising when the aims are listed as non-statutory.

In a study of science teachers' (n=320) choice of activities in their teaching of the National Curriculum, by far the most frequently reported activity was 'practical work in groups' closely followed by 'scientific investigations for assessment' (Donnelly and Jenkins 1999). The authors conclude that 'the priorities identified by teachers in this study are those which have characterized secondary school science teaching in England and Wales throughout much of the twentieth century' (Donnelly and Jenkins 1999: 6). This finding suggests that the focus of practical work in science is identified mainly with assessment, which narrows the range of strategies and activities to which pupils are exposed.

In view of the changes in society over, say, the last fifty years, in the growth of our understanding of the natural world, our ability to manipulate the living and non-living world, the extraordinary developments in communications technology and in access to information, the stability of the science curriculum is remarkable. It is hard to see how *Science 2000* can be any more attractive to pupils now than its predecessors, one effect of which was to turn pupils away from studying science post-16. An added factor is the pressure placed on pupils (and teachers) to perform well in public tests, which has led to more intensive 'teaching for the test' than before. Responding mainly to pressures of examinations is not a good way to develop interest and excitement in any subject, much less promote understanding. The 1995 NC science and *Science 2000* implicitly support the continuation of traditional methods of teaching science despite the rhetoric of ministers that teachers and teaching methods must change. If, for example, ICT is really to have an effect on teaching and learning, this is possible only if the curriculum changes. The emphasis on recall of a narrow range of facts needs to be replaced by a teaching and assessment framework which allows teachers to use a wider range of strategies and skills. In this way, pupils may develop enthusiasm for, and improved understanding of, science.

What do teachers think of NC science?

OFSTED inspections focus on the performance of science teachers. An OFSTED inspection is a one-way exercise and does not report the views of teachers about the curriculum, their resources or their perceived conditions of work.

In a recent study of secondary schools (n=500) the views of teachers of history and science were sought concerning changes in their practice since the introduction of the National Curriculum (Donnelly and Jenkins 1999). Some views of the science teachers are reported here. Science teachers recognised some positive features arising from the introduction of the NC but far more negative factors were cited. One finding was the wide range of experience and views expressed by teachers, which may reflect the particular circumstances of each school, its pupils and staff.

Among the positive features of the effects of the NC has been the improved coherence of the science curriculum. Other positive effects included increased collaboration between science staff and more demands placed on technical staff. The authors suggest that the NC has led teachers to clarify better their lesson objectives, spend more time planning lessons and using Schemes of Work. Teachers now pay closer attention to record keeping and monitoring of pupil progress, with better feedback to pupils suggesting improved accountability. These are all features of progress but, as the authors point out, by themselves these factors do not constitute progress unless learning is enhanced.

Science teachers (n=358) were asked to rate the importance of aims in teaching science in secondary school, selecting from a list (generated from interviews with science teachers) using a four-point scale ranging from irrelevant to very important. The aims listed in order of importance were:

- the teaching of skills and processes
- pupils' enjoyment of science
- establishing good relationships with pupils
- success in examinations

- 'teaching science content'
- 'making science relevant'

All six items were rated between important and very important.

When a smaller sample of science teachers were interviewed and invited to identify their own aims, as distinct from selecting from a list, a different order of priority appeared (see Table 1.1).

The data show that teachers hold a wide range of opinion about the aims of science teaching. More importantly, the differences in priority suggested by the two sets of data might also point to differences in what science teachers believe to be important in the teaching of science as opposed to what is important in their daily work under the NC. They may also be influenced by what they think is expected of them when selecting items from lists.

If we extrapolate from the small sample to include most science teachers, then clearly the effect of the NC on teaching science is to focus on the content and process of science in order to pass examinations with less importance attached to the social setting of the classroom. Enjoyment of science lessons and establishing good relationships is a low priority among the sample of teachers interviewed (less than 20 per cent of teachers expressed these aims (see Table 1.1)). It is of interest that when teachers were asked to select aims from a list, the importance of social factors was given a high priority as well as that of passing examinations, suggesting that to these teachers the former are a necessary prerequisite to the latter.

In the same study, teachers (n=358) were asked to rank factors in lesson planning which were important to them, again selecting from a list. Top of the list was mental planning, closely followed by a requisition list to technicians, resources and a SoW. All four items were rated as important to very important. A written plan was identified as important by far fewer teachers. The choice of requisition list underscores the emphasis placed by teachers on practical activities as the means of teaching science. It is not surprising, then, that when teachers were invited to rate the frequency with which they used particular strategies in the laboratory, practical work, Sc1 investigations and the provision of pupil worksheets were rated as important to very important. We return later to the role of practical work in science teaching. However, it is interesting to note that, in this study, 'using Sc1 investigations

Table 1.1   Teachers' aims for science (n=31)

Aim	Percentage of teachers expressing this aim
Teaching scientific content	52
Making science relevant	52
Success in examinations	39
Teaching scientific processes	35
Promoting enjoyment and interest	17
Establishing good relationships	13

Source: Donnelly and Jenkins (1999): 4

to teach skills and processes' was ranked equally with 'copying from the board'. The use of ICT was rated between not very important and irrelevant; information technology was used about as frequently as taking pupils on industrial visits.

One of the crucial findings of this research relates to the attitudes science teachers now adopt in relation to their role in teaching science. Science teachers reported their loss of fun in teaching science and reduced enjoyment by pupils. Whereas the criterion of enjoyment may not be a national priority it is of concern that science teachers in this study report an inability to respond to individual pupils, especially those with special needs. The reported loss in teachers' capacity to pursue science of interest to the pupils – for example in their locality – is also worrying. The statements used by these teachers to describe their feelings about teaching the National Curriculum are revealing. For example:

- pupils jumping though hoops
- teach much more academic science (now) to the lower ability groups
- much less time to teach the relevance of science in their (the pupils) everyday lives
- I am totally de-motivated by the constant reference to target setting, monitoring and evaluation.

(Donnelly and Jenkins 1999: 10–14)

An evaluation of the Key Stage 3 Tests in English, mathematics and science has drawn attention to the constraints placed on teaching and learning by these tests. The report raises doubts about the reliability and validity of the tests and their fairness towards pupils with language limitations (ATL 1999).

The picture painted of teaching science under the National Curriculum, together with the associated assessment demand and the use made of it by government, is of a curriculum made narrow by the pressures to succeed, and a teaching force which sees itself as being deskilled by the constraints placed upon it and less able to respond to pupil needs and interests.

Science content and teaching strategies

At the same time as the revised National Curriculum for Science was published, a leaflet was published describing a programme called 'New Frontiers of Science' (Royal Society 1999b), designed to attract young people to science. The programme included:

- trying your hand at surgery using a computer designed to test the skill of surgeons;
- discovering and testing your own botanical knowledge with a revolutionary way of studying plants;
- discovering how the Halley polar site monitors 'space weather' in its extreme and remote environment;
- studying the bones of people who lived centuries ago revealing new insights into diseases that are still common today.

There were seventeen other topics as well. Contrast this programme with some of the science content of the school curriculum under National Curriculum guidelines. Pupils may wonder about the connection between school science and the exciting, contemporary science described above, as well as that seen in many national television programmes. How to connect 'frontier science' with science teaching has been a dilemma for some time (Follett 1997: 15). However, it is not just the content and relevance of the curriculum which causes concern but the strategies used to teach it. A weakness of school science is its perceived dullness, in both presentation and content (Millar and Osborne 1998: 24).

The following description of lessons is based on the author's experience of watching many student teachers working in school under the guidance of experienced staff. It is suggested that the situations described are not isolated ones, but may occur in many schools and are not just attributable to teachers in training. Most schools have a scheme of work to which all staff refer and has, almost certainly, received the approval of at least one OFSTED inspection. The purpose of introducing these examples is to illustrate the effects of the pressure on teachers, through crowded syllabuses, tight examination demands and the need to produce substantial evidence of pupil performance.

It is not unusual to see a lesson which sets out to teach pupils the classification of vertebrates and which encourages pupils to use their own observations to classify selected animals. The process objectives are given high profile in lesson planning. Pupils are given first the characteristics of amphibia, birds, fish, mammals and reptiles, and after some discussion and exemplars are asked to place new animals in their class, using photographs. In practice, pupils often know from experience in which class to place the organism, and if they do not, they ask someone. Close questioning of the pupils often reveals an inability to identify from the photograph the distinguishing features which would allow the correct classification of the animal. The pupils know this and believe that the exercise is one of knowing the correct class in which to place a named animal.

This teaching situation seems to be absurd and may turn some pupils away from science; others may feel that they cannot do science because they cannot do the task as set. If this example were rare it could be ignored, but my experience suggests that this approach is a frequent feature of teaching in some schools. One reason why the lesson is taught this way may be lack of time to deal with the topic in more than a superficial way. Another reason cited by teachers is lack of resources, which may be due to lack of time to identify them.

Another area of school science which is poorly understood by pupils is physical and chemical change. This classification has been essential for 11–16 year-old pupils for decades. Some practical activities used to teach this topic do not provide clear evidence of change that can be interpreted using the criteria for physical and chemical change. Even where evidence is sound, the interpretation some pupils place on it shows the difficulty pupils have in building an adequate conception of the difference between these categories (Driver *et al.* 1994: 85–9).

The combustion of iron filings in air using a Bunsen flame is one example. It is popular because the ensuing cascade of sparks is lively and can be linked to a fireworks display. The difficulty is to show that the iron has changed into iron oxide and to convince pupils that a new substance has been formed. Pupils see little change in the iron filings; some colour change may be noticed but it rarely convinces. An explanation by the teacher that 'a non-reversible and energetic reaction' has occurred, as I heard recently, leaves much to the imagination.

Another change that is poorly presented is making salt from brine. This change is often described 'as obviously a physical change because no new substance is formed', but may avoid discussion of the large energy input needed to transform salt water into salt and water vapour. It is not obvious to pupils that no new substance has been formed. Labelling evaporation as a physical change does not enhance understanding unless accompanied by extensive discussion. One criterion for distinguishing physical and chemical change is the magnitude of the accompanying energy change. The problem with using energy change in this way is knowing, without recourse to quantitative work, when a lot or a little energy has been transferred.

The criteria for placing change in one or other category are not obvious to pupils and much depends on teacher intervention. It begs the question of why some practical work is carried out since it is often inconclusive. Why do we try to divide the variety of changes in matter into physical and chemical, categories which practising scientists themselves rarely use? The most important reason may simply be tradition; another reason may be the ease with which knowledge of changes in matter can be tested by using the categories of physical and chemical change. Rarely in science lessons do you see good discussion about changes in matter and what might be going on; more often there are hurried arguments to foreclose on the 'right' answer.

Similar issues can be identified in relation to the teaching of energy. The National Curriculum science describes energy change in terms of energy transfer between systems. However, many schools continue to teach energy and change using the concept 'forms of energy' and flow diagrams showing energy transformation, for example, 'light energy to heat energy'. Others pay lip service to 'transfer' and talk confusingly of 'transferring energy from one form to another'! Once again, the reasons for a continuation of this practice seem to be ones of tradition, with many teachers having taught that way for a long time and many new teachers having been taught that way themselves. In addition, some textbooks retain the use of 'forms of energy'. A further reason for retaining 'forms of energy' may again be the ease with which the topic can be tested. If pupils need to explain how energy from the Sun heats the Earth, then the pupil can select from a list of forms of energy and say, 'light energy is changed to heat energy', which is short, simple and either right or wrong. The disadvantage of this description is that it carries little explanation and is labelling without clarification.

The transfer model describes light as an energy carrier and pupils need to construct sentences in order to explain the change:

> Light carries energy from the Sun to the Earth. Light interacts with the Earth's atmosphere and transfers energy to it, making it warm.

Explaining change in this way requires a more sophisticated use of language than selecting suitable energy terms from a list. The process takes longer and assessment is more subjective.

Requiring pupils to explain what happens either orally or in writing is a better way to identify their understanding of science than checking the correct choice of labels or a score from a test paper. However, teachers under pressure to complete the syllabus and get pupils through examinations may have little time for discussion but are, I suggest, manoeuvred into 'pulling pupils through hoops'. The National Curriculum science syllabus is too full.

In the examples above, practical activities are a prominent feature of teaching. Pupils experience the phenomenon but by itself this does not necessarily help with explanations. Other examples come to mind:

- Explaining why large animals survive better than smaller animals in cold climates. Investigations with large and small cans of warm water do not help much with the explanation through arguments about the surface area to volume ratio.
- Explaining the differences between heat and temperature by giving the same amount of energy to different masses of water at the same starting temperature. Although pupils accept the smaller mass gets hotter, they also say that the hotter body has the most energy.

Several points arise through consideration of these examples.

- simply telling pupils the conclusion does not guarantee learning;
- carrying out an activity does not necessarily improve understanding;
- unless pupils are given opportunity to talk through the findings and their implications, understanding rarely develops.

In the case of heat and temperature, it is not the practical outcome that causes difficulty but the concepts involved in the explanation. Some years ago a former distinguished colleague wrote:

> The slogan, 'I do and I understand' is commonly used in support of practical work in science teaching … In many classrooms I suspect, [it is] 'I do and I am even more confused'.
>
> (Driver, 1983: 9)

However, while the place of practical work in schools remains as strong as ever the role of discussion in developing ideas and giving meaning to data is less well developed. The pressure on the teacher to complete the SoW often prevents meaningful learning and may limit pupils to recall of factual material with minimal understanding.

The science curriculum is overloaded and summative assessment plays an important role in driving the way teachers works. The outcomes of that assessment are vitally important for a school's standing in the community and in relation to other schools. One consequence is that teachers may cut corners in their teaching.

The development of understanding and the deeper satisfaction of comprehending the explanations in science are both sacrificed to the twin targets of completing the syllabus and getting high marks in public examinations. Much is said about raising the levels of literacy and numeracy in pupils, but to what purpose? If pupils cannot use these skills to grapple with new ideas, or with results from practical activities, then that development is wasted. Examinations which ask for one-word answers or short phrases to complete a partially formed sentence do not need very high levels of literacy.

Ways forward

The previous sections have drawn attention to advances in teaching and learning achieved through the introduction of the National Curriculum Science and to some of its deficiencies. The gains are important, in particular that science, alongside English and mathematics, is a curriculum entitlement of all pupils 5–16. Issues of access remain. Science represents one of the great cultural achievements of humanity, not only by changing dramatically the way we live but more importantly through what it says about our understanding of ourselves, our past, present and of possibilities for the future.

The development of a science curriculum, by contrast with a set of separate science subjects, has produced a measure of coherence, which is advantageous to the learner. It has brought science staff together and been a unifying force in many departments. Set against that gain are the concerns of some graduates teaching outside their specialist subject, a minority of whom regard such demands as an imposition. The increased focus on experimental and analytical skills through investigations has been beneficial. The presentation and assessment of investigations has improved with each version of the curriculum but, for many teachers, that framework still encompasses a too narrow range of inquiry and little time to make the best use of it.

The most serious criticism of the National Curriculum Science is overload. The volume of material to be taught, coupled with a demanding assessment system, taxes teachers and has led to superficial coverage of content and skills. The system forces pupils and teachers to rehearse for testing, limiting the scope of the curriculum and the enterprise of teachers. Summative assessment drives teaching. This position was predicted by commentators at the time of the second revision (Jennings 1992: 36) and deplored much earlier by HMI (DES 1979). The much-valued improvements in literacy and numeracy among pupils cannot be exercised. An important way forward is to reverse the relationship of teaching and assessment; we need to decide first what we want to teach and why, and only then devise a system of assessment which reflects that decision.

There was a glimmer of hope in this direction in the late 1980s when extensive research was undertaken to develop new ways of assessing pupils in experimental science, developing out of the work of the Assessment of Performance Unit (Murphy and Gott 1984). Patience ran out (and elections were looming) and the work was abandoned without publication (Swain 1991a). The tests were deemed to be unnecessarily complicated; in the words of the then prime minister, 'let us go back to simple paper and pencil tests', which we did! The development of mean-ingful tests takes time, needs adequate funding and must undergo trials. These requirements cannot be linked to a political agenda but are the mid- to long-term aim of any decent education system.

As to what we should teach, this has been a long-standing issue and frequently discussed (for example, Ingle and Jennings 1981; Association for Science Education 1992b; Jennings 1992). Most recently, the Nuffield Foundation organ-ised a series of seminars to which science educators from schools, universities, LEAs, learned societies and government officers were invited. The seminar report (*Beyond 2000*) offers a long-term view of how the curriculum might be developed in the light of ten years experience of the National Curriculum (Millar and Osborne 1998).

The outcomes of these seminars were expressed through ten specific recom-mendations. The key recommendation identifies the fundamental weakness of the current science curriculum as the *lack of clear aims*. This deficiency causes funda-mental problems in trying to justify any content or approach offered for inclusion in a curriculum. As mentioned earlier in this chapter, much of the current science curriculum is there because it has always been there, despite some tinkering over the years. There appears to be no link between desired outcomes and the choice of content. Other recommendations arising from the Nuffield seminars included the broadening of the range of teaching strategies used by teachers, the encouragement of literacy in all its genres and the widening of the ways in which pupils are assessed.

Other commentators have offered views about the ways that the science curriculum could be developed. Some have drawn attention to the connection between science and technology (Macaskill and Ogborn 1996). They stress the importance of teaching about capability (technical competence), of knowing about the importance of technology in our lives and the connections between science and technology. Others have drawn attention to the need for developing scientific literacy in the population (for example, Millar 1996). Indeed, if the aims of the science National Curriculum expressed through the 'distinctive contributions of science to the school curriculum', referred to earlier, were given serious considera-tion then a very different science curriculum would emerge.

There is a need to develop skills in the population that allow individuals to access scientific information, either for personal use, for work-related demands or for participation in wider debate. An increasing source of information is the World Wide Web. A serious drawback to the current science curriculum is that it is not necessary to use ICT to achieve the standards of SATs and GCSE, thus opposing one aim of the ICT curriculum.

A further important issue is the relationship of the compulsory curriculum to the post-16 curriculum. It was mentioned at the beginning of this paper that the science curriculum has its origins in the grammar school curricula for the separate sciences, intended to prepare pupils for further training in science. Despite the fact that most pupils will not be scientists and the country needs only a small number of trained scientists, the curriculum remains driven by the needs of this minority. How to disengage the compulsory curriculum from the demands of the post-compulsory specialist curricula needs urgent attention and perhaps 'thinking the unthinkable'. We have worked this century on the assumption of a necessary continuity between a school leaving qualification, a higher specialist qualification (GCE A-level) and degree courses. Do science undergraduates need to start their courses with such substantial pre-university courses in their subject? Perhaps if we rethought what knowledge, skills and abilities we need of the trained graduate scientists and research scientists in the next millennium then a different view of post-16 education might emerge with a downward beneficial effect on the compulsory school science curriculum. See, for example the critique of the assumptions underpinning current science education practice (Osborne 1999). The stumbling block to school curriculum reform remains the high value placed on GCE Advanced Levels. The maintenance of A-levels as the 'gold standard' is having a profound and deleterious effect on the development of an attractive science curriculum appropriate for citizens in the twenty-first century.

2 Teaching science in a multicultural, multi-faith society

Michael Reiss

Introduction

Suppose that the following three statements are true:

- there is no doubt as to what science is;
- the role of teachers of science is to teach pupils what science is;
- science teachers do not need to take much account of pupil diversity in their classrooms because all pupils of a certain age and ability come to science lessons with much the same knowledge and understanding of, interest in, perceptions of and expectations of science.

The job of a science teacher would then be a lot easier. However, it would also be a lot less satisfying for a creative teacher. This chapter is written with the conviction that none of these three statements is true, and that by analysing further why these statements misrepresent pupils, science and the job of teaching, science teachers and science educators can be helped to find richer ways of teaching science in schools at both primary and secondary levels.

The chapter will address four questions. The first three relate to the three bullet points above; the last is to do with one aspect of teaching science in a multi-faith society:

- What is science?
- What is the purpose of teaching science?
- Why do science teachers need to take account of pupil diversity and how can they do so?
- Should questions to do with scientific origins – of the Universe, of life and of the human species – be introduced in science lessons and, if so, how?

Aspects of the first three of these questions are also considered from different angles in other chapters in this book, but they need to be considered here to prevent multicultural science being seen by some as a sort of marginal extra in science education, something that it would be nice to do if we had the time and resources or if we had a different sort of pupil intake.

What is science?

First, there is not one science; rather, there are sciences and there are ways of undertaking science. Worldwide, many school science curricula pay, at best, lip service to this. For example, ever since the introduction of the National Curriculum in England and Wales in 1989, the notion that there is a single best way of carrying out a scientific investigation has been enshrined in legislation. Although the 1995 revision of the Science National Curriculum slightly improved matters, it remains the case that most pupils end their mandatory science education with a very narrow understanding of what science is and how it is carried out (Driver *et al.* 1996; Donnelly and Jenkins 1999).

Let me be personal. In my own brief career as a research scientist, I worked in the Zoology Department of a reputable university. Yet I carried out two quite different types of scientific work. One involved field work on the behaviour of red deer. Here, being a good scientist meant such things as being able to find particular deer (which might take an hour or more), identify them, record their behaviour using techniques adapted from field anthropology and so on. The other type of scientific work involved constructing mathematical models to try to predict why animals were the size they were. Trying to explain why both types of work could be carried out in the same Zoology Department is quite difficult. Apart from the fact that each involved original work on animals, they had little in common. Interestingly enough, neither bit of work would have got me a high level on Attainment Target 1 (Sc1) of the Science National Curriculum. Authors who have argued for the need for, and feasibility of, having pupils conduct genuine classroom investigations include Woolnough (1994), Albone *et al.* (1995) and Roth (1995).

Writers about multicultural science often include something about the nature of science to try and persuade the reader that pupils generally leave school with only a narrow model as to what science is. Indeed, historians of science, sociologists of science, philosophers of science and a growing number of science educators accept that there is no such thing as '*a* science' or '*the* scientific method' (for example, Feyerabend 1988; Woolgar 1988; Chalmers 1990; Aikenhead 1997).

For example, the current strong consensus amongst historians of science is that what we call science has changed greatly over the centuries. Fascinatingly enough, this does mean that, in the words of two historians of science, 'On this view, the history of science becomes a relatively short and local matter: extending back less than 250 years, and largely confined to western Europe and America' (Cunningham and Williams 1993).

Such an assertion seems to fly in the face of what writers about multicultural science (including myself) commonly maintain, namely that other cultures have had flourishing examples of science that should be much more widely known by pupils (Peacock 1991; Solomon 1991; Reiss 1993; Thorp *et al.* 1994; Reiss 1998). However, this 'de-centring the Big Picture' can serve to free up school science education. Instead of comparing the scientific achievements of other cultures against the canons of late twentieth-century Western science, pupils can be helped to see that science is a cultural activity, and it is inevitably the case that different cultures produce different sciences.

There are two main reasons why such an apparently innocuous assertion can prove so disconcerting, even unbelievable or threatening, to many science teachers. One is simply that most of us were not taught, at school, a view of science which saw it as a cultural activity. The implicit message we were given was that, to parody Hebrews 13:8, 'Science is the same yesterday and today and for ever'.

The second reason why the notion that science is a product of human culture can be so troublesome is that it can appear to give credence to a theory of absolute relativism. It may be thought that once it is admitted that scientific truth is cultur-ally bound rather than absolute (the same for all times and in all places) this is not only to eschew a doctrine of logical positivism or scientism but also to embrace a belief that scientific 'truth' is meaningless.

A way out of this apparent dichotomy is to steer between Scylla and Charybdis, lashing oneself to the mast of reliable knowledge. In other words, science provides only provisional truths but nevertheless these truths are often robust. This is most obviously the case when considering how we can use well-established laws in physics and chemistry to determine, for example, how much fuel an aeroplane needs for a flight. But even in contemporary areas of public debate, science can often help. For instance, we cannot yet be certain about the long-term health consequences of eating genetically modified foods, but the knowledge provided by feeding such foods to two or more generations of rats provides information which is trustworthy to a certain extent.

What is the purpose of teaching science?

The question of the functions of science teaching has been extensively debated in recent years both in the UK and internationally (Black and Atkin 1996; Millar 1996; Millar and Osborne 1998). Increasingly, it has been agreed – largely for reasons to do with justice rather than with the design of school curricula or with pedagogy – that school science education should serve the needs of the whole school population. That is, it cannot exclusively or even primarily restrict itself to the interests of that small minority of pupils who will go on to become scientists.

For this reason, scientific literacy, however this term is construed, is seen as the prime aim of science teaching (see also Layton *et al.* 1993; Irwin and Wynne 1996). Generally, scientific literacy is seen as being a vehicle to help tomorrow's adults to understand scientific issues. This understanding of scientific literacy is acceptable as far as it goes, but it can be taken further by considering the three axes of 'the here and now', 'space' and 'resistance'.

For a start, we should not only think of school science education providing skills and information for the citizens of tomorrow; it should be absolutely relevant to the pupils being taught today, that is, in the here and now. Obvious examples of topics pertinent to pupils that could be meaningfully taught in school science include ones presently covered (though often in only a rather cursory fashion) in health education and environmental education within science.

For example, the issue of cigarette smoking is typically covered in school science lessons by means of a practical demonstration that cigarettes contain tar and a series of polemics (often backed up by the making of posters by pupils) that smoking is bad for you. More time in science curricula would allow for both a more detailed and a more nuanced treatment. For instance, pupils could be taught more about the addictive nature of nicotine, about possible health benefits of smoking (for example, there is some evidence for a negative relationship between the risk of developing Alzheimer's disease and the number of cigarettes smoked) and about the reasons why people take up smoking. They could also, in science lessons, PSHE lessons or citizenship lessons, consider whether the aim of education about smoking should be one of beneficence (doing good, such as by persuading pupils not to smoke) or one of the promotion of autonomy (enabling pupils to make their own informed choices) (see Reiss 1996). It would also be worth seeing whether pupils' writings could have audiences beyond their teacher and peers. For example, instead of only constructing posters about smoking, destined never to leave the confines of school laboratory walls, pupils could produce desktop published leaflets for distribution in GP surgeries or, failing that, at least in the school visitor area.

A second way in which school science education can be taken further is by accepting the idea that education can help provide pupils with space in which to live their lives. This idea has its roots in the work of Solomon (1992), who looked at how pupils learn about energy. She found that pupils do not simply learn a single meaning for the term 'energy'. Instead, they get to know about its several meanings in a variety of ways. Indeed, pupils are perfectly capable of holding a number of alternative understandings (today they might be called 'mental models') simultaneously.

From such work it can be argued that the job of school science lessons about energy is not to provide pupils with only a single model of energy. Rather, we should aim to provide pupils with a variety of models that can be used appropriately in different contexts. Pupils should be helped to develop a plurality of intellectual spaces which they can inhabit as occasion requires. We all know the stereotype of the scientist who can only see a rainbow in terms to do with the reflection and refraction of light. Such knowledge is incomplete. A fuller understanding of rainbows in the culture I inhabit comes with seeing Constable's watercolours, reading the poems of Wordsworth and knowing about the story of Noah's flood.

Finally, science education has the potential to serve as a platform for resistance, a notion just beginning to be explored in some science education writing (see Rodriguez 1998) though well-established in anti-racist education circles (for example, Ahmed *et al.* 1998). For example, in a paper about teaching science to homeless children in an urban setting in the USA, Barton writes about 13 year-old Gilma. Gilma took the lead in a project, developed by the children themselves, to study pollution in their local community. Barton concluded that the main reason for Gilma's enthusiastic participation in this project in her community was 'to figure out how to make it better for herself, her friends, and her family' (Barton 1998).

Why do science teachers need to take account of pupil diversity and how can they do so?

As every teacher knows, pupils differ in all sorts of ways. They arrive at school with different ways in which they prefer to learn and learn best; they arrive knowing different amounts as a result of their lives to date; and they arrive expecting to learn different amounts that day (Reiss 1998).

What is a teacher to do faced with this diversity? To what extent are different curricula, resources and teaching approaches needed for different categories of pupils? It seems obvious that different science resources would be provided for a pupil with a physical disability (such as severe sight impairment) and a pupil without such a disability. However, should both pupils receive exactly the same science curriculum? This question is a harder one. And what of girls and boys? Should they receive identical teaching approaches? Some people argue 'No'; others 'Yes' (Reiss, 2000).

Over the last twenty years or so, issues to do with equality in science education have, encouragingly, been taken on board to an increasing extent by professional associations, textbook authors, publishers, examination boards, individual teachers and other science education professionals (Thorp *et al.* 1994; Cobern 1996; Guzzetti and Williams 1996). No longer is it implicitly assumed, for instance, that physics is largely an activity undertaken predominantly by white middle-class men interested only in car acceleration and the motion of cricket balls. More generally, a greater number of teachers realise that the content of what they teach and the way they teach can turn pupils on to, or off, science.

However, despite such improvements, much remains to be done. Though under-researched, differences in educational attainments in science and other subjects are very strongly related to class and economic position (Croxford 1997; Robinson and White 1997; Strand 1999). In the UK, certain ethnic minority pupils, notably African Caribbean, Pakistani and Bangladeshi pupils, continue to underperform relative to other pupils in many LEAs, whereas in other LEAs these patterns are reversed (Gillborn and Gipps 1996). While gender inequalities in the UK are considerably less than in many other countries (Harding and McGregor 1995), girls continue to be several time less likely than boys to continue with the physical sciences once they have the option, while boys are more likely than girls to leave school with no qualifications.

Should questions to do with scientific origins be introduced in science lessons, and if so, how?

Should questions to do with scientific origins – of the Universe, of life and of the human species – be introduced in science lessons? This issue has, to date, been less controversial in UK schools than in the USA. However, it is possible this could change and even if it does not, there are good pedagogical and pastoral reasons for teachers of science thinking carefully about how to deal with the issue, especially given today's multi-faith society.

There are very strong arguments for teaching about origins in science lessons.

Accounts of the origin of the Universe, of life and of the human species lie at the core of cosmology and biology. For two main reasons, such topics need to be handled differently from teaching about equations of motion or chemical bonds. First, the evidence in favour of the currently accepted scientific theories about origins is less strong than the evidence in favour of many other aspects of science. This means that teachers need to ensure that they do not give the impression that currently accepted scientific views about the origins of the universe and of life on Earth are 'proved'. Indeed, introduced carefully, teaching about origins and evolution can be a valuable way to teach about the provisional, even tentative, nature of scientific knowledge.

The second reason for handling topics about origins in science lessons is that for a number of pupils, the issue will be of great personal significance for them. There are many science teachers for whom the notion that the Earth is only a few thousand years old and the direct result of a miraculous creation is difficult to imagine, even bizarre. Yet many pupils either hold such beliefs or come from homes where family members hold such beliefs as core aspects of their being. For such pupils, attempts in science lessons to disprove their beliefs may be personally threatening (Jackson *et al.* 1995; Roth and Alexander 1997). It ill behoves science teachers to trample on such personal values.

At the same time, I consider it inappropriate to deal with this issue by omitting all serious discussion of origins from the science classroom or laboratory. To do so is to lose the heart of much of science. Possible learning approaches when teaching about origins in science are discussed in Reiss (1993).

Conclusion

Although many people (though not young children) are disillusioned with science and its promises, we still live in an age where science has tremendous cultural and technological significance. Science education has the potential to aid pupils in engaging with the world of science and in understanding both its powers and its limitations.

Science is not a homogeneous whole and pupils are diverse. There is a diversity of sciences and pupils differ with respect to such characteristics as gender, ethnicity, class, the extent to which they may have special needs, their preferred learning styles and other aspects of their personality and home culture. What is a science teacher to do with this diversity? This chapter argues that to take account of this diversity leads to teaching that is both just and a better form of science education.

There is more to science education than coping with pupil diversity and introducing pupils to the idea that science is culturally bounded. Science education can also help pupils to resist and to create space. However, before pupils can do these, their teachers may need to do the same; see the constraints of imposed curricula as borderlines within which meanings are to be constructed rather than as tramlines to be followed routinely.

Finally, the question of the teaching of origins (the origins of the Universe, the origins of life and the origins of human beings) in science lessons raises important issues about the nature of scientific knowledge, the pedagogy of science education and considerations such as parental rights and the relationship between home culture and culture in society more generally. A balance needs to be struck between omitting such topics from science lessons, for fear of upsetting people or 'causing problems', and tackling these topics in a cavalier manner which fails to understand their cultural significance.

Questions

1 To what extent are different science curricula and pedagogies needed for different categories of pupils?
2 How can science teachers provide science lessons that are relevant to the here and now and enable pupils to find space and develop resistance?
3 Should science lessons consider such controversial issues as the origins of life and the evolution of humans?

Further reading

Blackmore, V. and Page, A. (1989) *Evolution: The Great Debate*, Oxford: Lion.
A balanced introduction to the controversies around the theory of evolution.

Dawkins, R. (1986) *The Blind Watchmaker*, Harlow: Longman.
A beautifully written account which argues that the diversity of life with all its wonderful adaptations does not require the existence of a creator.

Hodson, D. (1998) *Teaching and Learning Science: Towards a Personalized Approach*, Buckingham: Open University Press.
A carefully argued book which explores how the goal of critical scientific literacy can be achieved by all pupils.

National Academy of Sciences (1998) *Teaching about Evolution and the Nature of Science*, Washington: National Academy of Sciences.
A robust defence of the argument that evolution should be taught in school science lessons.

Poole, M. (1995) *Beliefs and Values in Science Education*, Buckingham: Open University Press.
A valuable book which examines ways in which beliefs and values interact with science and science teaching.

Reiss, M. J. (1993) *Science Education for a Pluralist Society*, Buckingham: Open University Press.
A book that argues that there is no such thing as 'science' but rather a collection of ethnosciences, and explores the implications of this view for science education and classroom teaching.

Siraj-Blatchford, J. (1996) *Learning Technology, Science and Social Justice: An Integrated Approach for 3–13 year olds*, Nottingham: Education Now.
A passionately written book which shows how global perspectives and social justice can be incorporated into technology and science teaching.

3   The irresistible rise of the nature of science in science curricula

Bert Sorsby

Introduction

This chapter concerns the steady rise in importance of nature of science as a curriculum component, in spite of many controversies that surround the subject. The controversies have arisen for many reasons, for example there is poor correlation between the culture of practising scientists and that of school science, especially with regard to different emphases on the procedural understanding of science (Gott, Duggan and Johnson 1999). The central theme of this chapter is that teaching the nature of science (NoS) is an important bridge between these two cultures. Somewhat paradoxically, the NoS bridge itself is full of flaws, which add to the controversy, and these too are explored in the first part of the chapter.

My first aim is to present an overview of NoS as a component in science curricula for education at all levels, and to consider the reasons behind its growth and durability as a curriculum component. The next is to consider some strategies for how the subject may be taught and learned, both in school and in teacher training. Finally some of the challenges facing NoS as a curriculum component are discussed.

What are the features of the nature of science and why are there tensions?

Nature of science is a relatively new curriculum component, which has grown out of an earlier imperative to teach 'the scientific method' (*sic*). Its current place in curricula at all levels of education has fuelled disagreements between, and among, professional historians, philosophers, sociologists, research scientists and educationalists. Nevertheless, as a component in the National Curriculum of England and Wales, the subject has showed considerable tenacity, surviving all school curriculum revisions since 1989 (QCA 1999a), and becoming established in the teacher training curriculum too (DfEE 1998b). Its place as a component in science curricula is now well established throughout the world, and is found in education policy statements of many countries in Europe, Australia and the USA (Matthews 1994; Jenkins 1996; Alters 1997).

In spite of this inclusivity, there remain many concerns, not least that the correlation between NoS in the school science curriculum in England and that for initial teacher training could be much closer (Sorsby 1999a). Yet another challenge is the low priority given to teaching this aspect of science in schools, and this is found both in the USA and in England (Alters 1997; Nott and Wellington 1999).

Part of the challenge involved in turning this particular bit of curriculum theory into practice lies in the diversity of meanings of the phrase 'the nature of science'. This remains largely unresolved because of the broad scope of the phrase, since the nature of science can include all the elements of science and technology in society, social studies in science, liberal studies in science, public understanding of science as well as the history, sociology and philosophy of both science and technology. It can embrace spiritual, moral and cultural dimensions as well.

The elusiveness of a crisp and concise definition has led to critical discussion from many professions who feel a special ownership for what they feel the phrase 'nature of science' should cover. There have been efforts to promote a rapprochement, especially between history and philosophy of science (Matthews 1994; Duschl 1985), but there are still many controversies and misunderstandings between the professional scientists; and this term includes philosophers, sociologists, and historians of science as well as research and applied scientists, engineers and technologists. Many educationalists (for example, Osborne 1996) are concerned about philosophers' and sociologists' use of constructivism in relation to the nature of science. Science historians have considered that approaching the teaching of nature of science through historical studies is basically flawed, since it cannot satisfy both generalist and specialist demands (Pumfrey 1991).

The breadth of vested interests suggests therefore that NoS in science curricula must involve a study of the wide web of relationships and interactions, between science, technology and society, both in historical and present day settings. Its study should incorporate philosophical dimensions too, which relate to the validity of science knowledge claims. Before about 1985 the educational concern in school-based NoS was with questions such as, 'how does/did science and technology affect society?', and teachers illustrated this by using anecdotal oddities, with stories about scientists, the 'ripping yarn' approach. These are still part of the content of NoS, but more recent historical and sociological scholarship places greater emphasis on the subtle, multiple interactions of society, technology and science, including the effect of society upon scientific and technological developments, the effect of technology upon science, as well as vice versa. Recent philosophical studies suggest that NoS should include study of how and why scientific knowledge and understanding is (and has been) gained and validated through the application of rigorous appraisal by the scientific community, by involving stringent and parsimonious logic, within social settings.

The result of these diverse influences is to steer NoS to a broader role within the science curriculum, but these pressures too have ensured that the gap has grown between what the curriculum requires and what teachers now feel able to teach in school. NoS requires much more than stories about scientists and their discoveries, and teachers have to rely on a greater range of subject knowledge and pedagogical skills, for which they have not been trained. It is not surprising that these aspects of the school science curricula are just not taught (Watts and McGrath 1998; Nott and Wellington 1999).

So why is nature of science included in the science curriculum?

There are at least two answers to this question, and both relate to the potential of NoS to act as a bridge between the culture associated with the community of scientists and the rest of society (Figure 3.1). Firstly, because NoS is now more broadly interpreted, it is increasingly important as a focus for exploring a common meeting ground for professional historians, philosophers, educationalists and scientists. The view of Nott and Wellington (1996), that science teachers are a part of the community of professional scientists, gives teachers an important role in these debates, and they are also the ones who are required to teach NoS as initiators of pupils into some aspects of the scientific culture.

Secondly, there is a political dimension as governments, urged by academics (for example, Millar and Osborne 1998), seek to steer and control school curricula in order to promote a better public understanding of science, raise scientific literacy, and thereby improve the understanding of science in relation to democratic citizenship (AAAS 1993; SCICentre 1998; QCA 1999a).

Figure 3.1 shows the parallels which can be drawn between the ways in which scientists and non-scientists (including children) learn science. In both cultures

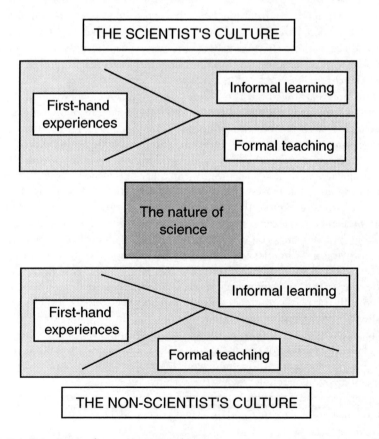

Figure 3.1 Scientist's and non-scientist's cultures

the learner gains direct, first hand experiences of science, they learn by being exposed to informal learning experiences and thirdly they learn as a result of formal tuition. However, it is clear from many research studies that non-scientists have misconceptions about the ideas held by the community of scientists, as well as many misunderstandings about the way science proceeds. I have discussed these points in greater detail elsewhere, especially the role of argumentation studies within the nature of science (Sorsby 1999a).

How should we approach teaching the nature of science in schools and in teacher training?

The finding that NoS is generally not taught in the classroom is serious, but there is currently a lack of emphasis on NoS as a subject in the training of science teachers too (see for example: Palmquist and Finley 1997). In addition there are only a few examples in the research literature about how the situation might be remedied for pre-service and in-service teachers, although there are occasional descriptions of undergraduate education courses (for example in the review by Matthews (1994)).

How can we approach teaching NoS to both adults and children? Lipman (1988: 27) considered that 'by and large teachers should be taught by the very same procedures as those they are expected to employ in the classroom'. Lipman's view underpins the following section, and approaches to teaching NoS to both pupils and teachers are considered in tandem.

Teaching and learning about the nature of science can be approached through philosophical contexts, especially using methodologies which involve argumentation. Working from a teacher education perspective, Lipman (1988) presented a three-stage strategy for developing a greater awareness of pedagogical approaches to philosophical issues namely, curriculum exploration, modelling and observation/classroom research. It is clear that at all stages discussion, logical argument and persuasion are vital. For child and adult learners alike, it is important to give time and structures to explore the nature of science through dialogue, and discussion both *in* science and *about* science (Sorsby 1999b, 1999c; Newton et al. 1999).

A second approach draws on sociological studies of the nature of science and this involves bringing out the relevance of science to pupils and to teachers. For some aspects such as ecology and health related issues, it is relatively straightforward to place the science within a human context. In other areas, such as those typically associated with the physical sciences, the human connections are less obvious, but in all, the role of discussion and argumentation is again very important. Ratcliffe (1998) recommended the following approaches to ensure good practice in science lessons: clarify the purpose of the discussion; make the science base overt; emphasise the nature of the evidence; use a framework for analysing discussion; value pupils' opinions; group pupils carefully; review the activity.

The longest-established approach uses socio-historical case studies to help pupils understand the nature of science and these may cover both biographical and thematic studies and some good support materials for schools have been produced (see for example Shortland and Warwick (1989), Solomon (1991), Honey (1990) and Nott

(1994)). There is also available a thrice-yearly pack of photocopiable teacher resources, 'Breakthrough', which was reviewed very favourably by Buss (1999).

Historical and science-in-society approaches for pupils have much in common. They share a pedagogy with Lipman's approach to teaching philosophy which includes discussion about socio-historical case studies; reading about science and science in society issues (especially from primary sources); listening to and watching audio visual presentations; using dramatic reconstructions of social and historical conflicts where science is involved; replicating historical experiments; simulation and role-play. Experience shows that it is reasonably straightforward to transfer some of these approaches, especially reading and discussion, to programmes for pre-service and in-service education of teachers and other adults. There are, however, greater challenges with getting adult learners to become involved in role-play and drama, especially on in-service courses where participants are unlikely to know each other sufficiently well for the approach to be successful. A successful approach using a limited degree of role-play with adult learners uses argumentation around history of science case studies. The teachers as a whole group are reminded (or taught) the basics of a current scientific theory, and as a group they have to identify and marshal evidence to support that theory. The tutor adopts the stance of propounding an alternative theory, and uses the data gathered by the teachers, as well as additional data, to provide an evidence base for the alternative theory. For example, in a historical case study of the oxygen versus phlogiston theories of burning, teachers are asked to provide data from a series of practical exercises to establish what is observed and measured when burning takes place. The tutor provides a counter-blast to the teachers' evidence and provides additional evidence, which can be used to support the phlogiston theory. Other case studies have involved the heliocentric versus the geocentric theories and the four-element theory of matter versus the atomic theory. In all of these, the aim is to illuminate for the teachers more about the nature of science, and especially to emphasise the role of argumentation in the processes of science.

Another approach to NoS, is through open ended investigations in science which involve problem solving. Practical investigations in science are well established in both primary and secondary pupils' education, and experience has shown that this is a successful approach with teacher education too. Since 1990, a science assignment for pre-service and in-service primary science teachers at the University of Hull, has required the teachers to identify an investigable question, and then to work in collaboration with two or three colleagues to carry out a scientific investigation into that question. The assessment criteria are given in Table 3.1, and this provides an initial framework for students to begin the study. They are expected to discuss their findings with professional scientists within the university, and it soon becomes clear that not every type of investigation will match all the criteria perfectly.

Present and future challenges for the nature of science

In Europe, as in the rest of the world, there is a quickening in pace and intensity in arguments for study of the nature of science in school curricula. The White Paper

Table 3.1 Practical investigations: assessment criteria

Before the investigation:

1   Did the group co-operate to agree a problem to investigate?
2   Is the problem or question investigable?
3   Have predictions been made and have suitable hypotheses been formulated to explain the predictions?
4   Did the group provide appropriate materials to investigate?
5   Has the independent variable been identified?
6   Has the dependent variable been identified?
7   Have the controlled variables been identified?
8   Is it clear what measurements are to be made?
9   Is it clear how the measurements are to be made?
10   Is it clear how measurements are to be used in analysing results?

During the investigation:

11   Are appropriate measuring devices selected for the task?
12   Have measurements or observations been repeated to confirm observations or to 'smooth out' uncertainties by averaging?
13   Has the group persisted when things went wrong? Did they modify their procedure in the light of practical experience?
14   Has the group co-operated so that each member had a chance to do all the activities?

After the practical investigation:

15   Has the group discussed and reflected critically upon the validity and significance of the results?
16   Does the individual's report show all the above stages?
17   Is the style of writing appropriate?
18   Are the results presented clearly and in the most effective way?
19   Are appropriate patterns identified and are conclusions compatible with the evidence presented?
20   Are the conclusions fully discussed?
21   Is the methodology evaluated critically?
22   Has an understanding of the science concepts appropriate to the investgation been shown?
23   Has the place of such an investigation in science education been assessed?
24   Has there been discussion of all aspects of the investigation with a scientist?

on Education and Training emphasised the importance of encouraging a sense of citizenship as well as a social and cultural identity, stressing that: 'Any action taken by the member states to introduce the history of science and technology into schools and to strengthen the links between research and basic education should be encouraged' (Commission of the European Communities 1995: 11). As a result, there are a number of in-service courses in history of science and technology funded by the European Commission for European teachers. Details are in the

Comenius Action 3 Catalogue of Courses, obtainable from the Central Bureau for Educational Visits and Exchanges.

In England and Wales, it is no longer necessary to ensure that NoS appears in statutory curricula since legislation is now in place for pupil education across the 5–16-year age range and also in the initial training of science teachers at both primary and secondary level. The survey of over 400 schools by Nott and Wellington (1999) showed that the challenge is to ensure that NoS is actually taught, and they conclude that this will not happen to any large extent until the nature of science is part of the statutory assessment procedures.

The research of Driver *et al.* (1993) supports NoS in science education, and they consider that its study will produce scientifically literate citizens who are able to exercise their democratic rights from a sound base of knowledge and skills. This view is echoed in the development of the National Curriculum for citizenship in England and Wales (QCA 1999e), but again, NoS will only be taught in classrooms when it becomes part of the statutory assessment of citizenship.

To summarise, it is evident from developments throughout the world that the nature of science is strengthening its position as a curriculum component at pupil and teacher education levels. The challenge now is to explore *how* this can be done, both for teacher education and for pupil education. The debate over *whether* it should be done is now over, at least in the statutory curricula for teachers and pupils in England and Wales.

Questions

1   What is your own nature of science profile? Try out the self-assessment exercise in *School Science Review* 75(270): 109–12 to determine your own views about the nature of science. To what extent do you feel that your views of the nature of science colour the way you teach the subject?

2   What is the nature of a scientific investigation? Produce an open-ended question which could be investigated in a scientific way. Plan what you would do using the criteria in Appendix 1 and then critically review the extent to which your plans match the criteria.

3   What is the nature of science education? Examine carefully and critically the model proposed in Figure 3.1 which links the world of the child with that of the scientist. What is the purpose of science education as set out in this model and are there other purposes for science education? What bridges other than those associated with NoS could be used to link the two cultures?

4   How does science proceed? Read the letter 'Keyringology – is it science?' in *School Science Review* 71(257):144–5. What are the claims which might make you consider that the study of key-rings is a branch of science? Why would you reject these claims?

Further reading

Matthews, M. (1994) *Science Teaching: The Role of History and Philosophy of Science*, New York: Routledge.

This is a scholarly and wide-ranging treatment of many issues associated with history, philosophy and science education. It deals with the historical development of NoS in the science curriculum and also presents detailed analysis of some of the current controversies associated with constructivism, multicultural science education and teacher education.

Chalmers, A.F. (1999) *What is this Thing called Science?*, Buckingham: Open University Press.

This is an excellent introduction to the philosophy of scientific ideas which moves from a naïve empirical, inductivist view of science through to the theories of modern thinkers including Popper, Kuhn, Feyerabend and Lakatos.

Sutton, C. (1992) *Words, Science and Learning*, Buckingham: Open University Press.

The role of language in exploring and in forming scientific ideas is the theme of this important book. Sutton draws extensively from sociological and historical case studies and interweaves classroom practice with wider issues in science and science education.

Driver, R., Leach, J., Millar, R. and Scott, P. (1996) *Young People's Images of Science*, Bristol: Open University Press.

This is the book of the research project which studied 9–16-year-old pupils' understandings of the nature of science. It reports findings about views on the purpose of science, the nature and status of scientific knowledge and their understanding of science as a social enterprise. Implications of the study are discussed, with special reference to promoting the public understanding of science.

Solomon, J. (1993) *Teaching Science, Technology and Society*, Buckingham: Open University Press.

The contributions of Joan Solomon to teaching and learning in this area cannot be underestimated. In this book she covers the history of the development of science and technology in social contexts, as well as giving sensible and authoritative advice about teaching these aspects to primary and secondary pupils.

4 Primary science: a second-class core subject?

Judith Roden

Introduction

This chapter will revisit the reasons why it is important for children to encounter science in the primary classroom. Firstly, it will consider the fundamental role of science in the primary curriculum and the role of scientific enquiry in the development of scientific understanding; secondly, it will consider the current status of science in the primary curriculum; and finally, it will suggest ways forward into the new millennium.

In 1989, Harlen and Jelly wrote 'there is no longer any need to justify the place of science in the primary curriculum' (Harlen and Jelly 1989: 5). Further, they believed that 'the problem now is not one of convincing heads, teachers and others ... of the importance of science but of helping with the undoubted difficulties of getting started and keeping going' (Harlen and Jelly 1989: 5). This positive view was widely shared amongst those then involved in the promotion of science in the primary classroom. This was because the teaching of science had become a statutory requirement as a result of the National Curriculum, newly introduced by the Education Reform Act of 1988 (DES 1988a), which gave science 'core status' alongside English and mathematics. The National Curriculum for science reflected the then held philosophy of primary science, and was hailed as the nostrum, the sovereign cure. Optimism reigned.

There were, however, some who were doubtful about the newly raised status of primary science. Crebbin, for example, feared that although there was a need for quality science courses for all pupils in every primary school, there might be a 'dilution' in the quality of pupils' scientific experiences as a result of the directive, and that science might appear on some school timetables as a subject to be taught with little regard to *how* it was taught (Crebbin 1989).

Ten years later, on the surface at least, everything appears well. Children are achieving expected standards of science, as measured by performances on SAT's tests and teacher assessment at the end of Key Stage 2. Many people appear satisfied with the progress of children in science, but this comfort may mask a darker aspect. Evidence suggests that things may not be as comfortable as they might appear. While there has been much well documented progress in many schools and individual classrooms since 1989, the future of the 'right kind of science' appears less secure. Primary science may well be threatened in a way that echoes its position when activity learning went out of fashion after 1914, and could reflect its similar demise due to the focus on mathematics and English and the emphasis on rote learning following the 1944 Education Act.

Why should science be included in the primary curriculum?

Reasons for the inclusion of science in the primary curriculum have been well documented. The Schools Council 5–13 Project (Schools Council 1972) considered that science fostered 'an enquiring mind and a scientific approach to problems' – a much-featured statement in school science policy documents, whilst de Boo (1999: 2) implicitly justified science in terms of how it can aid enquiry where 'generic, transferable skills' are developed which 'equip children for effective lifelong learning'. Further, Harlen argues that science is important because the methods of science are used in the study and research of other subjects (Harlen 1996). Indeed, for many years, science educators advocated a cross-curricular approach to science and emphasised the way in which other subjects could be taught *through* the medium of science (Learning Through Science 1982).

However, science holds a much more important position in learning than these views suggest. Philosophers such as Hirst (Hirst and Peters 1970) and Phenix (1964) argued that science holds distinctive features which are found within no other discipline. Hirst suggested that science should be introduced alongside other forms of knowledge to enable children to become rational human beings. More recently, David Blunkett, the Secretary of State for Education, stated in his letter 'Achieving Excellence Through the National Curriculum' (Blunkett 1999) his intention to 'ensure a full and rounded entitlement to learning' for all pupils. He made the case for including other subjects in the National Curriculum alongside English and mathematics. Pointing to the distinctive contribution of other subjects, he placed science with history and geography, saying that these 'give an essential understanding of our place in the modern world, including the importance of sustainability' (QCA 1999a).

Further, QCA (1999a) exemplified the distinctiveness of science in terms of how it stimulates pupils' curiosity about the natural world. Moreover they emphasise pupils' engagement with scientific method as a form of critical and creative thinking which involves explanation, modelling and evaluation. Through science, they say, 'pupils understand how major scientific ideas contribute to technological change' and they 'learn to question and discuss science-based issues' (QCA 1999c: 82); overall, a powerful view of the role of science in children's learning.

The role of scientific enquiry

Scientific enquiry incorporates a variety of practical aspects, and has long been held as important in children's learning in the first stages of education. Traditionally, the practical 'hands on' approach has had much support. The Hadow Report (1931) suggested that primary school science should consist of more than a 'study of plant and animal life', and argued that the curriculum should be thought of 'in terms of activity and experience rather than knowledge to be acquired and facts to be stored'. Later, it was believed that science could make a contribution to the education of the 'whole' child (Isaacs, 1958; Nuffield Junior Science Project 1967; Learning Through Science 1982).

The Nuffield Junior Science Project (1967) and the later Schools Council 5–13 Project (1972) took a strongly child-centred view of primary education and emphasised the fundamental role of practical activity, especially that to 'do' science was more important than science itself. Materials developed for use by teachers arose out of, and reflected the perceptions of, the Hadow (1931) and Plowden (1967) Reports' views about how primary education should be, or was thought to be, progressing. Since then there has sometimes been heated debate about the role of 'content' versus 'process' in primary science (Hodgson and Scanlon 1985), but Harlen clarified the situation saying that:

> science cannot be characterised as being either content or process alone [and that] the ideas children create can be scientific if they are testable and falsifiable and the fact that they are often falsified by the evidence makes them no less scientific. Learning science and doing science proceed in the same way.
>
> (Harlen 1996: 5)

Harlen (1999a), in a review of research into science teaching in Scotland, identifies the approaches and techniques which have proved effective in raising standards of achievement in science. Whilst she reports that practical work 'often fails to serve a useful purpose and sometimes might obscure more than it helps understanding', she identifies three important functions of practical work, which enable pupils to:

- see a phenomenon or effect for themselves;
- decide what to change and then try it in order to test a theory or their own ideas;
- conduct an open-ended investigation, using the full range of physical and mental processes, and to gain some understanding of the nature and limitations of scientific knowledge and procedures.

(Harlen 1999a, 1999b)

Research has shown that children's existing ideas can be very difficult to change and particularly so by formal, didactic teaching (Driver 1983; Driver *et al.* 1994). The Children's Learning in Science (CLIS 1987), and Science Processes and Concept Exploration (Primary Science Process and Concept Exploration Research Reports, 1990 onwards), Projects, undertaken at secondary and primary levels respectively, explored effective strategies for dealing with children's misconceptions or 'alternative frameworks' and demonstrated that children's ideas need to be challenged, not only by verbal means but also by engaging in practical work which enables them to test their own ideas.

Recognising the need for pupils to engage with the scientific process, the intention was that it should be taught alongside aspects of content within the National Curriculum. Unfortunately, in practice, this appears not to happen as often as was intended and thought desirable. Currently, as Hollins and Whitby point out, 'process' and 'content' 'are supposed to be given equal weighting in the planning of activities – and in the assessment of pupils' (Hollins and Whitby 1998: 10). Further, referring to SCAA (1994), de Boo (1999) argues that recent statutory educational obligations have aided the use of didactic or non-practical methods of teaching at the expense of enquiry learning. Teachers often emphasise rote learning of 'facts' at the expense of learning through practical enquiry, thereby diminishing the role of practical work and reducing the opportunity for children to extend their understanding.

Evidence suggests that children are born with an ability to learn in the way that scientists find out about the world (see Roden (1999) for further examination of this). It is important, therefore, that children are given the opportunity to develop and refine the skills of observation, question raising and investigation, continuously and progressively throughout KS1 and KS2. Without encouragement and practice, a child may soon lose the ability to think 'scientifically' and fail to develop scientific skills. Children need opportunities to practise their skills, as scientists, continuously from birth to nursery, from nursery to KS1 through KS2 and to KS3, KS4 and beyond, if they are fully to benefit from a 'scientific approach' to the problems they will encounter in later life. Taught well, science can add richness to a curriculum which may otherwise focus merely on the acquisition of knowledge.

When the current and increasing emphasis on English, mathematics and information and communication technology, and the associated demise of the foundation subjects is considered, it is clear that science is the *only* core subject which offers children the opportunity to put forward their own hypotheses and test whether these are false or not, by setting up practical situations (see Harlen 1996).

What is the current evidence for concern?

Assessment at KS1 and KS2 relies heavily on teacher assessment (QCA 1999b, 1999c) which, in theory at least, holds equal status with externally designed and marked Standard Attainment Tasks (SATs). The focus within SATs largely requires recall of factual information which has led to 'coaching' and 'teaching to the tests'. Some aspects of the scientific process, such as interpreting data, are assessed within the tests, but these items tend to be those aspects of the scientific process that can be taught by didactic methods. Other aspects of scientific enquiry such as observation, the ability to ask questions or to record data accurately is currently assessed through more subjective teacher assessment. Whilst there is little formal evidence to suggest that teachers emphasise those aspects of science assessed through the tests, it is generally believed that this is the case at KS2, especially in Year 6.

Examination of official documentation reveals two other causes for concern about the state of science in the primary classroom: firstly, concerns related to pupil performance in National Curriculum assessments; and secondly, those contained within OFSTED reports on primary schools. Reports of pupil performance on SATs (QCA 1998c) suggest that children at the end of KS2 are, at least on the surface, achieving target levels in science. Performance judged in relation to Attainment Target level descriptions presupposes that the levels are gauged correctly in relation to the science Programmes of Study. Scrutiny of QCA Reports (QCA 1998b, 1998c,) however, provide food for thought. A comparison of pupil achievement for mathematics, English and science for 1998 reveals the following pattern:

Table 4.1 English, mathematics and science national results, Key Stage 2 1998 (percentages of cohort at each level)

Test Level	Below 3	3	4	5	6
English	6%	26%	48%	17%	0%
Maths	7%	31%	42%	17%	0%
Science	4%	23%	53%	16%	0%

Source: QCA 1998c

Analysis of the above table suggests that not only are children doing well in science in terms of test performance, but that they are performing better in science than in English and mathematics. Hence the lack of 'official' concern about children's performance in science and in the progress of science. This pattern is reflected in similar data provided for 1997 (QCA 1998b). In fact, there appears to have been an improvement in children's performance in science over those years and QCA(1998c) claim that:

> Raising standards of achievement is our top priority. The national targets of 80% of 11-year-olds reaching level 4 in English and 75 % in Mathematics by 2002 are both demanding and ambitious, but they are also achievable.
>
> (QCA 1998c)

That there is no similar target for science is interesting as pupils' performance at level 4 or above in science in 1998 was below 70 per cent. Furthermore, figures show that the proportion of children achieving level 4 and above has increased steadily since 1996. Why, therefore, given that science is a core subject, has no similar target been set?

Concurrently, QCA's (1998b) own analysis of data reveals disturbing gaps in pupil understanding of science at the end of Key Stage 2. These relate particularly to aspects of the processes of science. For example, 'describing relationships between variables' where 'just over a quarter of children, on average, produced full, clear answers ... a further 10–15% of children provided partial answers'. Regrettably, this leaves, at best, 60 per cent of 11-year-old children unable to describe the relationship between variables.

Later analysis of data reveals that 'as in both 1996 and 1997, questions assessing life process and living things were answered more successfully than questions related to materials and their properties, whilst questions assessing physical properties were answered less well' (QCA 1998c). This is a worrying finding, given that questions relating to 'life processes and living things' are more likely to be answered successfully by rote than questions about 'materials and their properties' or 'physical processes'. These are more difficult conceptually and less well answered merely by recall of knowledge.

Disturbingly, specific recommendations for future practice highlight significant weaknesses in pupil performance on SATs (QCA 1998b). Within the 'Implications for Teaching and Learning' section of the report, out of the three general and seven specific recommendations four suggest that pupils need more specific 'hands-on experience' in order to improve their understanding.

A worryingly small percentage of schools participated in the independent evaluation of the 1998 SATs (QCA 1998c). Out of 544 schools selected for the survey, 214 agreed to participate in the investigation. From these, 513 questionnaires were returned by teachers and headteachers from 138 of the schools, which was a 25 per cent response rate. Within the survey, aspects of teacher assessment were investigated. Evaluators found that teachers claimed to use the following techniques when making assessments. These are ranked in decreasing order of perceived performance:

- regular assessment of children's work during the Key Stage
- informal day-to-day observations
- assessment of specific tasks
- use of previous years' statutory tests and tasks
- children's results on teacher devised tests
- portfolios and samples of work
- performance on the 1998 tests

Evaluators commented that the 'list conceals the findings that different aspects are very important to different teachers'. It was suggested, for example, that about 30 per cent of Year 6 teachers found current statutory test results essential for producing evidence in making teacher assessments.

Evidence in OFSTED Reports suggests that much needs to be done to create improvement in many schools, especially in relation to scientific enquiry. There is a worrying, but officially approved of, discrepancy in relation to the amount of time pupils spend on English, mathematics and science. OFSTED (1999) reported that the 1994 Dearing Review of the National Curriculum had enabled schools to build up stable and appropriate patterns of teaching. For example, the report showed that primary schools were devoting 40–50 per cent of their time teaching the key subjects of English and mathematics, 10 per cent to science and other time spread evenly between other subjects.

In their most recent review of primary education, OFSTED (1999) report that standards of achievement in science had risen between 1994 and 1998 and that from their perspective, teacher confidence and expertise had grown. However, standards in experimental and investigative science were considered variable. Inspectors reported excellent investigative work in some schools, but that able pupils at Key Stage 2 were not always given the opportunities to achieve the higher levels of which they were capable. On the quality of teaching, the report stated that for some years after the introduction of the National Curriculum, science teaching was weaker at Key Stage 2 than at Key Stage 1. This was said to be because many teachers who lacked qualifications in science struggled with the concepts and methodology involved. Difficulties, they said, were greatest in physical science. However, 'a combination of training, self-help and the clarification provided by feedback from tests has greatly improved the knowledge base of teachers', but 'where teachers stay well within their sphere of confidence, this can result in narrow lesson objectives, a restricted range of teaching approaches and an undue emphasis of factual information' (OFSTED 1999: 13–14).

The review acknowledged and appeared to approve the fact that there had been a reduction in the time spent on science from 'up to 20 per cent' when the National Curriculum was first introduced to 'typically 10 per cent of taught time at Key Stage 1 and a little more at Key Stage 2'. The latter, they considered is 'sufficient to cover the programme of study'. The review admits that national tests have had an impact on the curriculum – 'they have given teachers a clearer idea of what pupils are expected to know and do and have sharpened teaching' – but 'many schools spend a substantial amount of time on revision for tests in Year 6; at best this consolidates pupils' knowledge and broadens their understanding but can, when too closely focused on test items, be unproductive' (OFSTED 1999).

Much colloquial evidence too, indicates that there is a lack of emphasis on scientific enquiry. Harlen's view is that:

> The preference given to assessing knowledge in the national tests has tended to push practice towards emphasising content … there is a tendency for teachers to give more attention to what is to be tested and so rather less to practical work and investigative skills.
>
> (Harlen 1998: 27)

Currently, The Nuffield Foundation is funding research into the needs of teachers teaching science at primary level. Researchers are looking at 'what is going on' in terms of teaching science in four geographical regions. They seek to identify the kind of support that teachers need to improve their practice. Murphy (1999a) reported seven identified trends:

- teachers plan by content, not by objectives
- science is embedded in plans, but not articulated in learning objectives
- QCA scheme of work (1998d) is used widely by teachers
- the emphasis on SATs has meant a separation of Sc1 from Sc2, 3, and 4, i.e. the processes of science from other programmes of study
- at KS1, science is served 'on a plate'
- at KS2, 'we sit them down and make them learn'
- the view that 'you don't need Sc1 to get good SATs results' is widely held

Findings of other work tend to support the above and led Cassidy (1999) to conclude that science is being 'sacrificed on the "altar of Literacy"'. Stout and Tymms (1999) researching on behalf of the Association for Science Education, undertook a national survey which sought to find out the impact of the introduction of the Literacy hour on the teaching of science in schools at Key Stages 1 and 2. Analysis of over 600 responses to the survey reveals that since the introduction of the literacy hour:

- the average number of hours dedicated to science at KS1 and 2 had declined;
- 60 per cent of respondents expressed concern about the adverse effect the literacy hour was having on science;
- 47 per cent of respondents reported that science based INSET had been postponed due to literacy training.

Specific responses were disquieting:

'Literacy takes a disproportionate amount of time. Science is rapidly losing its momentum and its significance in the curriculum.'
'I really feel the clock is ticking. If you don't understand a concept first time – well hard luck, as we're moving on without you.'
'Science is one of the most enthusiastically embraced subjects by primary children, but I am very worried about the future of science in primary schools.'
(Stout and Tymms 1999)

Since the introduction of the numeracy strategy in September 1999, it is likely that the situation in relation to science has become even more difficult as teachers concentrate their efforts on English and mathematics.

Conclusion

In theory, science is a core subject within the National Curriculum and thus forms an important part of children's learning at KS1 and 2. However, in practice science does not enjoy the same status as English and mathematics. Essentially, pupil learning and achievement in science depends on pupils' understanding and knowledge of English and mathematics, and increasingly upon aspects of information and communications technology. Science, though, offers a further dimension to intellectual development which is significantly different from any other subject in the primary curriculum. Unlike all other subjects, science provides children with the opportunity to hypothesise and test their ideas by practical investigation. Under the National Curriculum, children of primary age, have a statutory entitlement to engage with scientific methods while acquiring knowledge about scientific topics. Evidence suggests that entitlement to continuous and progressive exposure to this aspect of learning in science is frequently missing from the diet of many children, especially at KS2. Part of the reason for this is the current emphasis on English and mathematics. The reduction in the status of science, in relation to English and mathematics, within the National Curriculum and the decrease in time allowed for science are interrelated and have conspired against the inclusion of a more practical approach to science. Since the introduction of the National Curriculum in 1988, there has been a marked and officially approved reduction in the time devoted to science in the primary classroom at KS1 and 2. Simultaneously and indirectly perhaps, this has led to a significant reduction in the nature of the science taught, i.e. the emphasis on the acquisition of 'facts to be stored' at the expense of the more practical aspects of the subject. 'Process' and 'content' seem to have become divorced from each other, and teachers appear not to recognise the interrelated nature of these two aspects of science.

Time must be devoted to practical work, including scientific investigation, if it is to be effective in supporting children's development in science, especially if children are to have their ideas challenged. Unfortunately, evidence suggests that little time is devoted to the promotion of this aspect of learning in science.

Currently, the primary curriculum is assessment-led. Many teachers appear reluctant, or unwilling, to include the whole range of opportunities for children's learning in science because the assessment procedures relating to some aspects of pupil achievement in science are not specific enough and are not prescribed to the same degree as others. It may well be that some class teachers may not necessarily be aware of the importance of the development of process skills.

Four things need to be done immediately to improve the situation:

1 The status of science needs to be raised to equal that of English and mathematics.
2 Time needs to be ring-fenced to provide enough opportunity for practical work to be developed to its logical conclusion. That is, there needs to be a government recommended time allowance, per week, which equals or exceeds that of English or mathematics.
3 Teachers need to increase the frequency of assessment of pupils' performance in science process skills.
4 Compulsory practical tests should be introduced for all pupils at the end of Key Stages 1 and 2.

There might be some resistance amongst some teachers to these proposals. Many would need support to implement such changes, but these measures would immediately raise the status of science and increase the opportunities teachers provide for children to engage in the scientific process.

Questions

1 What strategies can be employed, in schools, to increase the awareness of teachers of the importance of the practical aspects of science?
2 How can teachers be helped, not only to provide appropriate opportunities for practical activity, but also to track the development of children's process skills?
3 How can the status of primary science be raised in a wider context?

Further reading

Harlen, W. (1997) *The Teaching of Science in Primary Schools*, 2nd edn, London: David Fulton.

In this book, Professor Harlen draws on her extensive experience and understanding of research into theory and practice in primary science. She not only examines the nature of science and primary science, but also provides readers with many ideas to challenge and extend the understanding of even the most experienced of teachers in the primary sector.

Newton, L.D. and Newton, D.P. (1998) *Coordinating Science Across the Primary School,* London: Falmer Press.

This book, aimed at those with a responsibility for the 'whole school' approach to science, provides advice about the complex issues of improving teaching and learning in science through effective management of science in the primary school. This book provides an invaluable aid to guide the whole school development of science in the primary school.

5 Balanced science
A battle still to be won?

John Sears

Introduction

The history of science education reveals a recurring conflict between the views of process-oriented and content-oriented protagonists; between specialists and generalists. For most of its history, science as a curriculum subject has not had an automatic place in the curriculum for all pupils, and today the argument continues as to whether all pupils should pursue a broad and balanced course of study to the age of sixteen. There is increasing pressure to reduce the amount of science in the curriculum and so it seems pertinent to look again at the arguments surrounding the idea of 'science for all from 5–16'.

Underlying all these debates is the fundamental question: 'Why should pupils learn science at all?' Science education has not always been seen to be important in the formation of an educated person, and even today there are many who think its importance is overrated in a postmodern world.

Assuming that we can justify the inclusion of science as a curriculum subject, the second most important question is: 'What sort of science should pupils be taught?' This includes questions of emphasis between different philosophies of science as well as the balance of the content of different science specialisms. More recently, this area has raised the issue of the purpose of science education, especially at KS4. Should we be tailoring different courses at this stage for pupils who are going to become technicians or artists from courses for those who are going to become scientists?

Finally, there is the question of the amount of science. This was one of the key questions the School Science Curriculum Review (SSCR) tried to answer when balanced science was first advocated:

> In what ways can a broad and balanced science education be provided for all our young people without distorting the balance of their overall curricular provision?
>
> (SSCR, 1987)

The historical debate

There is little new in the debate concerning balanced science for all. As far back as the great exhibition in 1851, debate had become focused on the need to provide science education for workers to help us compete with France and Germany. The profits of the exhibition led to the formation of the Science and Art Department, which established a system of science classes based around the idea of a 'science of common things' that was intended to give manual workers a good enough education to make them a more useful workforce.

Public schools, by contrast, had developed in a tradition dedicated to the training of the mind. In this tradition, few saw that an education in natural science had much to offer a pupil. As late as 1864 the headmaster of Winchester is quoted as saying: 'I think, except on the part of those who have a taste for the physical sciences and intend to pursue them as amateurs or professionally, such instruction is worthless as education' (quoted in HMSO 1960: 8–9).

During the latter half of the nineteenth century, the debate over the introduction of science teaching gathered pace. Supporters such as Herbert Spencer and Thomas Huxley from outside the public schools system and Dean Farrar from within strongly argued the case for the inclusion of science as part of a balanced curriculum, and that this science should cover all aspects of natural science. Huxley in particular had much to say concerning the justification for scientific and technical education as a means for people to 'get on' in society:

> no boy or girl should leave school without possessing a grasp of the general character of science, and ... the methods of all sciences; ... being familiar with the general current of scientific thought, and ... able to apply the methods of science in the proper way ...
>
> (Huxley 1869, quoted in Bibby 1971: 102)

H.E. Armstrong, who was also a strong advocate of the need to teach science experimentally, wrote about the breadth of scientific studies:

> In my opinion, no single branch of natural science should be selected to be taught as part of the ordinary school course but the instruction should comprise the elements of what I have already spoken of as the science of daily life and should include astronomy, botany, chemistry, geology, mechanics, physics, physiology and zoology ...
>
> (Armstrong 1884)

After the First World War, a committee of the British Association expressed surprise at the neglect of the teaching of science as a 'body of inspiring principles and truly humanising influence', and along with a committee chaired by Sir J.J. Thompson recommended broader based courses taking account of the interests of pupils. This attitude led to the vogue for general science courses that persisted for many years. At the same time the introduction of the Higher School Certificate in 1918 (a forerunner of A-levels) introduced a contrary pressure for earlier specialisation. These courses required a more detailed background than the general science that existed at the time. This top-down pressure was a strong force for the introduction of specialist courses in the separate sciences, and such courses were encouraged by the introduction in 1951 of GCE exams at age 16.

The introduction of CSE exams, the spread of comprehensive schools and the raising of the school-leaving age all contributed to concentrate educational developments on the 'less able' pupil. A variety of more vocationally oriented schemes were produced: the LAMP topics by ASE, Science at Work and the Nuffield Secondary Science Scheme are typical examples. All these schemes were based on modules or units of work which covered topics in familiar and relevant settings from across the broad range of sciences. Thus it was that by the end of the 1970s, most maintained schools were operating a system of separate sciences within an options scheme for the 'more able' pupils and a general, or integrated (usually modular), science course for the 'less able'. These developments provided a springboard of experience in the provision of a new type of general science and fitted into an increasing demand for science for all to the age of 16.

Most recently, changes from GCE and CSE to GCSE exams, the introduction of the National Curriculum (NC) and the devolving of financial power to schools and Governors has all affected science education. The major thrust of this has been that by 1993, 20 per cent of the curriculum was devoted to science at Key Stage 4 (KS4) and studied by 87 per cent of pupils nationally, and science for all existed from 5–16. This broad and balanced science has thus had a major impact on staffing, costs and the management of curriculum time. The NC basis of the science has also been developed with considerable input from science educators and its structure embodies a philosophical approach which, despite many revisions, still exists.

Why study science at all?

As can be seen from the brief history outlined previously, science education has been supported from a number of different perspectives. The debates over the purposes, audience and type of science education continue and the nature of the arguments would be familiar to Armstrong or Huxley.

The debate over purpose is fundamental. Why should children learn science? There are a number of strands of thought, not necessarily mutually exclusive, in answer to this question. There is a long tradition of the instrumental view that the country needs scientists to be able to compete internationally. Comparisons would seem to suggest that as a country we are good at producing top-flight pure scientists, but less good at producing engineers and skilled technicians. Many of those who in other countries go on in these fields drop out of science in the UK (Smithers and Robinson 1991). However, it is not clear that there is any direct link between the number of scientists and engineers and a country's success economically, so to justify science education simply in terms of instrumental purposes would seem to be a poor basis for including science in the curriculum.

A second line of argument is the 'science for daily life' view put forward since the mid-nineteenth century. On this view, children need to study science in order to understand the world around them. This is the view that considers science to be a system of well-established, non-controversial truths, which pupils need to know in order to understand the world in which they live.

Many of those who argued for science for all did so, however, in the hope that it would be based on a fundamentally different approach from previous syllabuses and programmes of study. West in particular argued that the current style of science education had failed:

> I have known people with good O- and A-level passes in science subjects get themselves sunburnt, mess up their marriages, go broke, buy the wrong food, spread gastro-enteritis, and generally fail to make sense of their fast-changing world.
>
> To what extent do existing science courses openly encourage lateral thinking, creativity, imaginative insights, the questioning of authorities, or any other form of scholastic 'deviancy'?
>
> (West 1981: 231–2)

As a result, West proposed a core based around five areas of scientific study: self, society, environment, self-sufficiency and creativity. Other authors have suggested different headings for the core, but whatever the suggested contents were to be, all are based on the notion that since people are surrounded by science, and since governments need to make decisions based on scientific research, then pupils should be taught enough science for them to participate in an informed way. This was a move away from just understanding your world, to the view that science is a value-laden human activity and that there is a need to understand the issues in a political context. Recently this view has been shown to have relevance in the debates on ethical questions raised by new technologies such as genetically modified foods. Much of the commentary in the media, written by people with little scientific training, has been hysterical and uninformed. Arguably, a better scientifically educated population would be able to have a more rational debate about technology.

A third argument for the inclusion of science is that it is a way of thinking. According to this view, the key point of science education is to encourage rational thought and a particular approach to the explanation of natural phenomena. Many laid claim to the underlying unity of the sciences in terms of its methodology or epistemology (Hall 1969; Richmond 1974; Prestt 1976a, 1976b). Historically, much of this debate became polarised around the issue of content and process, but at a deeper level was really a debate about epistemology. What is it that makes something a science? What kind of thinking or worldview characterises science?

In the past, some science courses have been based in a particular philosophical approach and view of what it is to be scientific. The Nuffield courses were based on the neo-heuristic view of 'learning by discovery', a Brunerian approach, but they were also influenced by Piaget's views of developmental stages. They clearly argued for a hypothetico-deductive approach, although this was rarely translated into practice for pupils.

It is perhaps surprising, given his influence on scientific thought, that Karl Popper's view of science does not appear to be the basis for any major educational development, although as Cawthron and Rowell say:

Nevertheless many students emerging from secondary science schooling ... respond strongly in the affirmative when asked whether scientific method is the critical testing of theories ... and the Popperian model ... is highly attractive ... as a view both of how science 'is' and how it 'should be'.

(Cawthron and Rowell 1978: 36)

Another approach to defining science as a particular way of thinking was provided by Paul Hirst. His notion of knowledge was that it consisted of distinct 'areas of experience' each with its own form of 'truth' and methods for arriving at and verifying that truth. In his scheme, the sciences were separated into two realms, 'the physical sciences' and 'the human sciences and history'. This division of the sciences was also pursued by Shayer and Adey, who argued that the methodologies and approaches of the physical and biological sciences are fundamentally different.

However we try to categorise scientific method, it is clear from the many recent sociological critiques of science that there is no definitive scientific method which is easy to uphold and teach and this in part accounts for a lack of clear epistemology in most published schemes of science education. Consequently, many rejected the notion of methodological unity but argued for a conceptual unity instead. Layton in 1973 put the case for 'the need to reassert the utility of science knowledge' and continued: 'the prime aim of science education is the induction of learners into the scientist's view of the world and the acquisition of scientific ideas and skills which will be serviceable in a variety of situations' (Layton 1973: 23).

In this view, there are simply current ideas and a variety of skills and attitudes to explanation that constitute being scientific, rather than a single unified method or approach. This is a much more Kuhnian view of science as a social activity, working for the most part within a generally accepted paradigm. A final part of this argument proposes the view of science as a cultural activity. In this approach, science education is seen as part of an overall approach to understanding not just the natural world, but the human condition.

What sort of science?

Assuming that we have established the need to teach science, the next question is what sort of science should we teach? One major group which influenced the development of balanced science was the SSCR. Its overall framework for balanced science had four strands. The first was *breadth*, which was taken to include factual information, concepts, applications and economics, skills and processes, and attitudes. The second strand was *balance*, which was taken to be the proper weighting of the factors in breadth, a range of teaching methods, equal opportunities, and to be considered in relation to the whole period of schooling as well as within a particular year. The third strand was *coherence*, which was a plea for making logical interconnections explicit to pupils so that proper progression could result. The final strand was *relevance*, being an attempt to base the curriculum on 'the environment and the experience of the pupils themselves'.

From its analysis, the SSCR came to produce a set of sixteen key proposals for science education. Importantly these suggested the following:

1   ... Every young person ... is entitled to science education ... up to the age of 16.
2   ... science studies ... occupy 10 per cent ... from age 11 to age 13, 15 per cent in the year from age 13 to age 14, and 20 per cent of the curriculum time across years 14–16.
3   ... The approach to science studies should display structural coherence, continuity and balance ...
8   ... content ... should be reduced radically so that ... The areas studied are thoroughly understood ... A better balance is achieved between content/knowledge and skills/processes ... Economic, environmental, political and social implications receive adequate attention ... Post-16 provision is enhanced ...

(SSCR 1987)

Accepting science for all from 5–16 raised a variety of issues. One of these was that few primary schools taught science at all. This was at the heart of the move to give pupils an entitlement to science education in the primary sector. HMI had a substantial influence on the thinking in relation to content and suggested the following for the primary school: 'pupils need to grow accustomed ... to the scientific processes of observing, measuring, describing, investigating, predicting, experimenting and explaining' (DES 1985: 8–9).

This notion that primary science is largely experiential, experimentally based and should 'arise from children's spontaneous interests', is one that became embedded in the early versions of the NC, although more recent revisions have placed greater emphasis on content. It seems right and proper to devote time and energy in getting children to approach relevant issues through investigation at an early age. The importance is to get them to think rather than just to memorise scientific facts.

At secondary school, early specialisation resulted in very different choices being made by boys and girls and more fundamentally the majority of pupils opting out of science almost completely. Consequently, the argument for broad and balanced science moved forward becoming incorporated into the issue of equal opportunity and a common core for all. In a study of curricular provision for boys and girls, HMI stated:

It may be that society can justify the striking differences that exist between the subjects studied by boys and girls in secondary schools, but it is more likely that a society that needs to develop to the full the talents and skills of all its people will find the discrepancies disturbing.

(HMSO 1975)

It is still not universally accepted that all children should be taught science from ages 5–16, and there is still a debate about giving an early choice to pupils.

This would allow pupils to take subjects they enjoy and not be forced to take aspects of science they do not like, or are not very good at. Chapman (1976) argued that a common curriculum to age sixteen was a denial of choice ensuring forced study of areas of little interest to pupils. He suggested that postponing choice did not make it easier or better. Thus separate grades in separate science exams will prevent a good biologist having their overall grades reduced by a poor showing in the physical sciences. The main argument against this is that choice allows pupils to opt out and reinforces stereotypes. Wallace (1994), in a survey for the Association for Science Education (ASE), found that where pupils were allowed to opt between single and double award science that many opted out of double award and that this was significantly more marked for girls than for boys. It is still the case that boys outnumber girls in the physical sciences by four to one at A-level, and there is no reason to believe this would not still be true at GCSE if choice were given.

Some arguments for changes at KS4 centre on the difficulty of science for all. Surely our less able pupils need a more vocational course especially tailored for their needs? Surely some pupils need to do less science because they cannot cope with what is on offer? This move has already resulted in some pupils being able to pursue vocational courses pre-16, and there is every indication that more flexibility will be allowed. This brings us back to the instrumental view of the curriculum and against this we need to clearly restate the idea of entitlement. As White, as long ago as 1969, said:

> If most children will later have to do jobs which are not intellectually demanding, there is no reason why they should be taught only those things which will make them efficient workers – and perhaps efficient consumers and law-abiding citizens as well.

Unless we are prepared to argue that we really believe that for some children education that is not job related is pointless after 14, we cannot argue for school based vocational courses that segregate out our pupils. It may be that the science curriculum for all should be more vocationally based, but that is a different argument.

Others have approached the debate from the need to produce good specialist scientists, arguing that balanced science does not provide a good enough base for A-level study. They would make the case that those who wish to go on and study science at A-level should take separate science GCSEs. Evidence does not support this view. A study of Hampshire Sixth Form Colleges (Macfarlane 1992) showed that there was no connection between GCSE science background and final results at GCE A-level. More recent evidence, which shows that those pupils from a double award background do less well in science A-levels than those from separate subject backgrounds, also concluded that this was not to do with the syllabus studied since these pupils also did less well in other A-level subjects. It was concluded that there must be whole school differences which accounted for differential performance at A-level (DfE 1994a).

How much science?

How much time science should occupy in the curriculum is problematic. At the moment, in primary schools under pressure from the literacy hour and the numeracy hour, the amount of time devoted to teaching science has dropped. Nonetheless, most pupils are getting between 5–10 per cent a week of their curriculum time devoted to science in their first six years at school. This is a significant improvement on the past, and gives grounds for optimism that science education is truly embedded in the curriculum.

At secondary level, most pupils study science for 10–15 per cent of the curriculum in years 7–9 and for 20 per cent in years 10 and 11. What then is the problem? The secretary of state for education recently asked people to consider ways in which curriculum time could be freed up at KS4, and the obvious solution (as the major user of curriculum time) is to downgrade the notion of 20 per cent science for all.

The main thrust of the argument is that we need to allow some pupils with particular aptitudes to devote more time to different studies such as languages or the creative arts. Provision of single award science already allows for such an option, although in the past it has been specified that this option would only be expected to be used by a minority of pupils. However, the single science option currently does not do justice to those who study it in terms of entitlement due to its bizarre content selection. Moreover we should defend the 20 per cent time allocation as being necessary for concept and skills development in what is a wide-ranging curriculum area. The subject matter covers the basic explanations and current beliefs of a major component of Western culture, and one on which much of our current wealth and comfort depends. It also covers an approach to explanation which requires rational thought backed by tested empirical evidence. These are high-level, abstract ways of working and require long periods of time to be developed successfully.

How then can we broaden the curriculum for the non-scientist? One way is to build much stronger cross-curricular links with other departments. Science has natural links with maths, geography and technology and it should be possible to teach aspects of these subjects through carefully constructed programmes. There are also links with the history of certain periods, and again this could be built into an imaginative curriculum. Science ought also to be one of the major vehicles for developing core skills without which pupils' own understanding of the science they study will be impaired. The answer, in other words, to the question of increased flexibility is imaginative curriculum design, not hacking about at the time allocations of entrenched subject empires.

Conclusion

The case for science as a core subject, as part of our main cultural tradition is clear. The need for such an extensive content area, derived from such a fundamentally important way of thinking, to require substantial periods of curriculum time is also clear. What is important, though, is that we do not just see science as an isolated, fenced-off part of the curriculum into which we as teachers smugly retire, confident of the importance of our contribution. Rather, we should be contributing to imaginative projects which will ensure the health of science in the curriculum and which will allow pupils to see science as inter-linked and inextricably interwoven with other aspects of our educational tradition.

The case for balanced science lies embedded in the arguments of entitlement and equal opportunities. If we want to give choice and opportunity to all at later stages in their career, we should not allow them to opt out of science early. Neither should we go along with the instrumental arguments that would segregate our pupils into vocational and academic, a distinction that is dubious at best, with each pathway having different esteem and social value. Gender stereotypes are also reinforced by early decision making and if we believe that education has any place in generating change then we should not revert to systems that disadvantage pupils by allowing stereotypical expectations to control their choices.

Questions

1 Is science for all still relevant from 5–16?
2 Should the type of science for all remain the same?
3 Is there a case for reducing content and studying examples of science at KS4, rather as historians study selected eras?
4 To what extent should arguments based on considerations of equal opportunity be the determining factor for the content?

Further reading

Chalmers, A.F. (1999) *What is this Thing called Science?*, Buckingham: Open University Press.
    An excellent introduction to the historical nature of science and how explanations of its methodology have defied definition

DES (1985) *Science 5–16: A Statement of Policy*, London: HMSO.
    Still one of the best explications of the basis of the science for all policy.

SSCR (1987) *Better Science*, London: Heinemann/ASE.
    An excellent set of books containing the arguments and philosophy behind the balanced science movement as well as strategies for teaching and learning.

6   Lifelong learning in science
Dream or reality?

Vanessa Barker

The need for lifelong learning in science was made clear to me by a recent conversation with a woman called Mary, who runs a travel recruitment business. She was intrigued to hear I worked in science education and, without warning, presented me with a bag of crisps, saying, 'You're a scientist, tell me if these are good for me!' Mary thought my science education made me an expert equipped to pronounce with confidence on crisps as 'good' or 'bad' food. I could be an expert in a completely unrelated area of science and so know nothing about the food value of crisps, but this did not occur to her. I had acquired competence in science, I used my knowledge in a professional capacity and would surely 'know' about crisps, while she felt incapable of making such a decision. Nevertheless, her asking the question suggests she was unsettled by a sense of ignorance about science, and wanted to 'know science' in a lifelong, useful way. Rather than equip her for life, Mary's science education had no meaning for her after school. Mary would perhaps agree with the statement: 'The things you do in school are to do with education and to get jobs. You're not really using them in actual real life' (A Birmingham 18-year-old, quoted in Bentley 1998).

This poignant remark reflects a key perception among young people of the role of formal education. An acknowledgement of this came from The European Commission (European Union 1995), which set out a vision for education to involve the extension of learning relationships to all stages of people's lives, suggesting that learning should become lifelong, rather than remain mainly school-based. Successive UK governments took up this theme, leading to the recent publication of *Learning to Succeed* (DfEE 1999a), which describes a new framework for post-16 learning. More specifically the discussion paper *Open Science* (ASE 1995) made the case that the post-16 curriculum should include science as a major area of specialisation and form part of everyone's lifelong learning. The issue debated here is the extent to which the current system and proposed changes will enable post-16 science education to participate effectively in the current fashionable drive towards lifelong learning.

How well does science suit lifelong learning?

In order to be successful in any lifelong learning model for education, science has to solve a major problem; how to be accessible as a subject to more people than the 'experts'. Mary's 'bag of crisps' indicated a belief that specialist knowledge beyond her own understanding was needed to obtain the answer to the problem. Thus, there is a tension between accessibility and the perception of exclusivity. In the UK, science education has attempted to improve the accessibility of science in one sense by first introducing a 'science for all' philosophy, the success of which has at least ensured 'bums on seats'. The merging of CSE and O-level into GCSE provided a science examination at 16 accessible, in theory at least, to all students. Yet despite these changes, science has retained its rather exclusive image resulting in a decline in recruitment to university courses in science relative to other subjects (Mason 1998). Few adult students opt to take formal science courses later in life. These points suggest that although access to science pre-16 has improved, the exclusivity remains. To suit lifelong learning, 'accessibility' must mean more than simply providing more science lessons in school.

Let us explore what 'accessible' might mean in a lifelong learning sense. The conversation with Mary provides a useful illustration by considering how she may have solved the problem herself. On realising that she wanted to know about the food value of crisps, Mary could have exercised a spirit of enquiry and carried out some research. This requires that she would know where to look, and what to look for. Next, she would need some understanding of what she might find out about crisps, so a level of technical competence and analysis in terms of food components, energy values, the role of fat in the diet, would be needed. Finally she requires an ability to process the information into an answer which was meaningful for her in the everyday sense. Thus, 'accessible' science would have three characteristics: a spirit of enquiry, acquisition of appropriate knowledge and everyday application.

Of course, there is another problem science must address: that of the 'need to know'. Knowledge and understanding of science is unnecessary in order to live. Unless she had some terrible problem metabolising fat, Mary would have lived perfectly well without ever asking me about crisps. In driving a car, we do not need to know that the energy for its movement comes from chemical bonds being made in a chemical reaction. We use computers and watch television without understanding the science behind electricity generation and how the equipment works. Although an unease with this situation can be detected, most people do not have a desire for scientific knowledge; the effort required to understand what are perceived to be 'technical' and 'hard' ideas is too much. So, lifelong learning in science must also capture a motivation for acquiring knowledge.

The influence of the science curriculum

> The day I went into physics class it was death. A short, dark man with a high lisping voice, named Mr Manzi, stood in front of the class in a tight blue suit holding a little wooden ball. He put the ball on a steep grooved slide and let it run down to the bottom. Then he started talking about let *a* equal acceleration and let *t* equal time and suddenly he was scribbling letters and numbers and equals signs all over the blackboard and my mind went dead.
>
> (Sylvia Plath, quoted in Claxton 1991: 21)

The pre-16 curriculum provides clues about the feasibility of science as a life-long learning subject. A typical science lesson provides an illustration. A competent beginning teacher, a biologist, was seen teaching a Year 10 physics lesson to a 'low ability' group, small in number, in a north London comprehensive school. The students spent much time plotting data obtained during an 'investigation' carried out in the previous lesson. The teacher showed the students how to use their calculators; to use the graph paper and finally to present the graph neatly, with a title, and write a conclusion. No one understood any aspect of the science concept involved: the resistance of wires. The exercise, collection of data by experiment, the writing up and the science behind this had lost all its intended meaning. Post-lesson discussion revealed that the beginning teacher was aware of the limitations of the lesson, but was following the 'scheme of work' and had felt powerless to prompt change.

A brief analysis of this incident suggests that the students were being presented with completely inappropriate science content knowledge: it was dominated by theoretical content and technical jargon, was wrapped in a complex procedure which obscured the meaning, and appeared to be completely irrelevant to any perceptible need or event they may have experienced. Inspection of the scheme of work showed the topic was organised through a series of lessons, each taking one aspect of the 'Physical Processes' section of the National Curriculum for Science (DfE 1995a). The approach did not generate lessons likely to contribute to lifelong learning. Science was presented as a body of knowledge comprising facts and theories (mostly ending up being presented as facts) to be 'learned'. Despite the work of curriculum developers from the 1960s onwards, much science taught today is not dissimilar to that experienced by Sylvia Plath. Robin Millar reflects:

> if teaching science is really the transmission of a body of consensually accepted knowledge, what is its value as general education? ... The pedagogical danger is that teaching becomes an arid business of rote learning of standard facts, theories and methods. The epistemological danger is that it makes science look like infallible, received knowledge.
>
> (Millar 1989: 58)

Of course, the National Curriculum makes no statement about *how* its content should be transmitted, only that it *should* be. Nevertheless, the content is a detailed, intense list with no reference to everyday relevance or sense of appropriateness for the recipients. Investigations form another strand of the pre-16 curriculum. Many schools now adopt a highly mechanistic approach to this, first by teaching the skills needed, then telling pupils with varying degrees of explicitness 'how to do it'. Teachers admit willingly to this from a concern to ensure the highest possible coursework marks for students and so maximise the possibility for their achievement of high final grades in the GCSE examination. The post-16 curriculum adopts a similar approach. The present curriculum does not meet the accessibility criteria established above. To achieve lifelong learning in science, change is needed: 'If learning science is to be part of a lifelong learning process, it has to be freed from the constraints associated with a body of knowledge and practice becoming a school subject' (Young and Glanfield 1998: 4).

School science at all levels is based around the theoretical content and abstract concepts perceived as acquired, required or used by practising scientists. Thus, the mystique of science as performed by 'experts' who understand these ideas is retained, because clearly the content and its presentation are too frequently far removed from the abilities and needs of the target audience. Even the most committed and able teacher finds students for whom science is 'too difficult', 'boring' and 'irrelevant'. Hence, adults such as Mary 'need' to ask a scientist, or remain content to rest with their ignorance. We cannot achieve lifelong learning in science with the present approach.

Young and Glanfield suggest that a curriculum framework capable of delivering lifelong learning in science be based on 'an analysis and prediction of what young people and adults will need to know to play a part in shaping the society of the future'. A similar view formed the basis for discussion among participants in a seminar series organised by the Nuffield Foundation. The report *Beyond 2000*, edited by Millar and Osborne (1998) on behalf of participants, begins:

> This report ... is driven by a sense of growing disparity between the science education provided in our schools and the needs and interests of the young people who will be our future citizens ... the rapid pace of technological change and the globalisation of the market place have resulted in a need for individuals who have a broad general education, good communication skills, adaptability and a commitment to lifelong learning. Our view is that the form of science education we currently offer is outmoded ...
>
> (Millar and Osborne 1998: 2001)

The report makes ten recommendations for a future science curriculum and suggests that the pre-16 curriculum be based around achieving 'scientific literacy', that is, a 'populace who are comfortable, competent and confident with scientific and technical matters and artefacts'.

They propose that this be achieved by presenting science as 'explanatory stories' focusing on the major ideas in science, rather than on excessive detail, together with the inclusion of relevant aspects of technology and applications of science. If scientists and science educators could agree on content able to achieve the literacy so defined, this may deliver the appropriate knowledge and a sense of everyday application necessary for lifelong learning. A variety of teaching strategies to permit research and the development of historical discussion, allowing students to gain perspectives of the place of science in the wider context would be required. Reduction in content, allowing it to be 'all right' for everyone not to know, for example, about the resistance of wires, would benefit many students and teachers, in theory making time available for the other aspects and approaches. *Beyond 2000* gives cause for cautious optimism. If the recommendations were adopted, further change post-16 would be inevitable.

The influence of assessment

> The assessment system should encourage the development of skills and capabilities which will be required for future employment in the 21st century … attention should be devoted to the assessment of those skills and competencies that are required in adult life both at work and for 'lifelong learning'.
>
> (Millar and Osborne 1998: 2025)

In England and Wales, GCE A-levels are the most popular examinations taken by 16–19-year-old students. Commonly, post-16 students select three related subjects. This has led to accusations of a narrow and too specialised post-16 curriculum. In the 1980s, the introduction of GCSE together with declining work opportunities led to increasing participation in A-levels. This was followed by a growing sense of dissatisfaction with the appropriateness of A-levels for the increasingly mixed ability clientele. To help address this, GNVQs were introduced in 1993 and in science in 1994 to providing a 'vocational' route to employment or higher education. The Further Education Unit survey (1994) showed that Advanced GNVQs have not achieved the objective set by the DFE's white paper 'Education and Training for the Twenty-first Century' (1991) to be of 'equal standing with academic qualifications at the same level'. Continuing debate about the relative values of these routes and the narrowness of the GCE A-level system culminated in the Dearing Report (Dearing 1996), which argued for the establishment of a National Qualifications Framework within which the academic and vocational (or 'applied') pathways were given equal parity of esteem, together with a broadening of the post-16 curriculum.

Although Dearing's proposals, in particular the complete merging of the academic and vocational pathways, have not been fully met, GCE A-levels changed from September 2000 in two significant ways. Two new one-year qualifications called Advanced Subsidiary (AS) and Advanced 2 (A2) have been introduced. AS courses are complete, allowing study for one post-compulsory year. Students may choose to continue a subject by taking the relevant A2 course which, together with the AS, provides a qualification equivalent to the current full A-level. In addition, A-level students will be invited to complete a Key Skills portfolio showing the development and use of communication, information technology and the application of number skills in their studies (Gadd and Sandford-Smith 1999). Although not compulsory, the Key Skills qualification will be examined in its own right and be accepted for university entrance.

These changes are likely to enhance the accessibility of science and could contribute to its development as a lifelong learning subject. In addition, the scope for post-16 science to begin to develop 'connective specialisation' will exist: 'overall curriculum goals in terms of knowledge, skills and attitudes to knowledge and learning, and the relationships that need to be developed between subjects in fulfilling such goals' (Young and Glanfield 1998: 16).

The division of A-level into two one-year courses introduces an opportunity for students who would have completed their formal science education with GCSE to include science in their post-16 experience. It is likely that students may study up to five AS courses. Thus, the long-sought opportunity to broaden the post-16 curriculum by increasing the range of subjects studied is now achievable, as students with an arts/languages/humanities bias could take an AS science course and vice versa. The success of this innovation depends on how students' choices are to be structured and on providing suitable courses. Students specialising in humanities could take an AS science to study wider societal issues, balancing their thinking and gaining wider perspectives. Courses such as *Science in the Environment* (OCR) or the *Public Understanding of Science* (NEAB) may meet these needs. Connective specialisation for these students could be a reality, as these combinations would enable relationships between science and other subjects to be developed.

Students with a strong interest in science will study AS chemistry, physics and biology in whatever combination best matches their interests, and may include one or more arts/language/humanities subject. These students too will have achieved more 'breadth' in their post-16 choices than was possible previously. However, the main benefit for our discussion here is that the new system provides an opportunity to increase the numbers of students studying science post-16, and hence permits consideration of the appropriateness of post-16 science courses in lifelong learning terms. Science AS courses must make the subject accessible, and the new proposals provide an incentive to ensure this. Having completed a one-year AS course in chemistry, physics or biology, any student may decide not to continue. Thus, teachers must offer stimulating, exciting, interesting and relevant AS courses, or risk losing all but the most committed students for the A2 year.

The introduction of Key Skills also merits discussion as an influence on a lifelong learning approach to science. Key Skills originated within GNVQ courses as a strategy for developing abilities transferable from school or college to the workplace. Opportunities to assess these were developed within the courses, contributing to the criticism that this was partly at the expense of developing conceptual understanding (Spours 1995). The Fitness for Purpose Project (Coles and Matthews 1996) assessed the importance of key skills to employers and higher education tutors, finding that communication, team working and mathematical ability were deemed essential (Coles 1998). In consequence, the Dearing Review recommended the adoption of key skills across the post-16 sector.

Teaching Key Skills within GCE A-levels is an entirely new venture which could make several contributions to making science suitable for lifelong learning. First, teaching and learning key skills means that a wide range of strategies must be employed to satisfy the requirements. For example, the 'communication' key skill requires students to 'participate in a group discussion about a complex subject' (C3.1a), 'make a presentation about a complex subject' (C3.1b) and 'write two types of document' (C3.3). These cannot be achieved by a teacher standing in front of a group of students wielding chalk or a board marker. *Beyond 2000* advocates introduction of a wide range of teaching strategies for use in pre-16 classrooms. Key Skills delivers this for the post-16 curriculum and their introduction into pre-16 courses would be beneficial.

Second, Key Skills would help foster a spirit of enquiry and acquisition of appropriate knowledge. Although this may not be in the sense of the formal 'process' of science reflected in experiments and 'investigations', the approach offered by Key

Skills is nonetheless valid. For example, skill numbered IT3.1 – 'Plan and use different sources to search for, information required for two different purposes' (Gadd and Sandford-Smith 1999) – is entirely applicable to Mary in solving her 'crisps' problem. Development of the key skill would enable her to gain access to appropriate scientific knowledge and take her towards applying the information in an everyday sense. This is entirely in accordance with the criteria for accessibility of science.

Third, the skills are genuinely transferable to the workplace. Young and Glanfield (1998) estimate that 25 per cent of the UK workforce have some post-compulsory science education. Assuming this proportion is maintained in future employment statistics, if Key Skills are implemented widely among A-level students, then this means that a high proportion of the workforce are likely to be able to combine acquisition of science knowledge with the abilities which reflect a stronger motivation and more positive attitude to learning.

The influence of attitudes to science

> I am going to make some accusations about science teachers and science teaching. First I accuse you science teachers of devoting your energies to the mere conveying of scientific knowledge and principles – to being, in other words, animated textbooks ... to the point where your pupils think that that's all science is ... Secondly I accuse you of giving your pupils a false idea of the essence of science ... My third accusation is that you haven't done much to help your average and below-average pupils to distinguish science from non-science'
>
> (W.J. Fletcher, quoted in Claxton 1991: 148)

The attitudes of two key groups of people will influence whether science can become a subject capable of meeting lifelong learning demands: students and their teachers. We may be able to supply a pre-16 curriculum which meets some, many or all of the recommendations of *Beyond 2000*, and have an assessment system which is motivating and appropriate, but unless attitudes are positive within both these groups, then change in the other areas will not yield results.

Ramsden (1998: 132) posed the question, 'Can anything be done about attitudes to science?', and by doing so acknowledged that students' negative attitudes to the subject present a problem to science educators. In answering the question, she describes the general case for attitudes research as, 'a desire to create the climate which best helps young people make sense of and feel positive about their experiences in science lessons'.

Evidence indicates that pre-16 students do not feel very positive about science. For example, the Royal Society of Chemistry (RSC) Report (1996) on career choices in chemistry notes that less academic 15-year-olds consider the subject to have little relevance to their future life outside school. More able and confident students give chemistry a more positive image, but perceive that although a post-16 chemistry qualification is worthwhile, it is difficult to obtain. Seventeen-year-olds participating in the same study describe chemistry as 'one of the hardest subjects post-16', and even those confident of their ability were unsure whether to study the subject further. Fitz-Gibbon (1994) found that chemistry and physics A-levels were at least one grade harder than other subjects, adding to the image of science as inaccessible and only suitable for the most able students. For science to feature as a lifelong learning subject, this must change. We need to promote a willingness among students to want to know, to be able to know, and to enjoy knowing, about science, in order to achieve lifelong learning.

The single most important factor influencing students' attitudes towards science is their teachers. When applied to teachers the term 'attitude' needs a little redefinition, since one could reasonably assume that professionals involved in science education like their subjects. The attitude requiring change is rather one of approach. Science educators of all types represent scientific success. We have learned our trade by meeting the detailed knowledge and abstract concepts comprising our subjects with varying degrees of success, but in every case sufficient for us all to be called 'scientists'. As such, we are guardians of the subject which we complain students do not like. We must take responsibility for their attitudes, for the curriculum and as far as possible, for the assessment system. Science teachers in school by and large enjoy teaching the subject as they themselves were taught, and in which they enjoyed academic success. This brings a sense of professional comfort, through delivering 'my subject', and remains among beginning teachers a major reason for their wanting to join the teaching profession. However, for science to become a subject learned over a lifetime under the criteria established here, teachers and other science educators must be prepared to change the attitude of teaching science as the preserve of scientists. Young and Glanfield state:

> science teachers will have to go beyond their traditional forms of insular specialisation that are devoted to protecting and improving existing science syllabuses and staying out of any wider curriculum debates.
>
> (Young and Glanfield 1998: 19)

Lifelong learning in science: dream or reality?

At present, the analysis here indicates that lifelong learning in science is a dream for two main reasons. First, the present curricula are content-laden and present science as the exclusive preserve of scientists. Second, teachers teach as scientists and adopt the attitude that students should learn as scientists, rather than as people needing 'science for life'.

Three distinct changes are needed. First, we must be prepared to release content. There is no need for young people to know the level of detail in the present National Curriculum for Science. To achieve lifelong learning in science, we must be ready to accept that the content we present pre-16 should be drastically reduced and replaced by a curriculum which permits challenge through a wider range of approaches and gives time to develop understanding of key concepts on which later science studies can be developed. Second, post-16 teachers in the new, September 2000 system must be prepared to give as much attention and care to students who will not study science beyond AS level as they do to those who will. If schools adopt courses such as the *Public Understanding of Science* and *Science in the Environment* to broaden the post-16 curriculum, science teachers should take a positive approach, seeking to share and extend their own experiences of science to students, helping them develop attitudes and understanding of science for life. Third, the adoption of key skills in A-level sciences must be grasped as an opportunity to develop a wider range of strategies post-16 than is used currently.

Of course, lifelong learning in science could be a reality. Changes in the post-16 assessment system must be regarded as positive moves towards this. The introduction of two one-year courses to comprise one GCE A-level presents post-16 science with the opportunity to increase numbers studying the subject to the age of 17, together with the chance to develop approaches to teaching science in the wider, societal context. Key skills within GCE A-levels gives educators the challenge of developing transferable skills through science subjects. This alone may help to foster positive attitudes and enhance motivation for knowing about science after leaving school.

However, as ever, the success of any change and the progress towards the development of a new pre-16 curriculum depends largely on the educators at the sharp end. For the dream to become reality, teachers need to release themselves from the primary role of scientists teaching pure science, thus ensuring that: 'Learning about science becomes much more a dialogue between common sense and scientific understandings, and less a question of "experts filling empty vessels"' (Young and Glanfield 1998: 15).

If this could be achieved, then science would be well on the way to meeting the broader test for education set out by Bentley (1998). He refers to two 'tests' which education must 'pass' in order to be effective: the first is to produce students able to apply learning beyond their formal experience, and the second is to prepare young people to solve problems and continue learning throughout the rest of their lives. A person worrying about the food value of crisps would not then need an 'expert' to generate an answer: rather s/he would be able to find out for themselves.

Questions

1   How else might lifelong learning in science be defined?
2   What other influences might affect if lifelong learning can be achieved?
3   What might be the benefits of science being learned in a lifelong way?

Further reading

Bentley, T. (1998) *Learning Beyond the Classroom: Education for a Changing World*, London: Routledge.

In this general text, Bentley argues a strong case for recognising learning taking place beyond the formal sector. For education to meet the challenges of the 21st century, we must make better and more effective connections between what happens in schools and wider opportunities for learning. Bentley describes and discusses the effectiveness of a wide range of educational innovations and challenges the reader to consider a radical rethink of young people's needs. The challenge in reading this is to consider how the arguments he raises apply to science.

Millar, R. and Osborne, J. (eds) (1998) *Beyond 2000: Science Education for the Future*, London: King's College.

The report recognises problems with the existing model of science education and suggests that a rethink of the aims is needed, including a need to encourage more students to study science post-16. Although *Beyond 2000* makes no formal recommendations about the post-16 curriculum, if implemented the proposals would have a significant impact on the development of science as a lifelong learning subject.

Higham, J., Sharp P. and Yeomans, D. (1996) *The Emerging 16–19 Curriculum: Policy and Provision*, London: David Fulton.

Although again a general text, the authors provide a stimulating account of the current state of the vocational and academic 16–19 curriculum. Chapters introduce hard data and draw on authentic accounts from those working in the system to arrive at answers to key questions relating to the development of the 16–19 system. The text provides useful background reading against which the development of lifelong learning can be considered.

7 Understanding evidence in investigations

The way to a more relevant curriculum?

Sandra Duggan and Richard Gott

Introduction

Investigative work in the UK science curriculum has had a bumpy ride. It has been criticised by many (for example, Donnelly *et al.* 1994) but there is nonetheless considerable support from a wide variety of bodies. One of its main problems has been, and continues to be, that the purpose of doing investigative work is poorly defined. In this chapter, it is suggested that the role of investigative work can be clarified: its main aim is that it is a means of teaching pupils to understand scientific evidence. The authors also suggest that understanding evidence should be an important part of the science curriculum of the future.

One of the main and widely acknowledged problems with the present science curriculum in the UK is that it is too crowded. What has happened is that, as new knowledge has emerged, each major area of scientific progress has fought for representation in the science syllabi. Looked at from the students' or even the teachers' point of view, the content of the present curriculum is not only overcrowded but it can also seem like a rather disjointed conglomeration of facts and knowledge required to be learned for assessment purposes. Not surprisingly, only those well-motivated students, usually with a particular goal in mind, engage with many of the current science courses and pass with a respectable grade, while the majority quickly become alienated from science, leaving it behind at the earliest opportunity. Of those who do achieve the higher grades, there is some concern that there is a lack of real understanding. A recent inspection of secondary schools in England reported that: 'Pupils' understanding of underlying scientific concepts frequently remains insecure, and they are insufficiently able to apply their knowledge in new contexts' (OFSTED 1998a: 132). The inspection team also noted a lack of coherence:

> chemists and physicists may have planned and taught energy transfer in chemical and mechanical systems without using the same vocabulary or drawing parallels. For pupils, what is received is therefore fragmented, and an intellectual leap is required to make important connections.
>
> (OFSTED 1998a: 132)

The growth of knowledge in science can be portrayed as a pyramid built upon agreed fundamentals by successive generations of specialist scientists. Once such fundamentals have been established, each generation of scientists adds in a vertical, more gradual and increasingly specialised way. Gibbons *et al.* (1995) refer to this as 'Mode 1', or disciplinary knowledge, which has been the dominant mode of knowledge production in the past. They suggest that there is an increasing move towards 'Mode 2' knowledge production, which can be viewed as horizontal or transdisciplinary in that it is generated by an interaction between people with expertise in a variety of disciplines. Mode 2 knowledge production is also charac- terised by an interaction between theory and the practical contexts where the new knowledge will be applied. If curriculum development is to keep abreast of these changes, then, in terms of science education, we need to incorporate more of the horizontal links that are common to all sciences as well as to other disciplines. Such linking may well enable pupils to make more sense of the subject of science by seeing its applicability across disciplines.

A further related argument weighing in against the current balance of content of the science curriculum is the advent of the information society, where scientific information in every conceivable form is becoming increasingly accessible to all. People will no longer need to know the facts themselves, since these can be obtained relatively easily. The opportunity is often there to access and examine the raw data, analyse it and interpret it for oneself. What people *will* need to know is how to handle all this information and how to disentangle opinions and interpre- tations from facts; the alternative being to accept interpretations, which may come from pressure groups or interested parties, at face value and so may not be free from bias. Young and Glanfield write that:

> under the impact of information technology, the skills needed in different occupational sectors are converging as more and more jobs demand *generic* and *abstract* rather than sector-specific skills.
>
> (Young and Glanfield 1998; authors' emphasis: 7)

They also suggest that recent government policy, with its emphasis on standards, narrowly specialist syllabi and externally marked written exams, is based on limited fundamental thinking about the science curriculum. In similar vein, the Institute of Biology criticises the high priority that assessment places on the acquisition of knowledge, pointing out that:

> Strategies that develop the skills of science such as encouraging learners to discuss scientific ideas with their peers, to evaluate evidence and to develop practical competence, as opposed to the knowledge and understanding of science, have been squeezed out.
>
> (Institute of Biology 1998: 27)

The impact of a centrally controlled curriculum has meant that we are trapped in an increasingly fact-bound recall-based science monitored by SATs and OFSTED inspections. This leaves little room for trying out radical ideas.

Students who do manage to grasp all the facts and knowledge that are required for current assessment and who then progress to careers in science will in fact use only a small part of the knowledge they have learned They are likely to enter a specialised area of science where they will have to acquire detailed specific knowledge and, understandably, they will soon forget the rest of their science education. So, from a functional point of view, one might ask as science educationalists, *what is science teaching for and whose needs is it serving?*

Young and Glanfield (1998: 15) argue for a change in the focus of the science curriculum, suggesting that the relationship between science and risk should be at the centre and that learning about science should 'become much more a dialogue between common sense and scientific understandings, and less a question of experts filling empty vessels'. The same authors write that: 'just as scientists need to know about society, so also do all the people that constitute society need to know about science, or more specifically, how society and science impinge on each other' (4). At the moment the relationship is rather one-sided, with scientists sometimes encouraging this by promoting an image of science which is remote and elitist. In the same way, school science perpetuates the myth of science as being difficult and inaccessible. The Royal Society, in relation to KS4, suggests that the gap between school science and pupils' interests should be narrowed:

> The large majority of pupils ... would also benefit from teachers being given increased flexibility to design courses which enabled pupils to study up-to-date applications in more detail and to pursue their particular local and personal interests via extended project-type investigations.
>
> (Royal Society 1999a: 3)

This would enable pupils to relate science to their everyday lives, empower them so that they feel able to deal with science and enable them to tackle meaningful issues.

In this chapter, we argue that science education needs a fundamental rethink if it is to prosper. The new millennium brings with it an opportunity for review: where is science education and where is it going? In many other countries, science education is in the process of reform so it seems timely to contribute to the discussion of how to address these issues. Young and Glanfield (1998) talk of a new era of 'flexibility, innovation and uncertainty', and suggest that the move towards lifelong learning and the need for a learning society call for a debate about the wider role of science education in future society.

A fresh start?

If a fresh start could be made, what would be the aims for science education? Instead of a top-down approach, a 'bottom-up' approach might be considered as the starting point for what the ordinary citizen needs to know about science in their everyday lives. We suggest that a student leaving compulsory education in science should know enough:

- to understand how scientific knowledge is used in science, engineering and technology in general terms so that citizens can engage in issues of current controversy involving science, such as the legalisation of recreational drugs or methods of birth control or euthanasia;

- to be in a position where they can obtain employment in science-based industry if they so wish or continue with higher level education in science or engineering if they choose to do so.

The order of these points reflects our priorities: while not denying that one of the aims of science education is to train future scientists, we believe that the priority in pre-16 science education should be to meet the needs of the majority of students who will not choose to study science at higher levels. We are also aware of other aims for science education, such as sustaining and stimulating natural curiosity about the world and how it works, but these are not the focus of this chapter.

What are the consequences of this position? Two case studies will be used: one to explore what sort of scientific knowledge is required to engage with a topical science-based issue in the public domain, and the other to explore what sort of understanding is needed in science-based industry.

What sort of scientific knowledge is needed to participate in a controversy about a science-based issue of concern?

This case study (Tytler *et al.* 1999a, 1999b) set out to determine how scientific knowledge was used in an issue which engaged the local community in a fiercely contested debate on the burning of recycled liquid fuel (such as paint thinners or ink solvents) in a cement kiln in a rural area. Previously, these waste products were disposed of in landfill or purpose-built high-temperature incinerators. Using them as fuel in cement kilns is attractive because the high temperatures and long 'residence time' of materials in the kiln leads to their effective breakdown and the energy produced is useful, allowing savings on coal. The less attractive aspect of the issue, and the main one which causes concern, is the nature of the kiln emissions, which include dioxins, heavy metals and volatile organic compounds.

By accessing all the relevant documentation (local newspaper reports, public releases from the cement company, information available on the public register and a House of Commons Report) and by interviewing members of the public who had participated in the debate at different levels, the sort of knowledge of, and about, science necessary for active and effective involvement in the debate was explored. The participants had garnered information from a wide variety of sources, including the Internet, but they claimed to lack the specific conceptual knowledge relevant to the issue, as stated by this participant who led one of the pressure groups:

> We knew nothing to begin with – we learnt a lot – a lot of that has been from reading documentation at the public register, finding out what the issues are, talking to people … but I certainly wouldn't claim to have any understanding of the chemistry.

(ibid.)

Such remarks have, of course, to be treated with some caution since it is possible that people have the basic knowledge of the underlying issues without explicit recognition of it. Nevertheless, the detailed specific scientific knowledge was sought out when it was deemed relevant.

The critical part of this particular controversy centred on the claims that were being made on the basis of the emission data which were available on the public register. One member of the public, 'Jim', who had a background in psychology and a good grasp of fundamental statistics, examined the data and realised that the basis of the claims was insecure. In some instances, the cement company had been selective in its use of data or incorrectly analysed and interpreted it. Jim explained that the issue rested on the fact that cement kiln emissions are very variable and that what was needed was to monitor the emissions 'a dozen times when you're burning waste and a dozen times when you're not burning waste and do a *t*-test – very simple basic stats' (ibid.). But what he found was that the cement company was 'measuring emissions on one day and comparing that with a measurement when they were burning waste on another day and saying well they've gone up or they've gone down and they were making huge claims on the basis of that' (ibid.).

This is one example of many which involved an understanding of how data are used as evidence. Other examples which emerged in the case study include selection of data to bias the result, or taking samples too early in the burning process (which would lead to underestimation of some of the emissions) or failing to sample all the emissions from a burn. All of these issues relate to understanding how data are collected, how measurements are taken and how data are handled and used as evidence.

It is true to say that, in this controversy, what mattered was having fundamental ideas about data so that pertinent questions could be formulated and answers sought. For example, the simple question, 'was the sampling procedure representative?' with the knowledge of what representative sampling entails, would have called into question several of the company's claims. Prior knowledge of the relevant scientific concepts did not appear to be essential since this knowledge could be, and was, accessed effectively.

What sort of scientific knowledge is used in science-based industry?

This question is confounded by the wide range of science-based industries but, nevertheless, if there is such a thing as knowledge which is useful across most science-based industries, then it should be identified so that it can be clearly defined. A survey by the Council for Science and Technology Institutes of over 1000 employers in industry (CSTI 1993) found that some 30 per cent of the workforce uses science or maths in some aspect of their work. The analysis of the results shows that industry requires employees to have three sets of 'skills': a central core concerned with the doing of science; communication skills and management skills. The first set is the most relevant to science education and comprises the ability to:

- generate own ideas, hypotheses and theoretical models and/or utilise those postulated by others;
- design investigations, experiments, trials, tests, simulations and operations;
- conduct investigations, experiments, trials, tests and operations;
- evaluate data and results from the processes and outcomes of investigations, experiments, trials, tests and operations.

Another study by Coles (1997) came to broadly similar conclusions and found that general capabilities such as decision-making by weighing evidence or 'scientific habits of mind' were often expressed ahead of any specific scientific knowledge, understanding or skills.

Although these studies have gone a considerable way towards defining the skills that employers require, neither of them provides the level of detail which would be useful to the teacher. We therefore decided to carry out a small number of case studies in science-based industries to see what sort of scientific knowledge is used.

One of these case studies, reported in detail elsewhere (Gott, Duggan and Johnson 1999), is taken as an example. The study was based in a small biotechnology company which manufactures and markets a range of medical test kits that are used in hospital and research laboratories in the measurement of picogram quantities of hormone or related biomolecules in a single drop of blood or serum. In order to understand the scientific knowledge required by workers at different levels in this company, considerable time was spent in discussion with management, in studying a range of documentation and in interviewing in order to establish the accuracy of the findings.

What emerged from this and two further case studies in quite different industries is that some understanding of facts, theories and concepts is needed in industry but that a lot of that knowledge is narrow, specific to the industry and often learnt through training provided by employers. What is also required, but is less easily identified, is an understanding of scientific data and its use as evidence. Examples include understanding ideas such as how different kinds of error occur and how they can be minimised, appropriate accuracy, repeatability and the significance of controlled conditions. All these ideas are interwoven and are an integral part of reliability and validity. Employers tend not to associate this knowledge with science but to regard it as 'common sense' or 'procedures'. At the same time, they recognised that many of the costly mistakes which occur in routine production could be attributed to a lack of such understanding. In some ways, it is not surprising that new employees do not understand ideas about evidence because it is rarely explicitly taught in schools.

Both these case studies have highlighted that the sort of scientific knowledge required both by the public in understanding science-based issues and by employees in science-based industry includes an understanding of data and data as evidence. Conceptual knowledge appeared to be less important. What does this mean for science education?

The implications for school science

From the above, it appears that teaching about scientific evidence should be a central part of a new 'fresh start' curriculum. In the past, science education has assumed that pupils pick up an understanding of evidence in the course of practical work. While some do, there are many who do not. Sc1 has served to highlight this lack of understanding. Many teachers will recognise the investigative practical in which pupils willingly, but perhaps superficially, engage with the task, collect data and hand in a report which serves only to show the teacher that the pupil has failed to make sense of the data or evaluate their findings: in other words, the purpose of the task has been lost. What is needed is a curriculum that explicitly addresses this sort of scientific knowledge.

What is meant by 'understanding evidence'?

First, a clear definition of exactly what we mean is needed: a content for a syllabus. With this in mind, some time ago, the authors began formulating a tentative list of ideas about evidence, which they called 'concepts of evidence' (Gott and Duggan 1995). In the light of subsequent research and ongoing studies in industry and public understanding, this definition has been considerably extended (now several pages long) and is under continuous review (see http://www.dur.ac.uk/~ded0www/evidence_main1.htm for the latest version). In brief, these concepts of evidence all relate to the overarching ideas of reliability and validity and they are relevant to each and every branch of science. Whenever scientific evidence is evaluated, the relevant concepts of evidence need to be considered. They include ideas about:

- design; for example, have all the relevant controls been considered?
- measurement; for example, have the measurements been repeated often enough to allow for random variation?
- data handling; for example, are the data represented (graphically or statistically) in an appropriate way?

How can pupils be taught to understand evidence?

Knowing that an understanding of evidence can be defined, the next step is to decide how best it should be taught. The authors have written materials both for schools (Gott *et al.* 1997; Gott, Foulds and Jones 1998; Gott, Foulds and Roberts 1999) and for colleges (Gott, Duggan and Jones 1998) all of which can be used to target concepts of evidence in various ways including practical work, written exercises, group and class discussions. The teaching of evidence using some of these materials has been trialled in a pilot study as a part of Intermediate GNVQ science. The outcome was a very positive response from the FE lecturers who taught the course:

> Basically you're teaching them logical ordered thought, which is what science is about isn't it? – deciding what you can and cannot conclude, designing a fair

test etc. Which is exactly the way you have to think if you're working in a laboratory.

These are not only thinking skills, they are important skills. They're important in science jobs but in other jobs as well.

I think you need this understanding – it doesn't matter whether they go on to do science or not – if you look outside, we live in a science world.

It seems that, if ways of teaching understanding evidence are presented to teachers, then it can be taught. Further, if teachers are given the opportunity to do so, then they readily realise the value of teaching this knowledge about science and recognise it as an omission from their previous teaching.

Where could this understanding of evidence be located in the National Curriculum?

It was argued at the start of this chapter that the current curriculum is overcrowded and heavily weighted towards facts and knowledge. Although understanding evidence is referred to in Sc1, there are a number of problems with the present arrangements.

Firstly, as has been argued elsewhere (Roberts and Gott 1999), Sc1 is under-specified in that the documentation does not make clear to teachers what, or how, to teach pupils about evidence. We acknowledge that these ideas may be taught but if so, it is in the face of the existing assessment requirements, which do nothing to address the poor experience of experimental work, and opportunities for understanding evidence, that some pupils receive. Until support is forthcoming from policy-makers in relation to assessment and examination boards, the current situation, where understanding evidence is afforded little attention is likely to persist.

The present curriculum is not only overcrowded, but it also supports the common misconception of scientific truth. Pupils are presented with 'facts' and are expected to find the 'right' answer in practical work. The notions of scientific uncertainty, probability and risk are largely overlooked. Yet these are the issues which lie at the heart of the public understanding of science and which should concern us all. Consider BSE, genetically modified foods or the multitude of health risks (smoking and lung cancer, or the risk factors associated with heart disease): these are issues which are often the most problematic, particularly when scientists communicate the state of the evidence to the public. The current situation is that the public expect a conclusive answer from scientists to each problem and this should come as no surprise given that they have been imbued at school with a science of facts and certainties. Here again the authors suggest that teaching pupils about evidence and providing them with ample opportunity to design experiments, collect, handle and interpret data as evidence in investigative work in Sc1 is the most obvious way to address these issues.

There is some light on the horizon. For example, a recent report entitled *Beyond 2000: Science Education for the Future* (Millar and Osborne 1998) suggests that 'Ideas-about-Science' which include an understanding of the reliability and validity of data and of statistical and probabilistic relationships be part of science education in the future. However, there is little to indicate that the authors regard such ideas as a body of knowledge in their own right which needs explicit teaching and assessment. The danger of this approach is that, in terms of the balance of the curriculum, it promotes the maintenance of the status quo. In this vision of the future science curriculum, scientific literacy is seen as enabling a passive understanding of topical science-based issues. The authors would suggest rather that it should be seen as empowering future citizens to actively participate in science-based issues. Although this is perhaps only a matter of emphasis, it is likely to affect the way such understanding is taught. The proposed new GCE AS Science for Public Understanding (AQA) appears to promote a similar content as the *Beyond 2000* report, but here there is a reference to active decision making.

A final note

It has been suggested in this chapter that the present science curriculum is urgently in need of reform and that the balance needs to be redressed with a greater emphasis on understanding the ideas underpinning scientific evidence. The research presented here has shown that these ideas are significant in public understanding (or scientific literacy) and in science-based employment.

In terms of motivation alone, understanding the principles of scientific evidence, particularly in relation to topical issues, is likely to have considerable appeal to students. Further, there is a general move in society towards evidence-based decision-making. For example, the Programme for International Student Assessment (PISA) (McGrath 1999: 27) focuses its science assessment on scientific literacy defined as:

> being able to combine science knowledge with the ability to draw evidence-based conclusions, in order to understand and help make decisions about the natural world and the changes made to it through human activity.

What is proposed is a radical rethink. There is a clear choice. Minor changes can be made to an outdated curriculum consisting of facts and knowledge quickly forgotten and of limited use to a minority of students. The outcome is likely to be the increasing alienation of the majority of pupils from science and the perpetuation of low levels of public understanding. Or, the balance of science education can be altered more radically. The outcome of changing the balance of the curriculum with a much greater emphasis on teaching an understanding of scientific evidence through investigative science would be that students would receive a science education which would not only better equip them to enter science-based employment but also enable them to participate and act on any issue of concern. The authors also believe that updating and reorientating science education in this way would engage many more pupils with the real nature of science.

Questions

1   How important do you think that a public understanding perspective grounded in participation is to science education?
2   Do you agree that the curriculum is too full? As an exercise, get a blank sheet of paper and write down what you would put in a curriculum for a particular year group. Then justify it.
3   How might the ideas put forward here translate into teaching schemes? Would, for example, a 'project' in which pupils devoted themselves full-time in their science lessons for three or four weeks to experimenting, data collection and analysis, and report-writing be one possibility?
4   What sort of topical issues would appeal to pupils of different ages and abilities? Which of them are accessible in terms of the understanding needed to get to grips with them and also have a good enough evidence base on which to base the 'project'?

Further reading

Atkin, J.M. and Helms J. (1993). 'Getting serious about priorities in science education', *Studies in Science Education* 21: 1–20.

This article explores the wide range of possible options for priorities in science education and suggests some guidelines for making a choice.

Chapman, B. (1991) 'The overselling of science education in the eighties', *School Science Review* 72(260): 47–63.

Chapman scrutinises the claims made for compulsory science education in a thought-provoking article.

Layton D., Jenkins E., Macgill S. and Davey A. (1993). *Inarticulate Science? Perspectives on the Public Understanding of Science and Some implications for Science Education*, Driffield: Studies in Education.

Layton *et al.* present the results of four case studies taking a detailed look at how the public uses science in issues of personal concern. The authors use these findings to make some recommendations for science education.

8 SC1

Beyond the fair test

*Rod Watson, Anne Goldsworthy
and Valerie Wood-Robinson*

Introduction

How do scientists carry out scientific investigations? There is no straightforward answer to this question. Scientists use a great range of investigative approaches. For example, they carry out laboratory tests, study patterns of behaviour, carry out surveys to try to correlate possible cause and effect relations, build models and test new theories, all of which is in stark contrast to the paucity of kinds of investigations carried out in schools in the UK. The first part of this chapter is concerned with the varieties of kinds of investigations used in schools and the problems associated with the dominance of fair testing. In the second part of the chapter, the pupils' experience of investigative work in schools is examined. Teachers see investigations as providing opportunities for pupils to make decisions, to think for themselves and to use scientific skills and processes to solve scientific problems, but do pupils see things in the same way? Do they have any idea of what they are supposed to be learning, or do they see investigations as just another school exercise to be done to keep the teacher happy?

Kinds of investigations

There are many different uses of the word 'investigations' in the literature. The meaning of the word used here is derived from data collected from teachers by the ASE-King's Science Investigations in Schools (AKSIS) project (Watson and Wood-Robinson 1998; Watson *et al.* 1999a). There was general agreement that:

- in investigative work pupils have to make their own decisions either individually or in groups: they are given some autonomy in how the investigation is carried out;
- an investigation must involve pupils in using investigational procedures such as planning, measuring, observing, analysing data and evaluating procedures. Not all investigations will allow pupils to use every kind of investigational procedure, and investigations may vary in the amount of autonomy given to pupils at different stages of the investigative process.

The model of investigative processes used in the National Curriculum (NC) has been heavily based on a structure in which students decide to change an independent variable, observe the effect on a dependent variable and control other key variables. This model is referred to in this chapter as the 'fair testing' model. This model has been 'softened' in subsequent versions of the NC (such as DfE 1995a) in order to accommodate a greater variety of approaches, but in spite of this the 'fair testing' model still dominates. The dominance of this model has led to the following problems:

- the investigations carried out in schools do not adequately represent the relationship between the development of scientific theories and empirical evidence;
- the variety of investigations used does not adequately represent the work that is carried out by scientists and presents a skewed picture of the nature of science;
- there is a tendency for some teachers to try to use fair testing procedures in investigations where they are not appropriate.

To help address these problems, a framework of six different kinds of investigations was proposed by the AKSIS project (Goldsworthy et al. 1998; Watson et al. 1999b). Many previous categorisations of investigations had been for the purposes of teaching (for example, Lock 1990; Watson et al. 1990) or assessment (for example, Gott and Murphy 1987; Ruiz-Primo and Shavelson 1995; Swain 1991b; Taylor 1990) and so concentrated on pedagogical characteristics that affect pupil performance (Song and Black, 1991, 1992). The purpose of the categorisation described here was different. It was to represent the range of investigations to which pupils are exposed and to consider whether this range is adequate.

The six kinds of investigations proposed are:

- classifying and identifying: classification and identification of rocks
- fair testing: which paper towel soaks up most water?
- pattern-seeking: do people with longer legs jump higher?
- investigating models: how do optical illusions work?
- exploring: what happens when different liquids are added together?
- making things or developing systems: design a road bridge for a model car to cross.

Table 8.1 summarises the different features of the different kinds of investigations.

Watson et al. (1999b) report the distribution of investigations used by over 1000 teachers of pupils aged 7–11 (KS2) and 11–14 (KS3) in England and Wales. Table 8.2 shows that at both key stages, particularly Key Stage 3, fair testing dominates and there is very little pattern seeking and virtually no modelling. There are more exploring and classifying and identifying investigations at KS2 than KS3, and there is some evidence of progression from exploring at KS2 to fair testing at KS3, in certain contexts, such as dissolving. Identifying is rarely carried out as an investigation. At KS2, a significant number of technological investigations (making things

Table 8.1 Stages in the process of different kinds of investigation

Classifying and identifying	Fair testing	Pattern seeking	Exploring	Investigating models	Making things or developing systems
Recognise characteristics to identify or classify	Identify independent, dependent and control variables	Identify dependent variable and possible causal factors	Observe phenomena for a scientific purpose	Identify what counts as evidence	Identify significant features of artifact or system to be designed
Select characteristics which discriminate, and develop a strategy	Decide how to observe and measure variables	Plan how to measure the variables as they occur naturally. Select a large enough sample to provide reliable data	Select observations to make and the number and frequency of observations	Collect evidence. This could be by classifying, identifying, fair testing, or searching for patterns	Plan designs and select the best fit to the design specification
Apply tests which display characteristics	Change values of independent variable and carry out observations/measurements under controlled conditions	Carry out observations and measurement. Note any uncontrolled conditions which may be significant, or carry out statistical analyses to look for strength of relations between variables	Use the observations to raise scientific questions	Critically evaluate in the light of the model(s)	Make the artifact or system
Draw conclusions by a process of successive discrimination	Interpret and evaluate the data to identify, describe and interpret relations between variables	Interpret and evaluate the data collected in order to seek for patterns of relationships		Use the models to predict. Collect evidence to test predictions	Test the artifact or system and evaluate its fitness for purpose
Identification can be used to gain access to information in secondary sources. Classification can be used to predict in new situations		If possible identify, through laboratory tests, causal links between correlated variables			

or developing systems) are done within science lessons, probably reflecting the fact that the links between science and technology are more easily made in primary schools where the two subjects are normally taught by the same teacher.

Table 8.2 Kinds of investigation carried out in Key Stages 2 and 3

Kind of investigation	KS2 (%)	KS3 (%)
Classifying and identifying	9	2
Fair testing	50	82
Pattern-seeking	2	2
Exploring	16	3
Investigating models	0	0
Making things or developing systems	12	4
No response or insufficient detail	11	7
Total	100	100

As well as being dominated by fair testing, the variety of investigations within the fair testing category tends to be very restricted. Thirty per cent of investigations across both Key Stages were accounted for by only four contexts: thermal insulation, dissolving, pulse rate (and breathing) with exercise and friction. This means that on average every pupil in England and Wales will have investigated the rate of a solid dissolving in water at least three times during KS2 and KS3. Over half the teachers said that they would like to use a bigger variety of investigations. Three factors seem to be constraining the variety of investigations: the way in which the curriculum is specified and interpreted, the demands of assessment, moderation and reporting and whether teachers know how to teach in different ways (Wood-Robinson *et al.* 1999; Donnelly *et al.* 1996).

Pupils' response to investigations

One characteristic that teachers feel is important in investigations is the amount of pupil autonomy. However, in a situation where more responsibility is given to pupils, it is important that they are clear about the educational purposes of what they are doing. Teachers' main justification for the inclusion of investigations in the science curriculum aim is to develop the use of the skills and processes of science (Watson and Wood-Robinson 1998), with teaching for conceptual understanding taking second place. Another aim is to develop pupils' understanding of the relation between empirical data and scientific theory (Driver *et al.* 1996). The effectiveness of investigations for achieving these aims is discussed in Watson (2000).

Watson *et al.* (1998) compared teachers' aims for specific investigation lessons with what their pupils thought they learned. The mismatch between teacher and pupil perceptions is striking. About half the aims of the teachers were concerned with scientific procedures, with only a third of them being about learning content. Pupils, on the other hand, concentrated on more obvious features of investigations and so for about three-quarters of the time saw the investigations as teaching them specific content, such as learning about dissolving. Only one-fifth of their aims were about procedures, and again these tended to be very specific, such as learning to operate a balance. A similar lack of clarity in understanding the aims was seen in a detailed observation study by Watson *et al.* (1999). The main focus of the lessons was in learning how to carry out fair testing procedures. The 12-year-old pupils were interviewed after the lessons:

Int:	What do you think you've learned from doing your investigations?...
R:	... that graph paper is stronger, that green one.
Int:	Right. Is that it?
R:	Um ...
Int:	You spent three lessons doing that, seems a long time to spend finding out that graph paper's stronger.
JA:	Yeah ... and we also found out which, um, which paper's stronger. Not just the graph paper, all of them.

Many pupils approached the investigation as a routine exercise. They saw the worksheets as guiding them through set procedures and many seemed to view satisfactory completion of the investigation as producing a set of completed worksheets.

Faced with such a lack of comprehension of the educational aims of an investigation, it is easy to see how teachers find it difficult to strike the balance between structuring an investigation to provide a framework for supporting students' thinking and structuring an investigation to drive pupils towards a predetermined outcome. Often teachers are unaware of how they are restricting pupils' choices, for example, by the way in which they introduce investigation or by the apparatus they provide (Watson and Wood-Robinson 1998). A useful way of analysing the balance between the decisions of the teacher and the pupils is to construct a decisions table. A decisions table for a visit to the zoo of a class of 8-year-old pupils is shown in Table 8.3. This is taken from a series of case studies carried out by the AKSIS project (Watson *et al.*, in press). The pupils were carrying out an investigation that involved them in classifying and identifying. They were using their observations of similarities and differences in order to decide what were good criteria to enable them to construct a key to identify a variety of animals. Before they went to the zoo, they had already had one lesson using pictures of animals to decide what characteristics to observe.

Table 8.3 Decisions table for zoo visit

What to decide	What is decided	Who decides
How many similarities to observe	5	Teacher
How many differences to observe	5	Teacher
How many kinds of animals to observe	3	Teacher
Which animals	?	Pupils
What to record	?	Pupils
How many individuals of each kind to observe	?	Pupils
Which criteria are useful for constructing a key	?	Pupils after class discussion

The decisions table shows clearly where autonomy is given to the pupils. It also shows where the teacher may have to ask questions to support pupils' thinking (How will you decide which animals to observe? What will you be observing? What will you record?) and also where it is possible for the teacher to encroach on the pupils' autonomy and make the decisions for them instead of supporting their thinking.

A tool, such as the decisions table, can be used effectively if a number of conditions for learning are in place. These are the conditions for formative assessment (Black and Wiliam 1998a, 1998b). The model of Black and Wiliam for the implementation of classroom-based assessment has been developed by the AKSIS project for use in investigational work. The model includes the following components:

1   The development of a model for progression within the particular investigation being used.
2   Procedures for sharing the educational aims of the work with the pupils. This includes both selecting and communicating aims and sharing the criteria used for judging achievement of aims with the pupils.
3   Procedures for assessing achievement of these aims leading to diagnosis of pupils' educational needs with respect to investigations. This diagnosis may be done by pupils or by the teacher.
4   Pupils knowing what they must do to reach the educational targets.

Items 2 to 4 are iterative; that is, it is not assumed that aims will be communicated at the beginning of the lesson and achievement of the aims will be assessed at the end, but rather that there is a continuing process in which all these components are present in helping students to construct their own learning.

These components are now examined in relation to the case study on the classification and identification investigation for 8-year-olds, described above. Before the investigation began the teacher and researcher examined the contents of the lesson, related them to the programme of study in the National Curriculum and translated these into aims that were specific to this investigation (component 1 above).

The investigation took place in the context of a topic on variation, classification and on living things in their environment. One lesson was spent preparing for the zoo visit, followed by a day at the zoo and then two follow-up lessons. During the preparation lesson, aims and the criteria used for judging achievement of the aims were shared with the pupils (component 2). Ways used to share the educational aims with pupils were:

•   Near the beginning of the lesson the teacher told the pupils the aims.
•   The teacher pointed out the aim written on the board, 'This lesson you will learn how animals are identified and classified by looking at how they are similar and different'.
•   Aims were written on worksheets.
•   At the end of the lesson the teacher recapped the aims.

The effect of explicitly sharing aims with pupils was striking. In an earlier investigation with the same class, the teacher used an investigation of the factors that affect how fast a person can run, to focus on particular skills of investigation. This focus was not apparent to pupils as illustrated by the following interview extract:

Int: What do you think you are learning in this lesson?
Pupil 1:   We are learning about running.
Pupil 2:   We are learning about the body.
Pupil 3:   We are learning about the body, skeletons and stuff like that.
Int: Is that what you think it is about?
Pupil 2:   Yes, body and skeletons. That's what we are doing: the whole class.
Int: So why are you doing an investigation?
Pupil 2:   To see how fast people can run and stuff like that.

The pupils focused on superficial actions and features of the investigations and searched for links with previous content studied. In contrast in the classification and identification investigation the vast majority of pupils were clear that the focus of the lesson was on the process of identifying and classifying animals:

Int: What are you doing at the moment?
Pupil: We are making a list of things that are bad to find out what they do, a list of things that are OK and a list of things that are good.
Int: To find out what they do?
Pupil: Yea. To find out how they are splitted up: how they are different.
Int: Right. How they are split and how they are different. What do you mean?
Pupil: Well, a fox isn't like a shark. And we are finding if it is good, the way we can split them.
Int: Yes, put them into groups: put them into classes.
Pupil: Yes, what makes … what things on that board (refers to the list of characteristics of a shark and fox on the board) make them different.

The criteria for judging achievement of the aims were communicated through the initial and final whole class discussion and during group work both in discussion between pairs of students and the teacher, and between students in pairs. The initial whole class discussion focused on why scientists classify animals and how animals can be identified. This was based on looking at similarities and differences in pictures of animals and making explicit the criteria for judging which observations were better. For example, some characteristics may vary between animals of the same kind, such as fur colour and size. Characteristics, which do not vary between animals of the same kind, are easier to use. Next, pupils worked in pairs and talked about what animals they would like to observe, what observations they would like to make and they completed a worksheet with their first thoughts about what to observe. The majority of the pupils interviewed were developing a good understanding of criteria that can be used to differentiate different animals.

The process of developing an understanding of the educational aims and the criteria for judging achievement of the aims was a process that took place throughout the lesson: sharing the aims of lessons cannot be done only at the beginning of the lesson. At the beginning of the lesson the pupils do not have the full picture and so can only partially grasp the aims.

In the first lesson after the zoo visit, after explaining how a key worked and discussing the qualities of good questions for a key in a whole class discussion, the teacher gave each small group a set of ten photographs of animals taken at the zoo on the previous day. Each group then worked on constructing key to identify the animals. This lesson provided opportunities for assessing achievement of the aims (component 3). The following interview extract shows how pupils were gaining direct feedback on the quality of the criteria being used to differentiate between animals, through discussion of concrete examples. Their difficulty in defining what is meant by 'furry', led them to seek for a better characteristic to differentiate their animals.

The interviewer asked the group how their key worked and then the discussion continued with the consideration of a giraffe:

Int: Is it furry? (referring to the first question on the key)
Pupil: Yes. No, because it is not too furry. It's got short hair so it's not furry.
Int: What do you mean by furry?
Pupil: It's not sort of like that (referring to a picture of an animal with long fur).
Int: It's got long fur but maybe this (referring to the giraffe) has short fur.
Pupil: and it's not like that (shows an animal with short fur) because that is hard.

After further discussion the pupils abandoned fur as a discriminating characteristic and looked for a different characteristic.

Apart from this self-assessment by the pupils, the teacher also carried out informal assessment of pupils' progress through discussion in groups and whole class discussion at the end of the lesson. Pupils' written work in the form of their keys also provided a focus for assessing pupils' progress. It was planned for the key construction activity to be followed by pupils swapping keys and using them to try to identify different sets of animals. It was envisaged that this would give feedback on the quality of the keys, give pupils and opportunity to adapt the keys to new animals and highlight what pupils must do to reach the educational targets. However, the activity of constructing a key proved to be much more demanding than expected and so this was carried forward to another lesson, which was not observed.

This series of lessons shows how the positive effects of formative assessment reported by Black and Wiliam (1998a, 1998b) may be achieved within the context of investigations. It gave these young pupils (aged 8) more control over their own learning by providing them with an insight into what they were supposed to be learning and what they needed to do to perform better.

Conclusion

The balance of different kinds of investigations shown in Table 8.2 bears little relation to the variety of kinds of investigations carried out by scientists. Many teachers are dissatisfied with the current variety of investigations. Biologists find ecological and classification investigations difficult to fit into the current curriculum and chemists find the same for identification and synthesis investigations. Gott and Duggan (1996) present a model for the role of investigative work in the curriculum. They separate two components in the content of science concepts, the theoretical and practical, and argue that there is a separate body of 'concepts of evidence' that should be taught. (The argument for a greater emphasis on teaching the understanding of evidence is developed further in Chapter 7.) Difficulties of separating concepts of evidence from the theory, in which they are embedded, have been highlighted by Millar and Driver (1987). Such difficulties become inescapable in some of the kinds of investigations discussed above (such as identifying and classifying) where the procedural understanding is inextricably linked with the theoretical concepts in which they are embedded. Another aspect that is under-emphasised is investigation of models. The normal procedure for carrying out fair testing investigations is to look for a relation between two variables and then after the investigation to explain the pattern of results in the light of pupils' current knowledge. It is very rare for pupils to be given the opportunity for deciding what kinds of evidence they might need to collect to test a model. Is it acceptable that most pupils in schools never have this opportunity? Can pupils understand the scientific enterprise without exploring the difficulties of testing scientific models?

The research about what actually happens in the classroom strikes a warning chord for the grand plans of science educators. If many pupils do not understand why they are doing investigations, can these plans be realised? Work in the area of formative assessment indicates that there is much scope for improvement. Putting formative assessment in place is very difficult and demands the careful co-ordination of various different components of the lessons, but the work of Black and Wiliam (1998a, 1998b) indicates that further work in the area of formative assessment should be a priority.

Questions

1   What is the appropriate balance of different kinds of investigative activities in the school curriculum?
2   How should the balance of different kinds of investigative work change through the different stages of schooling?
3   Investigative work offers the opportunity for more pupil autonomy. How can lessons be organised to give pupils more effective control of this autonomy?

Further reading

Watson, R. (2000) 'The role of practical work', in M. Monk and J. Osborne (eds), *Good Practice in Science Teaching*, Buckingham: Open University.
      This provides an introduction to the role of practical work in school science and its effectiveness for achieving different aims. The focus is on lessons from research for teachers.

Watson, J.R., Goldsworthy, A. and Wood-Robinson, V. (1999b) 'What is not fair with investigations', *School Science Review* 80(292): 101–6.

This article provides a useful discussion of the different finds of investigations.

Millar, R., Lubben, F., Gott, R. and Duggan, S. (1994) 'Investigating the school science laboratory: conceptual and procedural knowledge and their influence on performance', *Research Papers in Education* 9(2): 207–48.

This is an interesting paper on student performance in practical work. For those interested in looking further into this area, the work of the Assessment of Performance Unit (APU) is recommended (references to the latter can be found in Watson (2000)).

Readers interested in teaching and learning strategies for the school classroom should consult the AKSIS publications, Goldsworthy *et al.* (1999 and in press), or Foulds *et al.* (1997, 1998, 1999).

Watson, R., Wood-Robinson, V. and Goldsworthy, A. (in press) *Investigations: Targeted Learning – Using Classroom Assessment for Learning*, Hatfield: Association for Science Education.

9 Numeracy in science

Understanding the misunderstandings

Graham Lenton and Brenda Stevens

Introduction

Understanding in science relies heavily on an ability to handle mathematical concepts confidently. It has been shown that numeracy is an important area which pupils need to develop (Gill 1995; Lenton and Stevens 1999). This chapter looks at some of the key areas in science which are at risk if pupils are not numerate. It may be that some of these difficulties arise through not distinguishing between the teaching of facts and skills and the teaching through conceptual understanding. Suggestions both for student teachers and existing teachers of science in primary and secondary schools on how this problem might be addressed are discussed.

The National Numeracy Strategy for primary school pupils published by the Department for Education and Employment (DfEE 1999b) has produced a number of positive responses from different subject areas. Schools involved in the pilot project noted 'staggering' results with improvement figures of up to 9 per cent for Key Stage 2 (7–11-year-olds) (Rafferty 1997). This will hopefully help to improve pupils' numeracy but in the meantime pupils already past this stage in their education may still be at risk. Whilst it is focused through the core subjects of English, maths and ICT, it is clear that numeracy is of vital importance in other subjects such as geography (Davidson *et al.* 1998) and science. Although there appears to be a widespread lack of confidence in numeracy throughout the general public, this lack is perhaps not so evident in teachers of science, almost all of who will have had some mathematical training in their degree, irrespective of their specialism in science. Science teachers are thus in a stronger position than many to encourage pupils' numeracy development. Nonetheless, many science teachers also admit to difficulties with some mathematical concepts.

Numeracy and the national curriculum

Gill (1999) suggests that there is considerable overlap between the National Curricula for mathematics and science and in particular Sc1 and Ma1. He suggests that perhaps there should be more liaisons between the staff of the two departments in schools and even use science classes as a resource for data for Ma4 (handling data), thereby showing pupils the importance of such links.

The report on standards in science at KS3 (QCA 1998a) points to the poor interpretation of graphs by pupils and gives the example of how only half the pupils in the 1997 assessments could correctly interpret a graph showing colour changes with time, as tea dissolves in water. It was suggested that some of the errors in their responses to this question resulted from a failure to read the scale on the vertical axis.

Derived variables such as speed also cause pupils difficulties. In the same QCA report, 60 per cent of pupils were able to calculate distance from speed and time; however, a further 25 per cent of pupils attempted to do this by dividing speed by time. In a more demanding question in the same test, only a quarter of the pupils were able to use the information provided to calculate time from speed and distance. Compound measures are placed at Level 7 in both the Mathematics and Science National Curricula (DfE 1995a, 1995b), while the interpretation of time-speed graphs is Level 8 in Science.

At first sight, these levels may appear higher than science teachers might expect, which perhaps might account for some of the difficulties but also many of the ways in which some teachers handle number in science lessons demonstrate that they perhaps do not distinguish the difference between ensuring an under-standing of a particular concept and simply teaching the skill to produce a result. If pupils learn how to achieve a result from a conceptual viewpoint rather than only working to a set of rules (the skill) then it may be found that mathematical under-standing improves.

What is numeracy?

Many student teachers have a narrow perception of what is understood by numeracy. They do not realise how important it is to appreciate that pupils often have a fear of maths and an inbuilt barrier when anything mathematical is proposed, or when calculations are expected during science lessons. Numeracy is defined by the National Numeracy Strategy as more than knowing about numbers and number operations. It includes an ability or inclination to solve numerical problems, and familiarity with the ways in which numerical information is gath-ered and is presented in graphs, charts and tables (DfEE 1999b). Numerate pupils should be confident enough to solve problems without going to others to seek advice or help; they should also have a sense of size of number; be able to calculate accurately, both mentally and on paper; have strategies to check if their answers are reasonable, and be able to suggest suitable units for measuring. They should also be able to estimate to a reasonable degree of accuracy.

Why is numeracy so important in science?

Numeracy in science is an important issue since so much science relies upon an understanding of the underlying mathematics. It is therefore essential that teachers of science are aware of the inherent difficulties that some pupils have regarding conceptual understanding in mathematics. This is particularly important in those areas that relate closely to science and underpin understanding of science concepts. Some science teachers may have their own conceptual difficulties with mathematics, and recent observations of student teachers in science by the authors have supported this assumption. Many pupils exhibit an anxiety when confronted with using mathematical ideas in science. The language of mathematics uses many conventions and symbols that can inhibit pupils' understanding and handling of concepts. Often pupils will manipulate data or perform mathematical tasks effectively in a maths lessons, but when confronted with the same or similar task in science will not be able to transfer the skill. This may be due to the use in science of a different term, a different approach to a problem, or a lack of confidence in the pupils.

Key areas of numeracy in science

An enormous number of areas in science rely upon the use and understanding of mathematical concepts. The use of scale factors and place value, ratios and fractions, data in graph and table form, equations, patterns, approximation, probability, derived variables such as density and speed are just a selection of examples that necessitate the use of maths. If some of these examples are inspected, it is not difficult to find key problems associated with their use.

The number system

The understanding of decimals can be problematic. Research has highlighted some of the key difficulties (APU 1983). When some 15-year-old pupils were asked to choose the number with the smallest value from a series of numbers with decimal places such as 0.625, 0.25, 0.3753, 0.125, 0.5, many (36 per cent) chose the number with the largest number of digits (i.e. 0.3753) irrespective of the value of the number. This shows that they have a misconception, based on their belief that the number must be the smallest if it has the smallest place value (the ten thousandths in this example). The use of superscript to define the power of a number leaves many pupils mystified, and they cannot relate it to the same number with a decimal point (for example, $0.1 = 10^{-1}$). Similarly, zero and negative numbers produce misunderstandings. Often pupils find difficulty in handling zero, especially when subtraction is involved. However, it must be remembered that these skills are considered Level 8 in National Curriculum mathematics (DfE 1995b).

Ratios and percentages

Ratios and percentage present enormous problems for many pupils and yet the use of percentage is common practice and is assumed in the understanding in many science ideas. Pupils can, for example, find difficulty in translating percentages into real figures. Calculations with percentages are Level 5 in National Curriculum mathematics (DfE 1995b), while calculating using ratios is Level 6.

An interesting example from APU (1985) relates to the composition of anthracite. Anthracite is composed of the elements carbon, hydrogen, nitrogen and oxygen in the following proportions by mass: Carbon = 93.3%; hydrogen = 3.0%; nitrogen = 1.0%; oxygen = 2.7%.

There was only a 59 per cent success rate when pupils were asked what mass of carbon is contained in 100g of anthracite, a 46 per cent success rate when asked what mass of oxygen was contained in 200g of anthracite, and only a 34 per cent success rate when asked how many grams of anthracite contained a combined mass of 12g of hydrogen and nitrogen.

In an exercise using small plastic construction blocks, student teachers were asked to construct a model aeroplane twice the size of the one demonstrated by the tutor. A wide variety of models were produced, some doubling the width, others doubling the width and depth, others doubling width, depth and length. What do we mean by double the size? We are often not clear in our language, but it is not always easy to be clear.

Dilution of solutions in science can produce difficulties. For example if a 10cm³ solution needs to be diluted ten times, pupils will often add 100cm³ rather than 90cm³. An understanding of how dilutions are formed is an important concept for pupils to grasp. Practically mixing, measuring and discussing the dilutions could help consolidate the concept and the calculations required.

Graphs

Little research has been done on pupils' abilities to handle graphs since the extensive work by APU (1988), when the focus was on reading and constructing bar charts, histograms and co-ordinate graphs. They found that top-performing pupils were competent in both but, in bottom performance bands, pupils did far less well.

In some recent research by the authors (Lenton *et al.* 2000) looking at constructing and interpreting graphs, some Year 10 pupils, of a wide range of ability, found little difficulty in transferring data into graphical form. They were given an exercise of plotting co-ordinates for data from a table of results onto a pair of marked axes. However, the transferring of data to graphical form can often show that pupils do not use the best representation, when given a choice. For example, a group of pupils observed in a science lesson on heart beat rate had taken their pulse readings before and after exercise. They had taken readings at two-minute intervals after exercise and recorded the pulse rate for about 15 minutes, until the heart had returned to the normal rate. They were asked to plot their results on a graph (no mean feat, in view of having to place the records at the appropriate point on the time axis). Some pupils asked if they could use a bar chart rather than a line graph, clearly showing a misunderstanding of the use of these two forms of graph. These skills are considered Levels 5 and 6 in science and Level 6 in mathematics, whilst producing graphs with lines of best fit is Level 7 in science.

Interpretation of graphical information often produces poor or misconceived responses (Taylor and Swatton 1989). The authors also found that their Year 10 pupils had a number of problems with answers to questions about data presented in graphical form. The pupils were given a number of different graphs (e.g. straight line, curved line, axes beginning at greater than zero, different scale graphs to compare, bar charts) and four multiple-choice statements to assess if false or true. One question (Figure 9.1) with which the pupils did have some difficulty showed two graphs with the same information but on different scaled axes (one graph showed a greater gradient than the other). Another difficulty was encountered when questions were posed about a time distance graph depicting a person's journey on a walk. Here they were not able to clearly state whether the distance travelled between A and B was the same as between C and D (Figure 9.2). In discussion about this answer they recognised that they were muddled up by the two slopes of the graph.

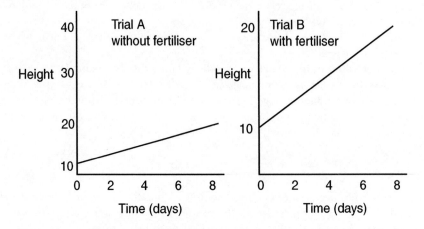

Figure 9.1 Two graphs, using different axes scales, showing the same data

The authors found that in many of these interpretation questions when pupils were allowed to discuss their answers after the event they invariably realised if they were wrong and quickly reasoned correct answers. This may mean that pupils answering such questions under examination conditions are doing themselves a disservice when they do not have an opportunity for deliberation before answering.

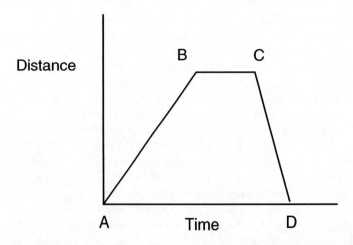

Figure 9.2 A distance/time graph of someone going for a walk

Measures and scales

Pupils studying science are regularly expected to read scales for collection of data during investigations (Level 4 maths and science). Rulers, thermometers and balances all cause their own particular problems (Strang 1989). Invariably, accuracy of reading or manipulation of the reading needs careful consideration. Tare balance reading often produces further problems, such as, when to use the tare and how to handle the reading on the balance once the tare has been used. Yet many top-pan balances in laboratories have this facility.

Once a reading has been taken, the interpretation of that reading may have further implications; for example, if a thermometer has risen from 200°C to 400°C, has the temperature doubled? Many pupils and student teachers will say 'yes' to this question (the authors' observations). One might ask in what sense is this doubling or not doubling? Even if it is not possible for a teacher to fully explain the answer, it is well worth raising the issue for pupils to consider the difference between interval scales (temperature in °C) and ratio scales (as in length). Offering pupils a comparison which is clearly an example of doubling (such as, 6cm is twice as long as 3cm) may help to clarify the issue.

Without practical experience of estimation, pupils will inevitably do it badly. How much does a pencil weigh? 0.4g, 4g*, 40g, 400g? (*correct answer). They could be asked to hold a pencil to experience the feeling of four grammes, not just told that it is that mass. Approximately how long is a million seconds? One hour, 12 hours, 1 day, 10 days* (*actually 11 days), 25 days, 1 month, 1 year? They could be asked to sit silently for, say, two minutes to gain a perception of 120 seconds, and compare this with how many they would need to reach a million.

The use of derived variables (compound measurements) such as speed and density rely on the conceptual understanding of the interaction of two variables. Concrete examples such as holding two blocks of metal (such as aluminium and iron) of similar size but of different density can alleviate this difficulty.

If a sheet of paper is rolled in two different directions (Figure 9.3) and pupils are asked if the two volumes enclosed by each cylinder are the same, many will say that they are the same. In fact they enclose very different volumes, obvious when trialled practically, and pupils who have answered 'yes' to the question may have a misconception in that the conservation of surface area does not necessarily determine conservation of volume.

Statistics

All pupils need to be able to use everyday statistics and to interpret common representations of statistics in our daily lives. Some of the basic statistics, such as averages and means, median and modes, are less understood and can be used to misinform unless the reader is fully aware of the differences. A manager might use the most favourable average wage of the work force by selecting from the median or mean to demonstrate what people earn in a company, while the union representative would almost certainly use the mode company wage (a lower figure) if a pay rise was requested. Both could be said to be average wages, but could be very

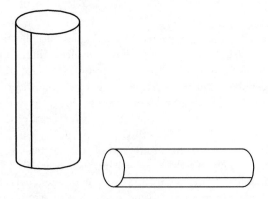

Figure 9.3 An A4 sheet of paper rolled into a column in different directions

different figures. Bar charts are commonly used in daily newspapers and by financial institutions selling investments. These can often misrepresent data if the reader misreads the vertical axis, the axis starts above zero or a large scale is used for an axis. In science, pupils often find the terms discrete and continuous difficult to apply to variables. If the terms 'measurement' and 'counting' are applied to the two terms respectively then there is usually no problem, but it is important for teachers to help and direct in these matters.

Facts and skills versus concepts

Many of these difficulties with mathematical concepts arise through not distinguishing between the teaching of facts and skills and the teaching through conceptual understanding. In many schools today, some mathematics may be taught by non-specialist teachers. Equally, science teachers may not have had a sufficiently mathematical background. For these people, one of the problems may be a lack of awareness of the nature of the conceptual problems that exist. It is important to teach from a conceptual point of view rather than from a rote-learned formula or process. Once a concept is secure, pupils are more likely to apply their ideas when solving problems or questioning data involving these. Most pupils can easily calculate an area if given the dimensions, but very few have a conceptual image of a hectare or of a thousand square metres, for example. Many pupils can draw a graph from data but find it difficult to interpret a graph when presented to them.

Pupils often have their own successful ways of solving problems mathematically but are often forced into using methods (skills) that teachers have used themselves. On the other side of the coin, sometimes pupils unfortunately make their own generalisations that do not always apply, and then arrive at incorrect answers simply because they do not understand the underlying concept. An example here is when the use of the addition of a zero for multiplying by ten is applied. It works well for whole numbers but when applied to decimals (2.3 X 10 = 2.30) it fails (Askew and William 1995). These generalisations can be counterproductive and mask understanding for the pupil. Unless the teacher makes specific efforts to uncover these misconceptions, they will remain hidden.

Too often, textbook examples assume too much from the pupil. In an example from a currently used textbook on acceleration a calculation was clearly shown, but then it continued to show how the force needed could be calculated from the acceleration. Although each step was clear to a mathematically competent person, to average pupils in Year 9 this may not have been the case. Additionally, they may not have linked this example to their own experience of acceleration. In a situation such as this, it may be necessary both for each step to be discussed and for a physical understanding of the situation to be gained. Support and guidance is clearly needed from the teacher.

Another example showed a nutrient list of vitamins measured in mg and μg, but there was nothing to say what a μg was or how it related to a mg. Points such as these can easily muddle pupils and give them less understanding. Surely all that is needed is a statement in this case explaining that there are 1000μg in a mg, followed by support from the teacher stating that m is always 1000 times greater than μ in all units. Perhaps also somewhere in the text, not necessarily at that particular point, there should be reference to the size of a μg in terms of everyday masses or units; for example, there are five million μg in a 20p coin (5g), or remember that one million seconds is 11 days.

Conclusion

It is important for science teachers not to reinforce negative messages about numeracy that are so often apparent with pupils and adults. Teachers should enthuse when using these skills and concepts to help understand science and positive encouragement should always be the focus. It is also important that science teachers should liaise with the mathematics department in the school and know how and when common skills are being taught and concepts developed, so that pupils can see some commonality and enjoy the differences in approaches used within the subjects. It is important to talk with pupils to find out what they understand and how they use their numerical skills and concepts to solve problems. Only by knowing what they are doing and how they are thinking can pupils be helped to understand, use and apply numeracy effectively in the adult world. Practical contexts often provide the basis of understanding in the mathematics needed.

As science teachers it is important to clarify to pupils:

- what needs to be *remembered* by them (facts, conventions);
- what they must *practise* (skills);
- what they can come to *understand* for themselves (concepts);
- when they have to make *decisions* about the approaches to use (strategies).

So, facts and conventions need to be learned and remembered. It is necessary to make sure that they have the skills of how to manipulate formulae, for example, and give them practice for fluency. Pupils need to experience the concepts in order to come to an understanding of them (for example, with a unit such as force) and also to be given opportunities to use their skills in solving problems, for example in *using* units of force. Moving between both they can then make decisions and learn which strategies are best to employ. If pupils are given time and opportunities to estimate, calculate, interpret, discuss with each other and with the teacher, then they will really gain a full understanding of the numerical and other mathematical concepts within science. Too often pupils jump to conclusions and use their facts and skills blindly, and do not put their ideas into context. It seems that there is a need to encourage pupils in such a way that they develop an expectation of the need to stand back and think before making a decision. Perhaps teachers should seriously think about introducing strategies that develop this aspect of their teaching; then pupils will be given the opportunity of achieving those higher levels of which they are actually capable.

Questions

1   How do we, as teachers, develop the notion of 'stand back and think' in pupils to improve their confidence in handling numeracy in science?
2   How do we develop strategies for discussion during science lessons that enable our pupils to explore their own ideas and understanding more fully?
3   How can we offer pupils more situations in which they are encouraged to interpret graphs produced from either their own class or other class data?

Further reading

Goldsworthy, A., Watson, J.R. and Wood-Robinson, V. (1999) *Investigations: Getting to Grips with Graphs*, Hatfield: Association for Science Education.

This is produced by the AKSIS Project and deals with handling graphs at Key Stages 2 and 3. It comprises a book and a computer disc and helps pupils to focus on different aspects of constructing graphs. There are activities and photocopiable worksheets for pupils and whole class teaching ideas together with discussion topics.

Swan, M. (1984) *The Language of Functions and Graphs*, Nottingham: University of Nottingham Shell Centre for Mathematical Education.

This is an older but still useful pack of activities and ideas for teachers in maths and science departments which would enhance teaching. It contains exercises, activities, worksheets, videos and OHTs.

10 Developing the literate scientist

Pauline Hoyle and Caroline Stone

Introduction

Recently, in education in England and Wales, there has been great emphasis on the importance of developing pupils' literacy skills in order to raise achievement. Within science education, the issue of language and learning has been discussed for a considerable period of time, and developing literacy skills has been part of this discussion. The 1999 draft revision of the Science National Curriculum has taken on the importance of language by incorporating communication into AT1. This may give added impetus to teachers addressing issues of language and literacy development through and within science (QCA 1999a).

Since September 1998, most primary schools have been implementing the National Literacy Strategy and some secondary schools have been piloting literacy projects in Key Stage 3. The National Literacy Strategy tries to develop pupils' understanding of language at the word, sentence and text level using a range of strategies. It places a great emphasis on developing literacy through patterning, modelling and scaffolding. Patterning work at the word and sentence level can help to make explicit, word meanings, spelling and appropriate grammar. Modelling is particularly useful at the sentence and text level by providing good models of listening, talking, reading and writing. Scaffolding is the process by which teachers provide appropriately differentiated and targeted support, which enables pupils to develop their literacy skills.

In addition to this, there is a great emphasis on the range and type of texts used in supporting and developing literacy. The text types include fiction and non-fiction, so it is possible to use texts on science topics as part of the literacy hour in primary schools. For some primary teachers, the emphasis on implementing the literacy hour, and shortly the numeracy strategy, has taken some adjustment. The practice in schools which have implemented the National Literacy Project has been to use a range of contexts, including science texts, in which to base literacy work. Feasey (1999) has produced a very useful resource which links primary science and literacy as have Lewis and Parkin (1998). The work of Lewis and Wray (1998) through the Nuffield Exeter EXEL Project has developed aspects of literacy, particularly writing frames.

Language, literacy and talk

It is important to consider how language develops and how it can be used to develop pupils' scientific thinking. The four main language skills: listening, speaking, reading and writing are needed to make a communicative and scientifically literate person.

Driver (1976) points out that although science teachers build courses around practical experience, this is of little value unless it takes account of pupils' thinking. Working with any young child will help us remember the importance of talk in developing pupils' understanding of the world and therefore developing their thinking

Vygotsky (1978) argues that the construction of knowledge and thought is based in social and cultural processes, often supported by the interaction between the individual learner and a teacher or more knowledgeable adult. Mercer (1991) suggests that pupil–pupil talk is an important part of the learning process as well as pupil–teacher talk. Bruner (1986) suggests the process of good teaching is one of providing a 'scaffold' for a child's learning. The learner does not stay forever attached to the teacher but, through effective scaffolding, professional judgement and successful 'handover', the child will learn independently.

We are therefore arguing that to develop a literate and scientifically adept child, we need to consider developing all four language skills within the science lessons, and that pupil–pupil talk combined with effective teacher interactions has a major role in developing literacy and raising achievement.

Developing listening and speaking in science lessons

How do we actually teach pupils science while supporting the development of listening and speaking in a classroom? As previously argued, we consider oral skills as the foundation on which reading and writing skills are based. Therefore the spoken word, particularly pupil–pupil talk, needs to be planned within a science scheme of work. We would suggest also that a variety of techniques to support oracy needs to be developed as part of the teaching and learning approaches to science. These techniques include:

- pupil–pupil discussion (modelling)
- teacher–pupil discussion (scaffolding)
- groups researching a topic and presenting their findings to the rest of the class (modelling)
- individuals or groups planning an investigation and sharing ideas with the rest of the class (modelling)
- role-playing, using simulation or drama (scaffolding)
- brainstorming (modelling)
- concept mapping (modelling/scaffolding)
- teacher questioning (modelling).

Patterning listening and speaking

Science has its own distinct vocabulary and technical terms. Pupils need to develop appropriate use and understanding of this terminology. For many pupils, there is confusion in their minds between the meaning afforded to words that have everyday usage and their scientific meanings, for example, for words such as cells, energy, weight, there are everyday *and* scientific meanings. This is particularly hard for pupils developing English as an additional language. Pupils' prior knowledge of the words that are common in everyday use can be ascertained by the teacher asking pupils for their definitions and understandings and by the teacher ensuring that pupils are alerted to the different meaning and use in a scientific context.

For example, to many pupils (and many adults) a cell is what you are put into at the police station or in prison. However, when we talk about cells in the body, we mean something completely different. This is a relatively easy word to redefine, as body cells can be seen or modelled. However, words like energy are much more amorphous and therefore it is important to focus pupils' attention on the different meanings. The teacher can support pupils' understanding and use of scientific terminology by using everyday terms alongside the scientific words such as kinetic and movement, see-through and transparent, until the children are confident in their understanding and use of the scientific word.

Modelling listening and speaking

The literacy hour is encouraging pupils to share their work at the end of a lesson so it may improve their presentation skills. Teaching pupils to ask well-defined questions of other pupils presenting their work can encourage the development of listening skills.

Part of science education is about pupils developing the skills of critical thinking. This involves an ability to ask questions and offer possible solutions based on theories. For pupils to learn to ask appropriate and scientifically valid questions, they need models of good questioning. For example in a nursery class learning about the seasons, the teacher can ask what colour a leaf is now, what colour the leaf was before, why the leaf changed colour and so on. Developing this type of questioning throughout pupils' science education, alongside pupils being given the opportunity to ask their own questions, is a good form of modelling.

The teacher, using good questioning techniques, can activate the pupils' prior knowledge which helps pupils recognise and express what they know. It can also give the teacher access to their thinking. For example, pupils can be given a limited amount of time to brainstorm in small groups, recording as a spider diagram on sugar paper what they know about a new topic such as forces. They can then use the rainbow technique (going to other groups) to share and exchange ideas before returning to the home group to add any further ideas which they have forgotten or acquired. At the end of the topic, pupils can return to their original spider diagram and add the new information which they have learned and then try to turn their diagram into a concept map by drawing together common areas and making links between different aspects of the topic. Other strategies that can be used are pupil discussion, using pictures and artefacts and deductive questioning.

Scaffolding talking and listening

Bruner (1986) suggested that the skill of the teacher is in using appropriate scaffolding and knowing when and how to 'handover'. So it is important for teachers to learn to listen to pupils discussing in small groups as well as judging when and how to interact and intervene. Some examples of scaffolding or structuring pupils' oral work include:

- pupils talking to their peers or their teacher about a piece of research or an investigation providing a useful rehearsal for writing the ideas down on paper;
- pupils being assisted in developing their ability to give oral presentations to a range of audiences by allowing them to practise in front of other children and receive constructive criticism;
- pupils who need support being given a structure to encourage them to make their oral feedback. For example negotiating with pupils some headings of what to cover or questions to address can provide the structure needed while other pupils need more intense teacher interaction.

Reading in science

Davies and Greene (1984) found that most of the reading, although minimal in terms of the amount of time used in secondary classrooms, is mainly associated with reading for meaning or abstracting information. There is little reading for pleasure or stories about science in secondary classrooms, although in primary classrooms the National Literacy Strategy will hopefully redress this balance. They classified the types of texts often found in science classrooms, which were mainly texts about activities, as instructional, or giving recipes, or texts associated with dealing with the following phenomena: classifying or categorisation; structures; mechanisms; processes; concept principles; and hypothesis–theory. Their work was particularly useful because it helped teachers move away from using formulae to determine the readability of the text, to considering how to make the reading active, particularly using directed activities related to texts (DARTS). Examples of strategies to support reading are:

- skimming, scanning and intensive reading of a text (patterning)
- model reading by using big books or OHPs (modelling)
- teacher questioning about the text before, during and after the text has been read (modelling)
- model how to use a glossary and an index (modelling)
- small group reading involving pupils of different aptitudes to reading (modelling)
- providing pupils with a variety of written genres (modelling)

- providing 'Know, Want to know, Learnt' (KWL) grids and 'Question, Answer, Details, Source' (QuADS) grids to support research skills (scaffolding)
- providing pupils with texts from different viewpoints to allow them to evaluate the information (scaffolding)
- allowing pupils to sequence a set of instructions prior to carrying out a practical activity to check their understanding of the task (scaffolding)
- Directed Activities Related to Text (DARTs), reconstruction tasks such as text completion and matching exercises (scaffolding)
- DARTs, analysis tasks such as agree and disagree, or sorting and categorising information (scaffolding).

Patterning reading

Pupils also need to be taught ways of looking at the words and sentence level of texts. Techniques such as skimming and scanning need to be taught. For example, when introducing a text to pupils, the teacher might invite them to look at the text for a few seconds and invite their predictions on what the text will be about. The teacher then asks the pupils if they saw any new words when they briefly looked at the text (skimming). The pupils can then be asked to examine the heading, subheadings and diagrams of the text for a longer period of time to get an overview of what it is about and to ascertain key words in the text (scanning). When the text is read word by word (intensive reading), the teacher can point out specific scientific vocabulary and the meanings discussed with the class. Often pupils will be developing a meaning for an unfamiliar or technical word, and they may not immediately be able to use the word in a new situation. Pupils need to be encouraged to create their own word banks, of scientific and everyday terms that are associated with the topic being taught, and to build up their understanding and use of the words.

Modelling reading

The National Literacy Strategy in primary schools has encouraged the use of big books to model the reading of a text and allows the teacher to point out ways of getting meaning from the text. Linking the reading to prior learning and asking pupils to explain in their own words what they have read are useful strategies to allow understanding of the concepts or thinking involved.

Modelling how to use a glossary and an index needs to be encouraged to help pupils use resources effectively in science. It is particularly necessary as pupils proceed through the Key Stages.

Enabling pupils to read together and to discuss in small groups (3–4 pupils) is an important strategy to support developing readers, especially EAL (English as an Additional Language) pupils. Pupils with different abilities in reading may or may not reflect their aptitude for science. By mixing pupils with different abilities in small groups, teachers can ensure that pupils share and build upon each others' skills, including the more competent readers, and it allows pupils to have reading modelled by other pupils as well as adults. It also lets the teacher spend time with a variety of pupils, not just those for whom reading is a difficulty, thus increasing the ways and levels in which a teacher can model reading. Alternatively, giving pupils with good reading skills a difficult or complex text can help them model reading for each other, and this really stretches them, but it is important to determine whether the science in the text is accessible or can be made accessible, as suggested earlier.

Writing in science

Purpose and audience of writing

The styles or genre that are used most frequently in secondary school science are reports, procedure and explanation. However, in recent years the scientific press has begun to write in a more personal way, rather than the traditional impersonal passive form. For some pupils, presenting information in a 'scientific format and register' may hinder them from communicating their understanding of the science. In order to expand the genre pupils use, it helps to widen the opportunities for writing. This can be done by creating different purposes and audiences for their writing. The purposes can be repeatability of an experiment, producing accurate instruction, presenting ideas argued in a logical way. Audiences for pupils' writing can include pupils writing about their investigation for different ages or members of the family, writing articles for a school or local paper, writing to scientists and so on. It is important that they get used to writing for different purposes and in different genres. This requires that teachers analyse a series of lessons and/or schemes of work to ensure that they provide a variety of purposes and audiences for pupils' writing.

Strategies to support writing include:

- encouraging pupils to spell scientific words correctly via marking and weekly spelling tests (patterning)
- providing a variety of purposes for the pupils' writing (modelling)
- providing a variety of audiences for the pupils' writing (modelling)
- modelling of how to write in different genre by the teacher (modelling)
- shared writing and group writing (scaffolding)
- teacher questioning to ensure the pupils understand the purpose and audience of the piece of writing (scaffolding)
- using writing frames to scaffold pupils' writing (scaffolding).

Modelling writing

For pupils to understand how to write in the different genres, they need to see a variety of text types and to use different models in their own writing. A class in a science lesson can discuss the structure of the text being used and the language features before and after reading it. It is also important that teachers model different tenses when talking to the class and then show how the tenses change when writing. For example, many instructions in science experiments are written in the present tense and pupils need to be taught to use the words in the instructions but to change them into the past tense for writing a report. By providing a list of connective words, such as 'before', 'then', 'after', 'next', the pupils can develop their writing and start to become independent report writers.

For example, in an experiment about using different filters to investigate muddy water, pupils were given the following instructions. Some pupils were given a help sheet to write up their experiment.

1 Make two muddy samples and label them A and B	We made two muddy ...
2 Sit each sample for 2 minutes	We let them sit ...
3 Make a solution of alum crystals and water	We made a solution ...
4 Add about 10cm3 of alum solution to the muddy solution A	We added about $10cm^3$ ...
5 Stir it in	We stirred it ...
Before each sentence use one of the connectives from the list below to make the sentences join together well:	
First, Then, Next, And, After, Finally	

Writing frames: scaffolding writing

The most common way to scaffold or support pupils' writing is to provide writing frames. A writing frame provides a series of prompts that helps make the structure of the text explicit to the writer. They can be used for drafting work and they take away the fear of a blank piece of paper. They are templates with starters, connectives and sentence modifiers that help the writer experience a range of generic structures. They can provide cohesive links, which allow pupils to maintain a sense of what they are writing. They offer a varied vocabulary of connectives and sentence beginnings, which allow pupils to move on from what they usually write. Writing frames can ensure some success at writing and therefore improve the motivation and self-esteem of the pupils. The appropriate way to use a writing frame is by the teacher firstly demonstrating how to use it. The pupils can then complete a frame as a joint activity. Next, pupils are able to complete the frame on their own, and finally they can complete a piece of writing independently without the use of a frame. Lewis and Wray (1996) have produced a number of writing frames that can be adapted for use in science. These include writing frames for the different genre: recount; report; procedure; explanation; persuasion; and discussion.

Below is a summary of the different types of genre used in science writing. It is based on the Excel project and work from the Nuffield primary science group (Lewis and Parkin 1998):

- Recount: text which is personal and story-like, written in the past tense, with events presented in chronological order. Most pupils are already familiar with this genre. Recounts usually consist of:

– orientation: setting the scene: 'We had to find out … '
– events: the events as they occurred written down: 'I measured the temperature with a thermometer'.
– reorientation: closing the scene: 'I found out that … '

- Report: text which is used to describe something in a logical way, written in the third person in an objective manner, usually written in the past tense and are non-chronological. Reports usually consist of:

  – an opening: 'Sodium is a metal.'
  – a more technical description: 'The symbol for sodium is Na.'
  – a description of the phenomena: 'Properties of this element are … '

- Explanation: text which is used to explain a process or how something works. It is often written in the simple present tense, using connective words such as 'then', 'next', 'after', 'because', 'therefore'. Explanations usually consist of:

  – an introduction statement: 'Kidneys are organs found in the human body.'
  – a series of logical steps explaining how something occurs: 'Blood goes into the Bowman's capsule where it is filtered then … '
  – the steps continue until the process is complete: 'The urine produced passes into the bladder.'

- Procedure: a series of steps written as instructions to describe how something is done. It is usually written in the simple present tense, in chronological order. A procedural text usually consists of:

  – a statement of what is to be achieved: 'How to neutralise an acid.'
  – a list of materials/apparatus: 'Beakers, measuring cylinders.'
  – a series of steps in order: 'Measure the acid.'
  – a diagram is often included.

- Persuasion: text which is used to promote a particular point of view or argument. It is usually written in the simple present tense with logical connectives such as 'however' and 'because'. Persuasive writing usually consists of:

  – the thesis: an opening statement in the form of a preview: 'Exercise is good for you.'
  – the arguments: consists of points with some explanation, such as, 'Exercise increase your strength and tolerance.'
  – reiteration: a summary and restatement of the opening statement, such as 'We have seen that … therefore all the evidence shows that exercise is good for you.'

- Discussion: text which is used to present arguments and information from different viewpoints. It is usually written in the simple present tense with logical connectives such as: 'because', 'therefore' and 'however'. Discussion papers usually consist of:

  – a statement of the issue with a preview of the main arguments: 'Should all pupils wear a reflector over their school coat?'
  – arguments for the supporting statement: 'Keeps pupils safe at night when crossing the roads.'
  – arguments against the supporting statement: 'Most pupils feel strongly that they do not want to wear a reflector over their coats (looks silly)'. (Arguments for and against can be in any order.)
  – recommendation: a summary and conclusion, 'We feel that … '

Differentiation

Writing frames can be overused or even abused in the classroom. Not all pupils in a class need a writing frame. Some pupils will be able to move from joint construction to independent writing without a writing frame. Writing frames are useful for reluctant writers, pupils with special needs, or in the early stages of EAL, or to scaffold the use of a new written genre. They should therefore be used with careful planning for differentiation.

Note-making

Another important skill in writing is note-making. Pupils do not find this easy and therefore need to be taught how to do it. They need to be shown the purpose of note-making. They can be given practice by providing a range of opportunities for note-making, such as making notes from text, notes from listening to a speaker, or notes from observations from their environment.

Strategies that can be used to support note-making are:

- model good note-making from the front of the class. Show them how to make notes in different formats such as lists, spider diagrams, flow diagrams.
- ask pupils to pick out three important points and make notes after reading a short piece of information. They will need to discuss examples of good notes taken and how to improve their own notes.
- ask pupils to make a list of the key ideas or features when shown artefacts.
- invite a speaker in and ask pupils to make notes. Get pupils to compare their notes and develop a set of class notes from the different notes taken by pupils.
- give pupils a science based article and ask them to underline the main points and then make a set of notes consisting of 4–6 key points. Get them to compare the notes they make from each source and discuss which are the best notes and why.
- provide a tape-recorder to make oral notes, for pupils who find difficulty in writing.

- give the pupils five different texts about a topic, restrict the time they can have to read the text and write one or two points from each one. When they have finished they can share their points with a group so that the group has five or six points. These points can then be shared with the class.
- Survey, Question, Read, Recite, Review (S.Q.3R.) is a useful strategy to encourage pupils to access text. The pupils need to be encouraged to make notes in a variety of formats, read the notes, recite them out loud, then to try and write them out again without looking at their original notes.

Summary

Development of literacy and science are interlinked. The point of science education is to enable pupils to better understand the world around them and to enable them to be able to adapt to a rapidly changing world and to developing technologies. We want to enable pupils to be scientifically literate, so we must use every opportunity when teaching science to develop pupils' literacy skills and knowledge. Science provides a wonderful context in which to develop new knowledge and therefore the need for new language to describe it. We need to develop all the four language skills: speaking, listening, reading and writing, within science contexts. We need to enable pupils to interact with each other, the teacher, other adults and resources to develop their understanding of the world and their ways of communicating that knowledge and understanding.

Questions

1   What examples of talk are there in your classroom?
2   How does the scheme of work you follow allow for variety of talking and listening, reading and writing?
3   How do you support the development of reading in your classroom?
4   How do you support the development of writing in your classroom?

Further reading

Davies, F. and Greene, T. (1984) *Reading for Learning in the Sciences*, Harlow: Oliver and Boyd.
   This book is an excellent summary of ways of making reading active and so supporting reading in science. It also gives teachers guidance on writing their own texts as how to make them accessible.

Feasey, R. (1999) *Primary Science and Literacy Links*, Hatfield: ASE.
   This book is an excellent resource, which demonstrates how to put the various issues discussed here and in the National Literacy Strategy into practice. There are lots of examples of pupils' work together with templates that can be adapted to support the development of literacy in the classroom.

Hoyle, P., Laine, C. and Smyth, S. (1990) *Science Kaleidoscope*, Oxford: Heinemann.
   This is a series of learning activities that can be used in KS3 or adapted to other Key

Stages. The activities are practical examples of how to model and scaffold reading and writing in a range of subject areas.

Mercer, N. (1991) *Learning Through Talk*, Milton Keynes: Open University, Article 1.2 in Course Materials.

This is an excellent and easy to read article which emphasises the importance of talk and teacher intervention in developing pupils language and thinking.

Thorpe, S., Deshpande P. and Edwards C. (1994) *Race, Equality and Science Teaching: Teachers' Resource Book*, Hatfield: ASE.

There are several articles in this manual which give guidance on developing language in science and the issues related to language development for bilingual learners in science education.

11 Health education is unavoidable

Sheila Turner

Introduction

Do you teach about any of the following topics?

- Animal-to-human transplantation
- Consumption of genetically modified foods
- Eating disorders
- Genetic engineering
- Genetic testing, such as for sickle cell
- HIV/AIDS
- Human genome project
- *In vitro* fertilisation
- Mental health
- Relationships
- Reproductive technologies

The answer is likely to be yes to most, if not all, of the above topics if you are a secondary science teacher, and some of these topics will also be covered at an appropriate level in primary schools. Therefore, it is almost certain that you and other members of your department/school/college are involved in discussions about health related issues with pupils. And you are not alone. The findings from a recent national survey of science teachers in England and Wales (Turner *et al.* 1999) indicate that most secondary schools/colleges and science teachers are tackling such topics in science. The majority of the science teachers in the survey were teaching a wide range of health related topics, including those listed above, to pupils aged 11–16 years and to students post-16. Some of these topics were part of programmes of work linked to the National Curriculum in England and Wales (DfE 1995a) or to examination syllabuses and were covered in some depth, others were touched upon in discussions in science lessons and/or Personal, Social and Health Education (PSHE) programmes. Interestingly, none of the science teachers in our sample questioned whether they should be teaching such topics as part of science.

The importance of PSHE in schools and colleges is now well recognised (DfEE/QCA 1999e), in marked contrast to the situation reported two decades ago by the former Department of Education and Science (DES 1978b) when few schools had teachers with responsibility for health education or planned programmes of health education. However, the DES noted that 'health education is unavoidable, even if its presence is denied' (DES 1978b: 29). Although the situation has changed, health education can still be marginalised or focus on a limited range of topics.

This chapter starts by considering a number of questions, including:

- What is health education?
- What are the issues?
- What is the role of science teachers in teaching and learning about health?

These questions provide a starting point for examining issues concerning the place of health education in the curriculum and, specifically, how issues linked to health education might be addressed as part of science teaching. The chapter goes on to consider how recent initiatives by government and projects undertaken as part of the Health Promoting Schools in Europe programme can be used as a basis for developing health promotion and health education strategies in schools and colleges. Suggestions for teaching and learning strategies are linked to research that has explored the views of teachers, student teachers and pupils about health education.

What is health education?

The response to this question is a personal one that will be influenced by factors such as where you teach and the age group(s) with whom you work, as well as your views about health and health education. The World Health Organisation (WHO) Constitution defines health as ' ... a positive state of mental, physical and social well-being and not merely the absence of disease or infirmity' (WHO Constitution, 1946). Despite being written over fifty years ago the WHO statement is still pertinent today and provides a useful starting point for thinking about health education. Health is not merely a question of hygiene and human physiology but encompasses all aspects of human life and lifestyles.

One way of introducing discussion about health education is to ask individuals (staff and pupils) to write down three sentences that begin 'Health education is ... '. Comparing statements can lead to a shared, common view of health education and stimulate further debate on issues of common concern and interest. This strategy was one employed as part of a recent study involving student teachers who were training to teach science in secondary schools in London and Stockholm (Turner *et al.* 1999). We asked students to write down their own definition of health education on two occasions during their Initial Teacher Education science course. The first occasion was before they had any experience of teaching in school, and the second after they had been in schools for some weeks. On both occasions, health education was conceived in very broad terms that included knowledge and understanding, for example about drugs and their effect on the body, and individual responsibility. The responses prior to and after teaching were similar but those given following teaching experience placed greater emphasis on pupils' teaching and learning, for example:

- teaching pupils about the hazards of drinking, smoking and drugs
- learning about drugs, safe sex and mental health.

Important aspects of health education raised by students after practical teaching included:

- the importance of raising self-esteem in pupils
- helping pupils to see the consequences of different ways of life
- influencing attitudes and values
- ethics.

There was a remarkable similarity between the responses given by student teachers in London and Stockholm. Furthermore, discussions with experienced teachers in both countries and elsewhere indicate agreement with the views expressed by these student teachers. Health education is described by teachers as embracing not just knowledge and understanding but also attitudes and skills.

Evidence for pupils' views comes from a number of studies (for example, Turner *et al.* 1999; Turner *et al.* 1997). The suggestions made by pupils about what topics should be included in health education are of particular interest. Secondary pupils in schools in London and Stockholm, for example, wanted to learn more about diseases, such as heart disease, cancer and inherited conditions (Turner *et al.* 1999). They wanted to know how these conditions were caused and what they could do to prevent such diseases. These pupils felt very strongly about what they wanted to know and were unhappy 'only learning about AIDS' (girl, 14 years). Some pupils indicated that they wanted discussions about mental health and bullying. They also commented on the approach to health education, indicating that they thought that health topics should be taught in an honest and open way. The pupils wanted relevant and practical advice about health, rather than being 'overloaded with details'.

The views expressed above by student teachers and pupils reflect changes in thinking about what constitutes health education during the past three decades. This change is apparent also in views about approaches to teaching and learning about health and science. Greater emphasis is now placed on the development of personal and social skills, including decision making. The development of such skills depends on the identification of appropriate contexts and suitable topics for different age groups.

Suggestions for topics that might be covered as part of health education in primary schools are shown in Figure 11.1. Many of these topics are also frequently addressed in secondary schools. A useful way of identifying what is taught in school/college is to ask colleagues and/or pupils to highlight the topics that are covered in different subjects and/or as part of health education: they will probably be surprised by the number and range of topics taught.

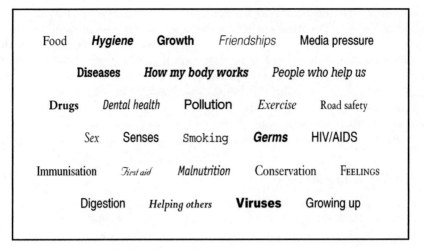

Figure 11.1 Topics that could be incorporated into health education programmes in primary schools

Source: based on *Health for Life 1: A Teacher's Planning Guide to Health Education in the Primary School*, Health Education Authority's Primary School Project (London: Nelson, 1989).

What are the issues?

Key issues in teaching and learning about health education include:

- the place and role of health education in the school curriculum;
- the role of teachers, including science teachers, in teaching about health-related issues;
- identifying appropriate teaching strategies that take account of young people's views, priorities, experience and understanding;
- identifying resources that are unbiased, reliable and up-to-date;
- the role of Initial Teacher Education (ITE) and Continuing Professional Development (CPD) in preparing teachers to teach about health related issues.

These issues are explored in greater depth later in this chapter. In many cases there are no easy ways of overcoming the more problematic issues. The aim is to stimulate debate rather than to provide solutions to specific problems.

A further issue is that health education in schools is no longer something that is decided solely by whim or in response to a particular situation by an individual teacher. During the past decade there has been increasing government involvement and direction in all areas of the curriculum, including health education, particularly in schools in England and Wales. An example can be seen in the plans to introduce the teaching of Citizenship into the curriculum in England and Wales (DfEE/QCA 1999e), an area that overlaps with health education, as well as the guidelines for Health Education that form part of the National Curriculum for England and Wales (DfEE/QCA 1999e). Regrettably, the PSHE guidelines are non-statutory. The discussions and rethinking of the curriculum that has resulted should be beneficial in many respects, in particular by raising issues and initiating rethinking of approaches to teaching and learning. The emergence of the Health Promoting Schools in Europe initiatives is further proof of the increasing importance of external factors and agencies. One outcome is that there are opportunities to think more creatively about science and health education, and their links to citizenship education, and how best to meet the needs of all pupils. Furthermore, there is money available from a variety of sources for local initiatives, including those by individual schools, to promote health education in new ways.

Health-promoting schools

The term health-promoting schools (HPS) has become increasingly commonly used during the past five years. However, there is still debate about what a HPS actually is and how one can be recognised. The questions in Figure 11.2 may help to answer this question. Such questions can be used to develop a 'health profile' of the school and to stimulate discussions with colleagues.

Current views about health education are based on ideas of the health promoting school/college, which envisages a whole school approach to health promotion that includes:

- the taught curriculum
- the 'hidden' curriculum
- the active participation of pupils and teachers, parents and governors

At the present time, as part of the move towards developing HPS throughout Europe, health promotion programmes are being developed as part of a joint initiative by the World Health Organisation (WHO 1993) and the Council of Europe (CEC) which aims to 'develop, and assess the effectiveness of, strategies for changing and shaping pupils' patterns of behaviour, with the aim of safe-guarding their long-term health' (Department of Health 1992). A key feature of HPS is that they actively involve all members of the local community in school-focused projects that range from improving the local environment and recycling of waste products to improvements in school canteens.

Young people's views

It is now generally accepted that young people come to school with ideas about scientific concepts and phenomena, including those related to the human body, that are based on everyday experience. There is a growing literature that suggests that some of the ideas that young people hold may be at variance with established scientific thinking (see for example Carey, 1985; Osborne *et al.* 1992; Reiss and Dale-Tunnicliffe 1999). There is also evidence that knowledge alone is not sufficient to ensure that individuals will act in ways conducive to the promotion of health (see for example Hochbaum 1979; Davies *et al.* 1982; Lucas 1987; Turner 1997).

My own research with pupils aged from 5–19 years over a period of many years

A. THE SCHOOL ENVIRONMENT **A1 The physical environment** – does the environment: 1. Have attractive, cared-for surroundings – interior and exterior? 2. Provide good quality conditions in which to work? 3. Have adequate facilities, e.g. a quiet room, rooms for recreation, exercise? 4. Offer access to a smoke-free environment?	A little ——————— A lot
A2 The school ethos – does the school: 1. Have clear social aims? 2. Develop and monitor health-related policies, e.g. for nutrition? 3. Have clear and consistent methods for policy making? 4. Actively promote the self-esteem of pupils by demonstrating that everyone can make a contribution to the life of the school? 5. Involve pupils in policy and decision making, e.g. through a School Council? 6. Encourage and enable *all* staff and pupils to contribute to innovation (i.e. including catering staff and caretakers)? 7. Encourage staff/student contact beyond teaching-related commitments (e.g. in the dining room/canteen)? 8. Consider the role of staff as models in health-related issues? 9. Have health guidance accessible to all? 10. Provide a counselling service for pupils and staff?	
B. TEACHING PROGRAMMES – does the school: 1. Provide stimulating challenges for all pupils through a wide range of activities? 2. Integrate health topics e.g. nutrition, across disciplines? 3. Demonstrate a commitment to active learning strategies? 4. Negotiate pupil-centred learning experiences and recognition of achievement?	
C. PARENTS AND COMMUNITY – does the school: 1. Have strategies for developing good links between the school, the home and the community? 2. Monitor and evaluate the way in which links are promoted and maintained between the school, the home and the community? 3. Have policies for promoting and sustaining good links between associated primary schools and, where appropriate, tertiary and FE colleges?	

Figure 11.2 Is your school health-promoting?

Source: based on ideas from A. Coles and S. Turner (1995) *Diet and Health in School Age Children*, and T. O'Donnell and G. Gray (1994) 'Tailor Made Training', in *The Health Promoting College*.

has indicated that the views of young people about health related issues are often refreshing, coherent and well articulated. Their ideas about health are influenced, as are those of adults, by many factors including personal experience, the family and the media as is shown in Figure 11.3.

Sometimes pupils recognise the influences of such things as home and parents, on other occasions they appear not to, as is apparent from a study in primary

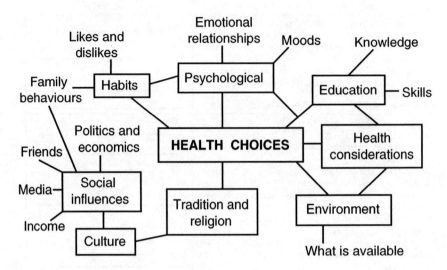

Figure 11.3 Factors that influence health choices

schools in London and Thessaloniki that explored the sources of the pupils' ideas about food and health (Turner *et al.* 1997). Families, in particular parents, appeared to be the most commonly identified source of information for children in both countries. The mother was perceived as being the main source of information in the family for a number of reasons, including who was responsible for cooking and parents' working patterns: 'I discuss more with my mother, because she usually cooks' (Turner *et al.* 1997)

Other sources of information included teachers, doctors and labels on food packages. When pupils were asked about what they learned about food in school they responded by describing what the teacher had said. Pupils frequently identified lessons, generally science, and the context of discussions about food, such as debates about food safety: 'all this trouble about the meat, we discussed with our teacher many times'; 'Our teacher advised us to eat fruits and vegetables' (Turner *et al.* 1997). It was apparent that television was an important source of information for all pupils, although they did not always appreciate that they 'learnt' about food from television: 'From the television we have not learnt many things' (Turner *et al.* 1997). The impression gained was that learning, in their view, was something that happened in school.

Whilst the views of pupils about health related issues may be different from the accepted scientific view, the reasons for this are complex and include misunderstandings, lack of experience and perhaps the context in which questions are asked. Pupils are also adept at giving the answers that they think teachers and/or researchers want! However, exploring the views that young people have is a useful starting point for discussion and teaching about health education. Journals, such as *School Science Review* and *Journal of Biological Education*, report on studies that have used a range of strategies including interviews about instances; draw and write (discussed later) and questionnaire surveys.

The outcomes of large-scale surveys can also be a useful starting point for teaching about such topics as diet and health, smoking, alcohol consumption, drugs and sexual behaviour and/or for collecting data in schools/colleges (see for example Department of Health 1989; Health Education Authority 1993a, 1993b). These surveys reveal the extent of young people's knowledge as well as their concerns and priorities. Thus, while the majority of 16–19-year-olds are aware of 'alcohol units' and sensible drinking behaviour, they tend to underestimate the strength of lager and beer (HEA 1993a). Young people appear to be aware of the risks associated with, for example drug abuse, but frequently fail to relate their own behaviour to these risks or choose to ignore the risks. There appears to be a feeling that the consequences of an unhealthy life style will not happen to them, or only in later life (HEA 1993a). These surveys suggest that health education can be helpful but needs to address more fully some of the issues raised by the studies as well as issues that young people perceive to be important.

The place and role of health education in the school curriculum

Health education, however it is conceived or taught, goes beyond the narrow confines of subject boundaries. Even when the NC was introduced in England and Wales in 1989 it was recognised that there were other aspects of the curriculum, such as health education, that should be an integral part of work undertaken by schools (NCC 1990). Although some aspects of health education might take place in science and other subjects, other aspects were more appropriately addressed through cross-curricular themes or topics. Furthermore, the boundaries between science and what can be considered as health education are not always easy to define. Thus discussions about, for example, the effects of inhaling cigarette smoke on the lungs frequently lead to more general debates about smoking and health.

The former National Curriculum Council (NCC) outlined different ways in which health education might be incorporated into the curriculum, including:

- permeating the whole curriculum
- as a separately time-tabled subject
- as part of themes or topics in other subjects such as science
- as part of programmes for personal and social development
- as part of tutorial programmes
- through opportunities arising from other activities

The ideal is probably a mixture of some or all of the above strategies, allied to careful record keeping to ensure that health topics are not forgotten or, conversely, repeated too frequently in an unplanned way.

Analysis of what schools actually do suggests that most use a variety of approaches and that there are differences between the ways in which primary and secondary schools tackle health related topics. Such analysis can be a useful starting point for schools/colleges and departments considering health education provision. The advent of citizenship as part of the curriculum in England and Wales and the provision of new guidelines for Personal, Social and Health

Education (DfEE/QCA 1999e) should lead to further rethinking of ways in which health education might be addressed in the future, as will the probable repeal of the controversial Section 28 of the Local Government Act (1988) in respect of teaching about homosexuality.

The role or science teachers in teaching about health: the science teacher as expert

The 'science teacher as expert' syndrome is prevalent in many schools/colleges. During discussions about health education with secondary science teachers many have indicated (Turner *et al.* 1999) that staff in other departments, who do not have a science background, as well as pupils, expect them to be sources of information about a whole range of health related issues from diet and exercise to drug abuse. The same situation can arise with science co-ordinators in primary schools. Science teachers frequently stress how important it is for pupils to understand the science underlying topics related to health, something that many feel they are in a unique position to provide. The expertise and knowledge that science teachers have is certainly important in developing and delivering health education programmes. However, it is obvious that none of us can be an expert or keep up-to-date in every field of science, let alone the more diffuse 'grey areas' of health education and this poses difficulties for even the most experienced science teacher. Furthermore, many science teachers teach outside their own discipline, for example, chemists teaching biology. Many also express lack of confidence in teaching about the broader social and ethical issues of topics such as those linked to biomedical research (Turner *et al.* 1999).

There is some evidence that the attitudes of teachers towards teaching about specific health related topics, such as nutrition, depend on how much time they spend teaching such topics. Teachers who teach such topics more frequently appear to be more positive and confident; a finding that is perhaps not unsurprising. However, it appears that teachers' knowledge and understanding is not the only factor that determines how they feel about teaching a particular topic, their attitudes and beliefs about health and health education are also important (O'Connell *et al.* 1981; Turner 1997). The study by O'Connell and her colleagues indicated the importance of teacher education programmes in influencing teachers' attitudes to teaching health related topics. This finding indicates a need for planned and co-ordinated CPD/INSET, with inputs by 'experts' in specific fields of health education such as drug education.

In my view, science teachers have an important role to play in health education programmes, not just because of their expertise, but because they have additional strengths such as those derived from working as a team in a practically focused subject. However, staff in other disciplines can, and do, make vital contributions to health education programmes. In secondary schools science teams sometimes need to be encouraged to break out of the prep room and develop creative partnerships with colleagues in other disciplines such as drama specialists. Ideally, planning for health education needs to involve all staff in cross curricular teams planning and implementing programmes for specific age groups. One example of good practice observed recently involved interdisciplinary teams developing programmes for specific year groups in a secondary school. Each member of the team was responsible for delivering discrete parts of the programme to each class in turn. The intention was to ensure that teachers were teaching topics in which they were interested and had expertise.

Teaching strategies

As noted earlier, health-related issues are frequently controversial and need sensitive handling at an individual and group level. A range of teaching strategies are required, some of which may be utilised rarely in science lessons, for example debates and role play, but are used frequently by colleagues in the humanities. The very nature and arrangement of science laboratories means that they may not provide an ideal environment for the type of strategies that are best suited to health education, including discussion of problematic issues.

The selection of appropriate teaching approaches is vital if the broad aims of health education, that include ensuring that young people have the knowledge and skills needed to help to them to make informed decisions, are to be achieved. Health education also focuses on raising self-esteem (DfEE 1999e) and there is general agreement that it includes young people taking responsibility for their lifestyles and health-related behaviours. How can this be achieved? One strategy that can be used is value clarification exercises that help pupils to explore 'values and attitudes that promote personal responsibility and that develop positive health behaviours' (Williams *et al.* 1990: 22). Such approaches require time for discussion and exploration of ideas allied to mutual respect and teachers adopting a neutral stance which neither promotes a particular set of values nor attempts to change attitudes (Tones and Tilford 1994).

Further strategies that can be incorporated into health education programmes include:

- debates/ discussion
- drama and roleplay: pupil/school-devised or theatre groups
- draw and write
- ICT: simulations, collecting and analysing data
- lectures/talks by visiting speakers and staff, parents and pupils with expertise
- literature, media and Internet reviews
- peer teaching
- presentations during assemblies
- practical and creative activities such as modelling or music
- 'puzzles' such as word searches or crosswords devised by pupils and/or staff
- writing, including creative writing
- visits

This list could be extended. Most of these strategies can be used with pupils of all ages, although some are more appropriate for pupils of specific ages. Guidance on how such strategies can be incorporated into health education programmes are available from organisations, such as the former Health Education Authority (1989), the Sex Education Forum (Thomson 1993) and the Wellcome Trust (1994), and in publications that focus on science education, such as Frost (1995, 1997), Reiss (1999) and Turner (1995, 1998).

Perhaps the ideal situation in developing programmes for health education is one where staff work across disciplines, thus benefiting from each other's expertise in using particular strategies, for example, role-play. In some cases, including peer teaching, schools may need to work in collaboration with specialist health education units in developing teaching approaches and materials. In one school I visited recently, sixth formers, who have been trained by specialist health educators, work with pupils aged 13–14 years (Year 9) delivering a sex education programme. The programme is very successful. Younger pupils find it easy to relate to the sixth formers and are able to ask questions that they might find it difficult to ask adults. The sixth formers also benefit from the experience; they have had to rethink their own views about sex-related issues, including relationships. There is evidence that peer teaching can be effective in many areas of health education, including teaching about substance abuse (Aggleton 1995), especially if a social and life skills approach is adopted.

The strategy of 'draw and write' has been used widely and very successfully in many parts of the world. It has been used to collect research data (Williams *et al.* 1989; Osborne *et al.* 1992; Mauthner *et al.* 1993; Reiss and Dale-Tunnicliffe 1999) that has provided information about ideas that children of different ages have about themselves and their bodies, as well as to explore attitudes to health. The strategy provides a good starting point for thinking about specific aspects of health, such as exercise and diet, with pupils of all ages. Younger pupils can be asked to 'draw yourself looking healthy and doing all the things you thought of that make you healthy and keep you healthy', and then to describe or write about what they are doing in the drawing (Williams *et al.* 1989). The drawings themselves, as well as the categorisation of drawings into groups, can be used as a starting point for teaching and as a basis for discussion.

Writing can have a number of purposes including:

- to explain experiences and learning;
- to share and communicate ideas;
- to reinterpret learning at a more personal level.

Providing opportunities for reflective writing for a specific audience can be a means of helping pupils to clarify their ideas in relation to health, including aspects of mental health, such as depression. Such writing has a place in science. Creative writing can lead to drama and role play, strategies that provide pupils with opportunities to explore ideas/situations in a safe environment, including:

- their own and others' lifestyles;
- health-related situations and problems with a range of outcomes;
- risk-taking and its possible outcomes.

Such strategies need to be used with care. Younger pupils especially may find it hard to distinguish between role play and reality. Discussions or collaborative work with colleagues with specialist experience in English and drama can be very valuable.

Sometimes the most visible product of teaching about health topics appears to be posters, for example, those indicating the dangers of smoking. However, there are other ways in which pupils' work can be presented and displayed including:

- wall stories or charts
- display boards
- class books
- videos
- CD-ROMs
- Internet presentations
- presentations in assemblies

Involving pupils in what should be displayed and how it should be presented is important, as is the sense of the target audience.

Resources and information

The topics listed at the start of this chapter illustrated the range of topics that might be addressed in health education programmes. Many of the topics identified are controversial and/or the subject of ongoing research and therefore having access to unbiased, accurate and up-to-date information about health related issues is vital. Government and independent organisations, such as the Wellcome Trust (1999) and Institute of Biology (1999), as well as industry, provide specialist information and the Internet enables such information to be accessed more readily than in the past. The information and resources available need to be evaluated critically – which takes time. Such evaluation is essential in the case of materials produced by industry, which may be biased and need modification before they can be used for teaching. Guidance such as that produced by the Department of Health (1996) for evaluating teaching materials produced by the food industry provides a useful checklist that can be used for other teaching materials.

Health education in schools; professional development and partnerships

The rapidly changing world of science and health is too complex and diverse for any one person to be an expert in many fields – or even one. We need to draw on many resources, including people and the 'new' technologies, to develop our understanding of the biomedical sciences at any one time. Programmes for CPD can have a vital role to play, provided they are targeted appropriately and meet the needs of participating teachers.

During the past two decades, the idea of partnerships has become an increasingly common one in education. The partnerships being forged across Europe in science education as part of the 'Science Across the World' initiatives by the Association for

Science Education are one example; the benefits are varied and encouraging. There are also many partnerships being developed at local level, including those between the community, involving parents, universities, industry and schools. The increasing use of ICT and the Internet will serve to broaden and extend these partnerships and can provide up-to-date information. How can we use such partnerships to develop knowledge and understanding of science and health?

One solution is to draw on biomedical researchers who are expert in their fields. Professional organisations such as the Institutes of Biology and Physics in the United Kingdom can provide opportunities for teachers and pupils to meet and work with scientists from industry and universities. We need to be imaginative about how we maximise the opportunities for dialogue with the scientific and education communities across Europe, through HPS for example, as well as at local level.

Such partnerships provide, in my view, a sound basis for developing knowledge and skills based on perceived needs. However, there is a 'health warning' attached to this suggestion. What is needed is not just up-to-date knowledge but a critical stance to enable teachers to interpret that knowledge and make it accessible and applicable in schools. Information can be up-to-date but biased, as is evident when complex issues are simplified in the media or Internet. There is a need for varied, scientifically accurate, resource materials for teaching beyond traditional textbooks and here the idea of partnership between 'experts' in complementary fields is worth developing further. There are many eminent scientists who are committed to increasing the public understanding of science through work with schools and teacher education programmes. There are also many scientists whose writings help to communicate ideas to those who are non-scientists.

Conclusions

As we move forward into the twenty-first century, it is evident that the science that underpins health-related issues will continue to change; indeed it is perhaps changing faster than at any time in the past one hundred years. Techniques involved in cloning and mapping the human genome, which until recently would have seemed the stuff of science fiction, are already a reality. Inevitably, the debate about the ways in which such advances should be applied in promoting health will be an ongoing one. The aims of health education in the coming decades will be, as now, to help pupils to live with change and uncertainty, to help them to adopt a critical stance, to be aware of the issues and to assess the risks involved in the applications of new technologies. Health education has a crucial role to play in developing the skills that young people need and in engendering positive attitudes to health, as also do science teachers. For science teachers, health education really is unavoidable.

Questions

1   What is health education? (Individuals could write down their own definitions before discussing these in small groups.)

2   How is health education organised in your school/college? What is the role of Personal/Social/Health Education and who is responsible for PSHE? Are there changes that you want to make?

3   What topics might be included as part of health education programmes for different age groups?

4   Who is responsible for teaching health related topics to different age groups? Are there other people who might be involved?

5   To what extent is your school/college 'health promoting'? (You may find it helpful to use Figure 11.2 as a starting point.)

Further reading

Coles, A. and Turner, S.A. (1995) *Diet and Health in School Age Children*, London: HEA.
This is one of a series of briefing papers produced by the HEA on health-related topics. It contains section on teaching and learning about diet and health plus relevant appendix on issues/questions that need to be addressed by health promoting schools.

Frost, J. (ed.) (1995) *Teaching Science*, London: Woburn Press.
A useful book that provides information about different teaching approaches that can be used in teaching science and health education, including discussion and role-play.

Thomson, R. (1993) *Religion, Ethnicity and Sex Education: Exploring the Issues*, London: National Children's Bureau.
A resource for teachers and others working with young people produced on behalf of the Sex Education Forum, this work provides a broad and balanced perspective about teaching sensitive and controversial issues. It raises pertinent issues for discussion and debate.

Williams, T., Roberts, J. and Hyde, J. (1990) *Exploring Health Education: Materials for Teacher Education*, London: Macmillan for HEA.
This resource provides comprehensive coverage of topics that are taught as part of health education in schools. It contains activities that can be used as INSET with colleagues as well as materials that can be used with pupils and ideas for teaching.

12 The use of cognitive ability testing to set targets

Pat O'Brien

Introduction

Schools and science departments need to be more scientific about the way they use data to assess pupils. Assessment is about attainment, progress and value added. Broadly, attainment is what has been achieved in the past; progress is a judgement of gain over a period of time; and value added is a relative measure of prior attainment to current attainment. Frith (1984) argues that assessment has a number of important roles:

- providing feedback about progress;
- communicating the nature and level of achievement;
- determining the grouping for learning;
- evaluating the effectiveness of teaching.

To perform any of these functions, we need good reliable information about the pupils and their basic skills and abilities, including their reasoning ability. However, assessment is not a science but a compromise. There are assumptions that need to be made in any form of assessment which always lead to assessment data being used cautiously.

White and Gunstone (1992) have argued that there are four key processes involved in school learning:

- memorising: recall of facts, sequences of ideas, or physical actions;
- decoding: making sense of pictorial, or symbolic, sources of information;
- creating: model building to represent a concept;
- co-operating: working together communicatively

These processes need to be linked to a pattern of working identified by Alkin and Kosecoff (1974), which involves four stages. These are identification of needs; using differentiated resources; monitoring by assessment; and informative feedback. How can such ideas be put into practice?

Sam and Chris: a case study

Sam and Chris are two Y8 pupils who joined their school in 1998. The school had been using Cognitive Ability Testing (CATs) to establish a baseline GCSE target. The general principle used by the school is that the tests give them some baseline idea of the possible outcome for the pupils. The CAT scores gives each pupil a standardised score for their verbal, quantitative and non-verbal reasoning skills. These three scores are aggregated and standardised to give a single score:

Aggregated Standardised Scores

Verbal Score + Quantitative Score + Non-verbal Score

It was noted that Sam and Chris had similar aggregated CAT scores, and their Key Stage 2 Test results were the same. They were placed in the same form for their science, and the expectations were similar. However, it was noted over the terms that Sam's behaviour demonstrated much frustration while Chris was a quiet hard-working pupil. The backgrounds of the pupils were similar, but teachers in the science department began to note Sam was very quick at seeing the solution to problems and talking about them, but was reluctant to record work in a written form.

A member of the Science Department had attended a course on the use of CATs to diagnose weaknesses and strengths in a pupil's reasoning abilities. He decided to use the CAT scores to help in the setting procedures. This required the department to make some clear distinctions in their procedures. The department adopted the following basic definitions:

- *attainment*, an appraisal of the pupils' experiences which can be affected by ability, motivation and basic skills capability;
- *ability*, which is intrinsic to the individual and is the potential of the person;
- *capability*, the basic skills and reasoning ability which relates to the use of verbal, quantitative and non-verbal reasoning. These are seen as the fundamental building elements of reasoning in a classical academic curriculum.

The department decided it was not possible to measure ability as an absolute, but only as a relative value. That value relies heavily upon the test and person conducting the assessment and the individual undergoing the test. Attainment and achievement are relative measures of what the pupil has demonstrated they know, understand or can do; they are not a direct measure of ability. To gain some relative indication of a pupil's capability, we need to use a range of information from any of the following:

- Cognitive Ability Tests such as CATs, YELLIS, AH2
- End of Key Stage Tests and public examinations
- teacher internal assessment
- reading ages
- records of achievement and portfolios of pupil work

The department decided that a pupil's efficiency in science depended upon their basic skills capability, and that the CAT score gave a good indication of the basic skill capability of the pupil and equated to the skill of the pupil to access the curriculum using basic skills.

When Sam's and Chris's CATs scores were analysed, it was noted that the verbal score for Sam was very low but that Chris demonstrated an average ability to understand words. Their quantitative scores demonstrated a very good reasoning capability using patterns in numbers, but a very low reasoning power in under-standing the concept of quantities. However, their non-verbal scores were different. Chris' scores were low across the full range, but Sam's were better. Some educational psychologists believe the non-verbal score is a good indicator of the innate abstract thinking ability of the pupil. A good score here could be an indi-cator of the capability to think in abstract concepts.

Using this premise, it is possible to see why Sam became so frustrated in his work. His verbal skills were low, so he found written work difficult and failed to see the logic when writing or recording ideas. In a subject like science, the skill of seeing a solution to a problem is often helped if you can visualise and model it. Sam demonstrated better skills at modelling than in using language to communicate ideas. Recent work using the Cognitive Acceleration in Science Education (CASE) Science Reasoning Tests (Adey *et al.* 1989) has shown a strong correlation between a pupil's results in the tests and the CATs non-verbal test. Chris by contrast was better capable at writing down what he understood and this lead to greater ability to cope with the style of work demanded. The use of the scores enabled the department to consider differentiated strategies to support the two pupils.

The rest of the chapter expands this short case study by documenting the pro-cedures being used by a number of schools and science departments around the country.

Cognitive ability testing

As teachers, we face the problem of how we define learning. Everyone has the capacity to think and all have strengths and weaknesses in their ability to reason. How do we as teachers design activities that allow pupils to improve their thinking, and how do we measure our success and their progress? Intelligence is many faceted and difficult to define, but we can learn something of people's abili-ties by the selective use of cognitive ability tests.

There are a number of cognitive reasoning tests on offer to schools, and all follow similar patterns. The analysis of the pupil responses to the tests can yield information about the pupil's basic cognitive skills. The tests are concerned with the decoding, use and application of formal systems using basic logical and reasoning skills without formal learned conventions and without embedding the question in a context.

In their learning, pupils rely upon a system of decoding various verbal and quantitative symbols, analysing patterns, systematically linking patterns into sequences and deriving meaning from these symbolic systems. To communicate, the pupil must use and apply these symbolic systems in a coherent and accurate way to convey meaning to others.

There is a fundamental strength and a weakness in that these tests are without context. For some learners, pupils with English as an Additional Language (EAL) or pupils from a poor social or cultural background, this is an inherent weakness because the assessment is not embedded in the learning environment and so does not furnish the pupils with cues. This leads one to a number of cautions about using and interpreting the results of these tests.

The tests cannot provide absolute figures, and at best appraise the reasoning of the individual. This implies that for a clearer interpretation of the capabilities of a pupil, the pupil will need practice to become familiar with the style and approach of the tests and to develop coping strategies. Therefore a low score does not always mean the pupil is necessarily of low ability, but that they may have a weakness or disadvantage due to lack of experience. For that reason, these tests should be used in conjunction with as full a knowledge about the pupil as is possible, and any analysis of the data should be weighed against that knowledge base. As Hedger and Jesson (1999) argue, it should be possible to establish a multi-level set of baseline achievements. Such a set of baseline markers would allow departments to calculate interventions for pupils whatever their current achievement.

Using CATs

The use of CATs by schools can present departments with enough data to attempt a multilevel analysis and supply information about groups and individuals. Used in conjunction with other pieces of data, the scores can act as indicators of areas of basic skill weakness for intervention and point to specific forms of action that could be taken with pupils with particular difficulties.

Some science departments are used to getting the aggregated CAT figure. It can be used to make some sense of the range of levels obtained by pupils in the end of key stage tests and in estimating chances of GCSE success. Using the end of Key Stage Test results as a device to group or gain some information about our intake of pupils is a crude measure, since they measure attainment and disguise a range of capabilities that may not serve the pupil in the next key stage. Some indication of the range of capabilities can be obtained by plotting the Key Stage Test level results against the aggregated CAT score. Where schools have done this they have found the range of pupils on Level 4 go from a CATs score of 81 to 115, and have a correlation for science between 0.65 and 0.75. This indicates the variability of the NC levels as measured by the SATs, and reflects the primary school's ability to teach pupils to attain levels that may not be a true reflection of the pupil's future potential.

Davis (1999) has identified the use of CATs as a good differentiating tool in forming groups on a whole school basis and some schools are now using them as a tool in differentiating groups in departments. They allow the creation of groups that have similar basic skills characteristics, which help in the management of their learning, particularly in the use of text. The groups are of mixed ability in subject knowledge which allows the pedagogy to be subject-based and gives some pupils, like Sam, the chance to attain a high level with the use of supporting basic skills strategies, for example, writing frameworks (see Chapter 10). This approach to setting can help to prevent the forming of a sink group based on poor behaviour through lack of motivation.

Other science departments are using the scores for verbal, quantitative and non-verbal reasoning. These are better tools for the determination of areas of weakness in the pupil's reasoning skills. Used together to demonstrate the balance of reasoning skills, they can be valuable tools in helping departments to identify their A* to C hopefuls and the C/D boundary pupils who, with four years of targeted intervention, will gain B and C grades. To do this a scatter plot of verbal against the non-verbal is made. By placing on the graph a line marking the national standard for verbal reasoning and a line marking the national standard for non-verbal reasoning, you create quadrants as in Figure 12.1. In this diagram, each quadrant shows a different balance of cognitive reasoning abilities. In the top left, pupils will generally show strength in verbal skills, find texts easy to understand and often favour text-style learning activities, but will sometimes have difficulties with spatial or pictorial models. Some of the pupils can be KS4 science dropouts because, although they found the language driven tests of KS2 and KS3 relatively easy and scored well, the change to more abstract ideas in KS4 makes a good performance at GCSE more difficult and some become frustrated with science. Some schools have found these pupils respond well to the use of CASE in Key Stage 3, teaching using concrete models and kinaesthetic approaches, and using photographs to help with interpreting pictorial work.

The top right and bottom left quadrants are reasonably obvious to deal with in that they identify clearly the A*–C students in the top right and the D–G students in the bottom left. To help in identifying specific groups, some schools add in their standard deviations for their school to identify their top and bottom 16 per cent, the more able and least able pupils. This can help to identify borderline pupils who, with specific intervention, could be more successful.

The bottom right quadrant contains some interesting students for science. These students are often able to see solutions to problems but find communicating about them difficult. These pupils benefit from intervention using writing frameworks and Directed Activities Relating to Text (DARTs) activities (see Chapter 10).

A similar analysis can be undertaken using the quantitative reasoning ability plotted against non-verbal reasoning abilities. Some departments argue that quantitative and verbal reasoning make a big difference to performance at GCSE, so it is valid to look at the balance of verbal and quantitative reasoning skills in this

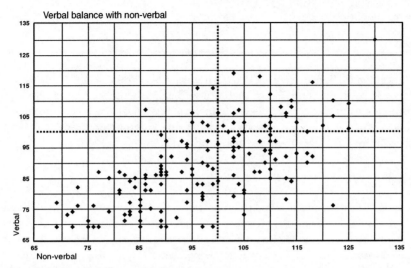

Figure 12.1 Verbal and non-verbal reasoning

way so they can target specific pupils more effectively. The clear information about the whole cohort allows departments to design teaching groups with more care.

Using the verbal reasoning batteries

These tests are made up of a number of specific tests that are indicators of a pupil's basic skill ability. Some verbal reasoning tests, test vocabulary and reasoning relating to structural factors. These tests rely upon a pupil's store and use of verbal concepts and with relational thinking in respect to a pupil's verbal skills.

A score in the verbal battery of below 90 could indicate a pupil who will need some intervention with text related work. Thomas and Mortimore (1994) showed that a pupil's verbal score made a significant difference to their overall points score at GCSE. On average, for every 10 points above the national mean (in verbal reasoning) the pupil gained 5 points on their total points score (in GCSE) and the reverse was also true. Knowing the overall verbal score indicates the possibility of intervention but not the style and form of intervention.

Vocabulary

In a vocabulary battery, the pupil is asked to link words with similar meanings indicating their ability to decode and relate words as concepts. Knowing the pupil has a score below 90 indicates they may have problems with appreciating the conceptual nature of words and will consider them to be largely tools for describing events without a consideration of the specific nature of the concept. This means that if assessments are about straight recall of definitions the pupil will be successful, but if the question requires the pupil to show understanding by applying the concept behind the word, they will find this a difficult task. This can be helped by using

DARTs with emphasis on pictorial representations of concepts linked to progressive development of concepts in text.

Sentence completion

A sentence completion battery aims to determine the ability of the pupil to use words by completing a sentence in such a way that the sentence makes sense. A low score – for example, below 90 – could indicate a pupil who will have problems with understanding the conventions of conveying information using text and could benefit from the use of writing frameworks in science.

Verbal classification

In this style of test, a pupil is asked to group words that have some link that would allow them to be classified. It is attempting to determine the verbal range of pupils and their ability to reason classifications based upon knowledge of a given group of words. A low score in this battery is more problematic to interpret since many pupils will perform badly due to a low experience base. However, teachers should be able to recognise from other evidence and knowledge of the pupil, when a low score is due to lack of experience and when it is an inherent problem. These pupils will need a good range of concrete experiences relating to classification and sequencing exercises.

Verbal analogies

This style of test looks at a pupil's ability to reason links between words based upon an example, indicating the ability to reason by decoding relationships between words. It requires the pupil to use a chain of reason. A low score in this battery could indicate a pupil who will have problems using text as a tool for arguing a case. They will need help with writing genres such as the use of writing frameworks plus help with the logic of writing by analysing the relationship of ideas in the text.

Using the quantitative battery

This battery looks at the basic store of quantitative concepts, but like verbal reasoning it is more about the perception of relationships and using that to reason. It is a good indicator of quantitative logical thinking and coupled with verbal reasoning is a good indicator of academic ability. Thomas and Mortimore (1994) showed that this cognitive ability affected the pupil's overall performance in GCSE by +/− 4 points for every 10 points above or below the national means.

Quantitative relations

This indicates the pupil's ability to deal with the concept of number or quantities and determining if one set of quantities is greater than, less than, or equal to another set. A low score in this battery could indicate a pupil who will need help with developing some appreciation of the concept of quantities. This can be helped by the use of number lines to develop a concrete feel for quantity. Pupils may also find computation and the concept of decimals difficult because of their limited understanding of numbers and their relationships. This would mean some concentration in science on the use of computation strategies.

Number series

This looks at the reasoning ability to complete a series of numbers by recognising the pattern between the string of numbers and then applying that pattern to determine the next in the series. A low score in this area could indicate a pupil who has problems identifying numerical patterns and could need help with learning common number patterns and their interpretation. These pupils could have difficulty with understanding changes due to related variables and so could benefit from work in CASE.

Equation building

This assesses the reasoning abilities needed to determine a computational pattern and apply it to determine the next in the series. Pupils are given a series of numbers and arithmetical signs, and they must use a reasoning chain with all the numbers and signs in any order to produce an answer. A low score in this battery would indicate a pupil that could have problems with algebraic processes and mathematical manipulation. These could be helped by the use of such devices as the equation triangle used to remember Ohm's Law.

Using the non-verbal battery

This battery makes use of shapes and the orientation in two-dimensional space of objects. The pupil must discover the relationships and patterns and use these to manipulate relationship patterns. It is generally a good indicator of the ability to use abstract ideas, and is sometimes called fluid intelligence since it is a measure of something not bound by formal school instruction. Thomas and Mortimore (1994) showed that this cognitive ability did not significantly affect the pupil's overall performance in GCSE – only +/− 2 points for every 10 points above or below the national means – but it does indicate pupils who will find abstract ideas difficult. A low score in this battery of tests could indicate a pupil who would benefit from concrete experiences to illustrate an event and who needs activities to develop an awareness of modelling systems in a diagrammatic way.

Conclusion

There is a considerable range of baseline assessments that can be used to support pupil learning. The use of ICT to correlate this data now gives us the ability to analyse specific strengths and weaknesses in pupils and to target our support. In all of our assessments we need to remember the following:

- The content taught is crucial and it affects attainment. Different pupils need content at different levels.
- Achievement takes different pupils different amounts of time. Teaching only has a limited amount of time, and so the need for baseline assessment early in the education system is important.
- Feedback will carry with it value judgements which may not match with a pupil's self-perception. This means that judgements based on hard evidence will be more compelling in supporting pupils. Giving feedback to pupils as a measure of progress, or value added, is more useful to pupils than an overall statement of level.
- The audience for our feedback must be kept in mind since the nature of feedback required is different for different groups, such as teachers, pupils, parents or governors.

Finally, it is important to note that whatever system a department uses, they should be convinced of its validity and reliability (see Taylor Fitz-Gibbon 1996; Gipps 1994a).

Questions

1   How might the use of CAT scores make sense of the spread of SATs results and help us to group pupils in teaching groups?
2   If we take notice of the CAT score as an indicator of the pupil's basic skill capability, what implications does this have for a science department trying to do something about literacy and numeracy?

Further reading

Davis, S. (1999) 'Reengineering the Classroom', in C. Bowring-Carr and J. West-Burnham (eds), *Managing Learning for Achievement: Strategies for raising Achievement Through Effective Learning*, London: Financial Times Pitman Publishing.

A carefully worded report of an SMT's use of CAT data to help develop a school facing difficulties with standards, it illustrates some of the difficulties and some strategies that can be used to help overcome those difficulties.

Thomas, S. and Mortimore, P. (1994) *Report on Value Added Analysis of 1993 GCSE Examination Results in Lancashire*, Lancashire Quality Development Division.

Although readable, this could be seen as for the enthusiast and statistician. It recounts the results of an LEA research project on the correlation between CAT scores and attainment at GCSE. Since 1993 there have been a number of LEA research projects involving the correlation of CATs and attainment but this still remains one of the most comprehensive.

13 Drowning in numbers?

The need for formative assessment

Pete Sorensen

Introduction

The drive to raise standards has been at the top of successive government agendas. Since the introduction of the National Curriculum (NC), a school's success in this regard has been judged in terms of the increases in SATs levels and GCSE and A-level grades. More recently the notion of 'value added' has been introduced to give some recognition to the fact that pupils start a given stage of their schooling at different achievement levels. This has been accompanied by the use of baseline assessment to establish such starting points, and benchmarking, as an indication of how well the school is doing in comparison to schools with 'similar' intakes. Along with this practice has come the idea that target setting *in itself* can act as a catalyst for improving performance despite the lack of research evidence to support this view.

In this chapter, it is argued that the concentration on simple numerical data, gathered from the assessment practices that currently dominate our schools, serves to undermine many of the aims and objectives of the science curriculum. Low-level cognitive skills are emphasised at the expense of other objectives. At the same time, the stress on the summative use of data undermines formative processes and the active involvement of pupils in the process. Alternative models of practice, which have been used successfully to support the development of pupils' all round scientific literacy, will be presented. It will be argued that these can support the objectives for Science 2000 (DfEE 1999c) more effectively, in particular the need to develop citizens who understand the processes of science and are able to analyse critically the contribution of science to society.

Purposes of assessment

Three main purposes for assessment have been identified:

- Formative (including diagnostic) assessment; where the emphasis is on aiding learning.
- Summative assessment; to allow for review of pupils' progress and possible transfer between classes within a school, transfer between schools and eventual certification in public examinations.

- Summative assessment; in terms of the accountability of departments, schools and LEAs.

(Black 1998)

Much has been written about the range of such purposes of assessment. In order to be effective Hayes (1998) suggests that these need to serve a number of purposes which include:

> provide information about the progress of pupils in relation to knowledge, skills and understanding...
> identify where emphasis needs to be made in relation to the next stage of learning for a group of pupils...
> identify specific learning issues for individual pupils and be the principal aid to target setting...
> be a positive experience for pupils...

(Hayes 1998)

Such lists as these clearly emphasise the importance of formative assessment in promoting learning. However, in contrast, reviews of teachers' practices have shown little evidence of their use (see for example Black 1986; Russell *et al.* 1994; OFSTED 1996). The most recent OFSTED report notes that 'Teachers spend a considerable amount of time on assessment ... but they make insufficient use of this to aid planning ... ' (OFSTED 2000). If we are to address this problem, we need to examine some of the reasons that lie behind current practice. We also need to be clear that it is worth addressing; in short, what is the evidence that good formative assessment can raise standards?

Historical background and current practice

The history of secondary education in this country up to the onset of the NC shows that the universities have been the dominant body in determining assessment practice. This resulted in a 'failure-led' system designed to select only a small elite who were deemed intelligent enough to go on to university. Despite various initiatives, including the Certificate of Secondary Education (CSE), with its attendant continuous assessment components, top-down summative methods based on external written examinations have predominated and it is these which have had the greatest time and effort devoted to them (Black 1986). Such examinations have tended to prioritise a narrow range of cognitive objectives. More innovative practices associated with the CSE tended to be lost in the search for 'academic respectability'; a grade one CSE had to be 'equal' to an O-level pass.

With the introduction of GCSE in 1988 and the NC in 1989 there was some hope that this situation might change. The guide produced to support heads and teachers in implementing the new NC, 'From Policy to Practice' (DES 1989c), gave equal prominence to formative and summative methods and the TGAT reports (DES 1988d, 1988e) stressed the need to involve teachers in formative assessment and give due weighting to their views. In practice, external testing arrangements have continued to dominate. Indeed, the increased government control following DES (1988a) was actually used to reduce the amount of course-work allowed (see Chapter 1). At primary level, too, the intention to embed assessment in the context of the primary classroom has been largely abandoned with the result that 'national assessment has come to use mainly traditional written test methods of the type originally devised for age 16, whilst leaving the assessment of practical and performance achievements to un-calibrated teacher assessment' (Black 1998). This has led many schools to adapt teaching and learning strategies to fit with the nature of the external tests. In short, we have continued to have an assessment led curriculum, with a narrow range of assessment tools predominating and, as such, this inevitably undermines some of the stated aims and objectives of that curriculum.

Prior to the introduction of the NC there had been developments towards more criterion referenced assessment systems. Such moves by some schools followed the example of the mastery learning movement in the USA (Glaser 1963). The work of Bloom and others developed hierarchies of learning objectives (see for example Bloom 1956) and examination syllabuses in this country began to reflect these, at least in relation to the cognitive domain. This practice helped to focus teachers more clearly on the objectives and some schemes (for example, those associated with the Nuffield movement) reflected this by defining specific learning objectives in behaviourist terms for particular units of work. However, the USA continued to take the lead and it was clear from various studies of mastery learning programmes (for example, Block *at al.* 1989), that setting clear, short-term goals for students led to significant gains in achievement. This contrasted with the more usual practice in schools in this country based on giving grades, such as A–E or numerical marks, without making the success criteria clear. Such practice remains the norm even today. Indeed, for many pupils the whole basis for their grading remains unclear. This makes it very difficult for them to take any action that may be required for them to improve their grades. It is rare for the grading to have any formative impact. The pupils themselves tend to see gradings of this kind as summative assessments for the school's or parents' benefit. In a study of primary pupils by Perrin (1991), the weaker pupils also saw the purpose as to make them work harder.

A crucial difference of criterion referenced systems is that they promote the active involvement of pupils in their assessment. Indeed, such involvement can be seen as integral to their use. Thus in-house or published schemes, for example GASP (Davis 1988), were developed based around the idea of judgements about what pupils knew, understood, or could do. This was given further impetus by the Records of Achievement movement (see for example the Oxfordshire Certificate of Educational Achievement (OCEA)), with the active promotion of pupil involvement in their own assessment.

One effect of this move to criterion referenced approaches was that other objectives started to be valued other than merely cognitive ones. Alongside statements such as 'I know that … ' and 'I understand that … ' appeared ones such as 'I can use a … to measure' (valuing manipulative or psychomotor skills), 'I can work as part of a group' (valuing interpersonal skills) and 'I enjoy the study of … ' (valuing attitudinal goals). Many schools that had adopted criterion referenced systems sought to continue them with the advent of the NC. The way the NC Attainment Targets, with the accompanying Statements of Attainment (SoA), were written seemed to support the use of such methodologies. However, there were so many statements (409 in the original version) that teachers found them to be unmanageable. At the same time, outside pressures and resources were focused on external tests. The result was little development of the formative use of such systems (OFSTED 1996). Teachers' practice was to use the statements for summative purposes. This contrasted with the arguments contained in the TGAT report (DES 1988d).

One major change in the NC for Science teaching was in the promotion of Investigational Science (Sc1). It was here that the use of specific criteria seemed most easily applicable and it is the area where criteria are used directly with pupils in some schools. However, even here it has been untypical to see much formative use made, with most energy being devoted to summative grading and 'levelling'.

The 1995 revision saw the move away from true criterion referencing with SoAs being replaced by more general descriptions of performance with attached levels and this move has been retained in the new NC (DfEE 1999c). The challenge now is to learn from our experience so that the assessment practices enhance pupils' learning as we operate the new NC.

Using assessment to improve learning and raise standards

The historical background outlined above shows how summative assessments have predominated in our school practice. However, we have an enormous body of evidence which suggests that it is the use of formative assessment that is the key to improving learning (see Black and Wiliam 1998a for a review of international research). We also have evidence that current formative practices are poor (Crooks 1988). This section draws on evidence of effective formative practices and looks at ways they can be applied in school science departments.

The starting point for assessment procedures should be the pupil

Models of teaching and learning in science have in recent times drawn significantly on the ideas of Ausubel and the constructivist movement ('the most important single factor influencing learning is what the learner already knows. Ascertain this and teach him accordingly' (Ausubel 1968: 36)). The logical development of this approach in terms of assessment is that the pupils themselves must be involved in the assessment process. It is through this that they are able to understand what the next step in their learning process is and how they might achieve it. In other words, good assessment practices include those which seek out the baseline for the student and establish a future target for that student. This is a much more useful version of target setting than those which seem to dominate government thinking. Global targets of, say, getting 80 per cent of students to a particular level in a particular AT are themselves of little value. They beg the question: 'why 80 per cent and not 75 per cent?' They also say nothing about how to get there. Setting a student a specific target, following establishment of their current position, and sharing the criteria for success is much more helpful. The outcome in terms of external criteria may well lead to some given increase in the percentage of pupils at a given level, but the key to the improvement is in the *dialogue* with the pupil.

Diagnostic testing should be a key part of the process

The current emphasis in most secondary school departments is on end-of-module or end-of-unit tests, with end-of-year tests to back them up. These tests are commonly based on the SATs questions (KS3) and GCSE past papers/module tests (KS4). We now see this model moving downwards into primary schools, with practice tests for the KS2 SATs. Such tests are rarely used for any formative purpose. At secondary level, pupils normally move on to the next module following a module test, with little time to do anything about things they have not grasped. Yet the way in which diagnostic testing can contribute to pupils' learning is well documented (see for example Simpson 1993). More use of diagnostic testing at the start of a unit is needed. However, it is also important to stress that such testing needs to seek to 'discover the underlying reasons for pupil failure' rather than simply being based on 'the assumption that learning difficulties are defined by the topic area in which they occur and they only arise from the pupils' own deficiencies' (Simpson 1993: 230). This means giving the opportunity for pupils to discuss and explore wrong answers and not just find out what they get wrong. This then helps to inform the learning experiences offered in the class. This approach lies at the heart of constructivist teaching strategies and can be seen in the CLIS project materials (for example, Needham 1987).

Diagnostic testing can also help in dealing with issues in relation to particular special needs and is a vital part of developing IEPs. However, it is worth stressing that such tests need to be separate from any summative arrangements and the pupils should be clear about this.

Assessment procedures should be integral to the curriculum

Formative assessment procedures need to be embedded in the curriculum. 'Building assessment into the planning stage is essential if it is to be truly an integral part of the learning process rather than a "bolt on"' (Bishop and Denley 1997: 65). This means ensuring that they are written into the department plans at Key Stage level, contained in Schemes of Work and an integral part of lesson plans.

Once again, the pupils need to be fully aware of the practice for it to be implemented effectively. 'In constructivist learning theory, students learn best by actively making sense of new knowledge' (Gipps 1994a: 22). Such learning leads to deeper levels of understanding and involves 'thinking about the meaning of what is being learnt' (Gipps 1994a: 22). This view is further developed in the concept of metacognition (Brown 1987), with students encouraged to think about their own thinking and 'The Thinking Curriculum' (Resnick and Resnick 1992). In this sense, students are seen as 'apprentice learners' and the assessment models required must of necessity be diverse and interactive (Gipps 1994a).

The work of Vygotsky has also led to further stress on more interactive models of assessment embedded in the curriculum. The notion of the 'zone of proximal development' is used to describe the gap between the student's unaided performance and that produced with the support of a teacher or capable peer. For Vygotsky, this 'interaction with more skilled partners' is 'conceived as the means by which children begin to use the intellectual tools of their society' (Rogoff 1999: 79). The process of support is one that involves assessment and interaction, with the support gradually being withdrawn as the student's performance improves. This can readily be applied to AT1 through the diagnostic assessment of skills in relation to particular criteria, with support given either verbally, through group work or via generic support sheets, and the gradual withdrawal of such support as the student is more secure in a given context.

The procedures must be manageable

For formative procedures to be workable it must be possible to manage them effectively in the time available. It is therefore essential that they *replace* existing practice. A number of problems arose in trying to implement the assessment procedures contained in the original version of the NC. The sheer number of attainment targets was one problem. However, there were two other issues that were also key. The first was that many departments sought to add new criterion referenced systems to existing practice. Older grading systems were retained while teachers sought to grapple with making decisions in relation to the targets. The second was the perceived pressure to use the day-to-day assessments as part of a summative process as well, with the accompanying worries about objectivity, validity and reliability. The effect of this was to convert a formative process into a tick-list system, which took on the usual summative format. A manageable system means organising Schemes of Work so that a small number of specific targets are included. These objectives should then be shared with the pupils in terms which they can understand, along with the success criteria to be applied. Marking practices must then be modified in the light of these objectives.

The assessment procedures must fully reflect the curriculum objectives

The new NC (DfEE 1999c) is clear about science education having a range of objectives across learning domains. This means that the assessment tools must reflect this range. The cognitive, affective and psychomotor domains must all be valued. Pencil and paper tests alone will not be sufficient to assess such a plethora of objectives. We need to be observing techniques and group interactions, and valuing oral contributions just as much as we do written work. Actions *can* speak louder than words. It is important that these procedures reflect the importance given to scientific enquiry in Curriculum 2000. Objectives in this area, as contained in the so-called 'Sc0' part of the 1995 version, were left out of previous assessment procedures and this led to little emphasis in classroom practice. However, the analysis of the work done by other scientists is an important part of considering the validity of evidence and understanding how we have reached our current view of the world. This must now be an integral part of our teacher assessment of the revised Sc1.

Pupils need to be involved in marking their own and each other's work

This is an important tool to help ensure that pupils fully understand what is required of them. It can help pupils to focus on whether objectives have been met. Such methods can be extended to looking at samples of work which have met particular criteria. The value of pupils marking their own diagnostic tests is clear (see for example Black and Dockrell 1980). Self-assessment can be developed further into daily classroom practice. As part of the OCEA procedures, pupils were asked to record their successful completion of objectives on prepared grids. The teacher's role became one of 'moderating' the claims. The beauty of this was that the pupils had to be clear about what they were seeking to achieve in order to make such claims. They also had more responsibility for their own learning. The motivational effect on pupils was clear to teachers operating the system. These methods have been particularly successful in helping to assess and develop skills. More recently self-assessment by pupils has been used successfully as a tool for teaching investigational science. However, it is essential to prepare pupils properly since, 'for formative assessment to be productive, pupils should be trained in self-assessment so that they can understand the main purposes of their learning and thereby grasp what they need to do to achieve' (Black and Wiliam 1998b: 10).

In marking work, written comments should be the norm, not grades

There has been an improvement in the consistency of policies in relation to assessment in schools as reported by OFSTED (2000). However, simple grades and numerical marks still prevail. Leaving aside the issues in relation to criterion marking, this is a strange state of affairs given that the evidence is that it is written comments *in the absence of grades* which have the most positive effect on pupil attainment (see for example Butler 1988). Observations of pupils given marks and comments show what most teachers readily acknowledge; pupils often ignore the comments if a grade is given. Moreover, grades tend to reinforce failure for those who do not do well, lowering self-esteem further and leading to further deterioration in results. Constructive comments relating to shared objectives, with action to be taken, are the key to success. Thus 'feedback to any pupil should be about the particular qualities of his or her work, with advice on what he or she can do to improve, and should avoid comparisons with other pupils' (Black and Wiliam 1998b: 9). Those who used the OCEA scheme, linking comments to achievement of particular criteria which the pupils knew in advance, also reported improved motivation. Pupils wanted to know why they had not achieved particular targets and then went on to do something about it once they understood the nature of the problem. Thus, 'effective feedback focuses on the work and does not make judgements about the ability of the pupil or comparisons with other pupils' (Harlen 1999a: 85).

Feedback should be positive and geared to promoting the self-esteem of pupils

The positive use of oral feedback (with care taken over the associated body language) is crucial for the effective use of formative assessment. Tunstall and Gipps (1996) have developed a typology of assessment which characterises positive feedback as being based on rewarding, approving (including positive personal expression and feeling, general praise and positive non-verbal feedback), specifying attainment (including specific acknowledgement, use of criteria and specific praise) and constructing achievement (mutual articulation of achievement, child role in presentation and praise integral to description). This work drew on research in the primary classroom but it is clear that 'all learners, of whatever age, need the same things: clearly described goals and/or tasks; praise and reward; recognition of achievement; and clear information, or guidance, on what might be done to improve' (Stobart and Gipps 1997: 22). In reporting to individuals and the wider community, it follows from the arguments made above that this must be done in a positive manner which supports an individual's progress.

The procedures must support progression

It is vital that the procedures which are in place show progression through the key stages. This issue is addressed elsewhere in this book, but it is worth noting that too many pupils do not even experience the same approaches to assessment within a key stage, let alone across the divide. At primary school, it is essential that teachers of science are using the same language and methodologies in respect of assessment, while at secondary level this should be based around a shared department policy. An example of the kind of problem that has hindered progression in learning can be seen in relation to the KS3 and KS4 divide and investigational science. Many schools have operated as if investigational science at KS4 is different from KS3. Pupils start again at KS4 as if nothing has happened at KS3. The different assessment formats in the pre-Science 2000 NC documents can be partly blamed for this. However, school systems that treat *any* evidence from KS3 as summative evidence from the past are perhaps the more major hindrance to continuity and progression (why?). In all sectors, we need procedures to support progression within a shared overall assessment policy.

Assessment procedures should be equitable

The assessment arrangements in place need to be accessible to all students. Science 2000 is very clear about this in its statement on inclusion. The three principles – 'setting suitable learning challenges', 'responding to pupils' diverse needs' and 'overcoming potential barriers to learning and assessment for individuals and groups of pupils' (DfEE 1999c) – clearly require the development of a range of techniques which allow all pupils to be included.

Whole school issues

Since 1997, schools in England and Wales have been expected to set overall targets for improvement in the core subjects, including science. In order to support this process, benchmarking arrangements were put in place in 1998, allowing schools to compare their performance against schools of similar intake (PANDAs). In addition schools have started to make use of a variety of baseline and cognitive ability data (for example, CATs, Yellis; see Chapter 12). This allows the progress of a pupil to be monitored across the curriculum, and this is clearly important if we are to deal with the whole pupil. Such measures have been used to predict examination outcomes and set targets. There are, however, a number of issues which arise from the use of this data. These include:

- The measures used still tend to narrow the focus to particular, generally low-level, cognitive skills. There is a danger that other important objectives will continue to be left out.
- The 'self-fulfilling prophecy' raises its ugly head. Low scores lead to low expectations. There is much use of the data for setting students. However, the dangers of the simplistic use of cognitive data for setting are explored (Chapter 19) and arguments for setting remain questionable (Chapter 18). There is little evidence that this translates into catering for individual needs.
- The age of a pupil can have a very significant effect. It is well known that winter-born children tend to achieve better.
- The data itself may not be reliable. The problems associated with the various 'intelligence' tests have been well rehearsed, while SATs tests are similarly flawed. In addition, the style of questions can differentially influence different races, classes and sexes.
- The data, in itself, does not inform the action which needs to be taken in order to improve achievement. In short, it has no intrinsic formative value.

Concluding comments

Huge quantities of time, money and energy have been invested in the assessment arrangements in place in this country. The balance of this investment has been towards the selection of pupils for particular purposes or, in more recent times, the monitoring of teachers and schools. The emphasis has also been in favour of a narrow form of pencil and paper testing used to collect data to support such summative purposes. In contrast, the surveys of research evidence drawn on in this chapter show that it is the use of formative assessment techniques that most benefit learning. It is time we changed our emphasis to reflect this evidence. This means a move away from 'top down' assessment practices to ones that are embedded in the science curriculum.

Questions

1   Does your school/department have a shared assessment policy for science? If so, where does the balance lie in the use of time and resources with regard to formative and summative practices? Do you think that the balance is appropriate? If not, how could you change it to reflect some of the ideas discussed in this chapter?
2   Does your school/department assess objectives in the science curriculum beyond low level cognitive ones? If not, how could practice be developed to give appropriate regard to meeting manipulative and attitudinal objectives, alongside some higher level cognitive goals, as well?
3   Does your school/department use diagnostic testing to inform lesson planning in science? If so, are pupils aware of this and active participants in their own assessment? If not, how could such practices be incorporated into Schemes of Work?
4   There is currently a considerable pressure to produce evidence on which to 'level' pupils, predict outcomes and set targets. How can formative assessment be used to inform these processes?

Further reading

Fairbrother, B., Black, P. and Gill, P. (1993) *Teachers Assessing Pupils: Lessons from Science Classrooms*, Hatfield: ASE.
     This is an excellent starting point for teachers wishing to develop their formative assessment strategies in the science classroom. It draws on work carried out in a variety of school contexts and identifies the key issues raised, together with the problems and successes.

Black, P. (1998) *Testing: Friend or Foe? Theory and Practice of Assessment and Testing*, London: Falmer.
     This book serves as a comprehensive, contemporary introduction to generic issues in relation to assessment. It is an excellent starting point for those wishing to study assessment further, written by one of the leading authorities on assessment in this country.

14 Between the idea and the reality falls the shadow

Provision for primary–secondary science curricular continuity

Ruth Jarman

Introduction

A decade ago, hopes were high. At least, they were so among those interested in the promotion of primary–secondary curricular continuity in science. The Department of Education and Science had introduced Education Reform in England and Wales with the assertion: 'A National Curriculum will ... help children's progression within and between primary and secondary education and will help to secure the continuity and coherence which is too often lacking in what they are taught' (DES 1987: 4). Similarly the Department of Education Northern Ireland, while somehow managing to omit mention of children at all, declared ' ... the new common curriculum (will) guarantee a continuity of curriculum content throughout primary and secondary education' (DENI 1988: 13). In Scotland, the document launching the 5–14 Development Programme (Scottish Education Department 1987: 7) indicated it would address ' ... curricular discontinuity, especially in the four years between P6 and S2'.

It could be argued, of course, that all this was government hype. Seasoned curriculum commentators, however, were happy to agree. Moon and Brighouse (1990), for example, concluded that the National Curriculum held out 'enormous potential' for overcoming the problems faced by children transferring between the phases of compulsory education. Of science, Jennings wrote:

> There is universal agreement that much has been gained by establishing a curriculum in science that spans the years of compulsory schooling ... The unified curriculum structure will help to ease transfer between schools and encourage primary–secondary liaison.
>
> Jennings (1992: 33)

Certainly there was cause for optimism. The initial proposals for science in the National Curriculum contained a number of features which could contribute to cross-phase continuity (Jarman 1990). The curriculum was presented as a single publication spanning primary and secondary schooling. Pupils were required to follow common Programmes of Study relating to common Levels of Attainment. It was anticipated that children would be assessed against these Levels of Attainment and their progress would be charted as a developing record of achievement that would pass from school to school. Elsewhere in the United Kingdom, centrally devised curricula were also being drawn up. The proposals for the Northern Ireland Science Curriculum were very similar to the National Curriculum. In Scotland, though not statutory, 'guidelines' for environmental studies were issued in 1993. All these arrangements addressed two key problems identified in the pre-1990 literature as major impediments to the promotion of primary–secondary continuity. Firstly, children's primary science experiences and achievements were often unknown by their secondary science teachers. Secondly, even when known, they were often so diverse as to make an appropriate response almost impossible.

So, there was widespread consensus, at their instigation, that the introduction of 'national' or regional curricular frameworks, whether statutory or non-statutory, had potential to improve primary–secondary curricular continuity in science. This prompts three important questions:

- To what extent *did* these centralised curricular frameworks promote planning for cross-phase curricular continuity?
- What explanations can be offered for their effects?
- What lessons can be learned for the future?

The impact of centralised curricular frameworks on teachers' planning for cross-phase curricular continuity in the United Kingdom

Across the United Kingdom, a number of key studies have been conducted which have had cross-phase continuity as a major focus. In England and Wales, for example, the National Foundation for Educational Research has undertaken three major surveys (including Schagen and Kerr 1999). The DfEE has just published an important review (Galton *et al.* 1999). In Scotland, a project to evaluate the implementation of the 5–14 Development Programme has produced a number of relevant reports (for example, Malcolm and Simpson 1997). In Northern Ireland, an investigation of continuity issues has been conducted (Sutherland *et al.* 1996). Furthermore, a few studies have focused specifically on science (Jarman 1995, 1997, 1998). Finally, HMI inspections, although not strictly 'research', give some evidence on the health of primary–secondary links in science (for example, OFSTED 1998a).

A reading of this literature reveals a remarkable level of agreement as to the impact 'across a variety of settings and situations' of these centrally devised curricular frameworks on teachers' planning for cross-phase continuity. The consensus is that they have prompted some, but not substantial, improvement in practice. Thus Schagen and Kerr (1999), while acknowledging some advance 'particularly in science', nonetheless write:

> The findings of this research project indicate that the National Curriculum has not had the anticipated positive impact on curriculum continuity and individual progression. [There is] a stark contrast between the rhetoric of the NC and the reality of the Year 7 classroom, where the 'fresh start' approach tends to predominate.
>
> (Schagen and Kerr 1999: 92)

Of those studies focusing specifically on science, the largest was conducted in Northern Ireland (Jarman 1998). This comprised a six-year longitudinal study, surveying secondary teachers' planning for primary–secondary curricular continuity in a 20 per cent sample of schools. Again, the research found some gains, but no great reform. More secondary science departments made contact with their associated primary schools in the five years following the introduction of the Northern Ireland Curriculum than had in the five years prior to its inception. Striking, however, was the low level of success of these activities, both in terms of sustainability and in terms of outcome. There was an increase in the number of secondary teachers who talked to their pupils about their earlier science experiences. Indeed, this constituted the main source of secondary teachers' knowledge of primary science practice. In contrast, fewer heads of department read the transfer documentation for their incoming pupils in 1995 than had in 1989. Crucially, however, while no teachers in the survey schools had claimed, before the introduction of the Northern Ireland Curriculum, to take any account of primary science in their junior courses, six years later, a third indicated that they had taken some cognisance of their pupils' earlier experiences. In only a few cases, however, did this amount to any material change in their practice. Typically, teachers continued to start their Key Stage 3 programme at a relatively low 'Level', as defined statutorily. Of the fifty schools in the study, there was only one example of an extended liaison project involving a number of primary schools and making a significant impact on the science curriculum in both phases. In respect of primary–secondary curricular continuity in science, then, the introduction of the Northern Ireland Curriculum has left the established order relatively undisturbed.

The limited impact of centralised curricular frameworks on teachers' planning for cross-phase curricular continuity: possible explanations

The literature on primary–secondary curricular continuity has tended to be characterised by a degree of 'sameness', both in terms of analysis of the problem and proposals for action. In the past, for example, many studies seemed to suggest that a lack of teacher time coupled with logistical difficulties were the principal constraints on the promotion of cross-phase continuity. More recent studies of Education Reform have, appropriately, pointed to problems of 'ownership' and 'overload' in its implementation. Significant as all these issues undoubtedly are, evidence from the Northern Ireland study suggests there may be other important factors at play. This discussion will focus on two: perspectives on cross-phase continuity, and issues of learning and teaching.

Perspectives on cross-phase curricular continuity

First, it is contended, difficulties exist in relation to the what, why and how of cross-phase curricular continuity in science. Surprisingly, there is little to suggest in official publications, or often even in the literature, that the term 'curricular continuity' is in itself problematic. This is not simply to say that its meaning is contested, rather that it is seldom considered at all. Certainly, the term was used freely in National Curriculum documentation with little guidance as to how it was to be understood (Kelly 1990). The Northern Ireland study, however, revealed no real consensus within the science teaching community as to what is meant by primary–secondary continuity. Among those who held a view, and not all did, two quite different definitions were found. One focused on 'starting points' and stressed the requirement to resume at an appropriate point along some pre-ordained learning sequence. This conceptualisation was strongly associated with, and indeed may have been promoted by, the National Curriculum construct of Levels of Attainment. Typically, it translated into the notion of a child stopping primary science at a particular Level and starting secondary science at the next Level. The second definition, on the other hand, focused on 'similarities' and stressed the desirability of a child recognising links between their learning experiences in primary science and those in secondary science. This finding has important implications. Exhortations to primary–secondary curricular continuity convey different messages to different people, and to some, no real message at all. Furthermore, those holding solely the 'starting point/level' position were delivered very quickly into the domain of differentiation, a practice that many considered extremely difficult if not impossible in the context of science. Significantly, perhaps, there was an association between offering a 'similarity' perspective and attempting, however minimally, to take account of primary science.

There are problems then, with the 'what' of continuity, but what of the 'why'? In the literature, if not always in official publications, it is recognised that establishing primary–secondary contacts and continuity require major investments of time and energy. It is important, then, that teachers perceive the benefits to balance the costs. Essentially, effort over outcome should not exceed one! However, the Northern Ireland study showed that the advantages of primary–secondary curricular continuity were not always self-evident to science teachers. Almost one-fifth of those surveyed indicated either that they believed the process brought little benefit or they were uncertain as to what the benefit might be. One can but sympathise. It is the case that in the literature the key argument for promoting primary–secondary curricular continuity in science, namely that the process enhances pupils' progress, remains, for all its face validity, at the level of unsubstantiated assertion. In truth, there is little evidence to which a teacher could turn.

If the 'what' and the 'why' of continuity are problematic, it is submitted that, despite all that has been written on the subject, the 'how' of cross-phase continuity remains just as problematic. When asked how primary–secondary continuity in science could be improved, it is noteworthy that the great majority of teachers in the Northern Ireland survey proposed what were essentially means, rather than, means and ends. That is, they suggested meetings between primary and secondary staff, observing teaching in the other phase, passing on documentation and setting up appropriate management structures. In so doing, they were echoing the guidance given in government reports and in the wider literature. But, as Benyon (1984) is among the few to point out, important as these activities are, they are only the first step toward the target of curricular continuity. Hence, perhaps, many Northern Ireland primary–secondary initiatives floundered. Though contact was made, continuity was not pursued. There were situations, too, where secondary teachers *were* eager to exploit their pupils' earlier experiences and yet still made no progress. Thus, for example, some teachers deliberately set out to discover what their pupils knew about particular topics but were subsequently uncertain how to act on the information. Nor is this surprising. Such guidance as exists is typically at too high a level of generality to support science teachers who wish to translate contacts into continuity, or information into action. Stillman and Maychell (1984) make the important point that continuity will be expressed differently in different curricular areas. Yet there is a dearth of subject-specific and action-explicit advice to assist science teachers in meeting the demands that are being placed upon them. Beyond the exhortation to 'build on' earlier experiences there is relatively little in the literature to indicate or illustrate what primary–secondary curricular continuity in science might actually look like in the classroom. Thus there remain profound conceptual, as well as practical, issues to be addressed.

Issues of learning and teaching

Startlingly, in the Northern Ireland survey, almost half of the secondary teachers interviewed asserted that, though their pupils had 'done things' in primary science, they did not 'know' them or they 'knew' them but did not 'understand' them. Hence, it was argued, it was impossible to take account of their earlier experiences. This view was so prevalent, even among those very positively disposed to primary science, that it deserves consideration.

It is suggested that at least four factors may be contributing to this 'done it but don't know it' phenomenon. First, Wragg (1992) asserts that one of the most difficult problems facing primary teachers is the considerable amount of subject knowledge they are expected to possess. Certainly in the United Kingdom, education reform placed heavy demands on them to acquire, in Shulman's (1986) terms, content knowledge, pedagogical content knowledge and curricular knowledge across a large number of subject areas. This was recognised (for example, Osborne and Simon, 1996) to be a particular problem in the case of science. Harlen *et al.*'s (1995) sensitive study of Scottish primary teachers' understanding of scientific concepts also probed the coping strategies that were adopted if and when knowledge was limited. These include teaching as little of the 'low-confidence aspect' of science as possible, relying heavily on workcards, underplaying questioning and discussion, and avoiding all but the simplest practical work. It may be that such processes are contributing, to some degree, to the 'done it but don't know it' phenomenon.

Secondly, research on assessment has shown the powerful ways in which testing affects what and how teachers teach (Black 1995). The higher the stakes, the greater this influence will be. In England and Wales, national test results in science contribute to primary school evaluation processes. In Northern Ireland, science tests form part of the transfer procedures within a selective system of secondary education. There is evidence to suggest that, in these circumstances, teachers tend to push children too far too fast, emphasising factual learning over conceptual understanding. Sutherland *et al.* (1996: 68) reported that, in their survey, many primary schools' respondents 'admitted teaching some of the more advanced topics earlier and faster than considerations of sound learning would lead them to'. There is the possibility, then, that the pressures of testing contribute to surface learning rather than more robust understanding.

It is contended that two further factors, however, each with profound implications for cross-phase continuity, may be contributing to the 'done it but don't know it' analysis. The first relates to the *accessibility of children's knowledge*, the second to the *characteristics of their learning in science*.

Most often, in Northern Ireland, secondary teachers' knowledge of primary science in their associated schools derives not from formal attempts to learn about their pupils' earlier experiences but from informal discussion with the children. Thus teachers are relying on their pupils' ability to describe their understandings and on their own ability to draw out these understandings. There are grounds for believing both processes are problematic. Children tend to underplay primary science (Jarman 1993). Some find it difficult to describe in teacherly terms what they nonetheless know. Then there is what I have christened the 'swaddling clothes effect'. This is graphically illustrated in a recent OFSTED report on Secondary Education, although it is not at all clear that the authors appreciated its full significance.

> the teacher of a Year 7 class investigating the cooling of a beaker of water was told by pupils that they had not done anything similar before. Later it was discovered that some pupils had investigated 'what material would be best to keep the baby Jesus warm', at Christmas in Year 5. Knowledge of this would have enabled the teacher to approach the activity rather differently so as to build on pupils' previous experience and existing understanding.
>
> (OFSTED 1998a: 131)

It seems that the circumstances of secondary science, with its unfamiliar laboratories, its sophisticated equipment and its decontextualised approach, are sometimes so different from primary science that pupils simply fail to see the connection.

From the secondary teachers' perspective, there are also problems. Class sizes are large and lessons are short, limiting opportunities for in-depth discussion. Furthermore, some respondents in the Northern Ireland survey acknowledged a difficulty in promoting dialogue. Significantly, a number of parent-teachers in the study made the point that they recognised a high level of science learning in their own children but failed to recognise the same in their pupils, though they knew it must exist. All this suggests secondary teachers have problems gaining access to their new intake's existing knowledge and understanding.

There are certain characteristics of children's learning in science that add to the difficulties of access for the teacher and for the pupil. Much early learning is deeply rooted in the experiences from which it derived. Tulving (1972, 1983) and White (1991) have proposed that its outcomes are stored as 'episodic memories'. These are pre-conceptual and highly context-dependent. Consequently, they can only be called up by specific contextual cues. As indicated, the circumstances of primary science and secondary science are often very different. They may be so different that contextual cueing fails altogether and the children make no link between their present and past experiences. This, it is submitted, is the 'swaddling clothes effect'. More likely is partial cueing, where the teacher's questioning fails to elicit a response, but the sight of a particular piece of apparatus does. This phenomenon was reported repeatedly in the Northern Ireland survey. Such effects cause secondary science teachers to underestimate the quantity and the quality of primary science teaching. They may contribute to the 'done it but don't know it' analysis and, in turn, to a downplaying of continuity concerns.

Finally, and shifting the focus from learning to teaching, it is pertinent to note, in the context of planning for continuity and progression, Basini's (1996: 5) claim that 'differentiation is a key concept in the National Curriculum'. Secondary teachers in the Northern Ireland survey were acutely aware of differences in their incoming pupils' primary science experiences and of differences in their attainment. Indeed, this diversity was considered to have increased following reform. It was also considered, however, to be the biggest obstacle to curricular continuity. Almost half of those interviewed reported that their pupils' increased science knowledge posed substantial or, as some saw it, insurmountable, problems for their management of the learning process. A number responded to primary science by covering the content more quickly or by omitting material from the course. While these teachers were happy with such whole-class approaches, differentiation was generally considered impracticable. Rather than take account of primary science, then, the majority saw no alternative but to ignore it.

Writing in 1985, Derricott, in his review of primary–secondary continuity, evoked Eliot: 'Between the idea and the reality ... falls the shadow' (Derricott 1985: 38). Fifteen years and Education Reform later, it seems the same can be said.

A way forward? Possible lines of development

It has already been noted that the literature on primary–secondary continuity tends to engage in much going over of old ground. There is a tendency, too, for its tone to be distinctly admonitory and exhortatory. Given the complexities of the issues, however, this seems less than helpful. What is needed is not more exhortation and certainly not more admonition (if such a statement does not itself constitute exhortation and admonition), but rather an acknowledgement of the size and nature of the challenge.

First and foremost, there is a strong case for opening up a debate as to how best, in the specific context of primary–secondary science, curricular continuity may be conceptualised. To date, too often, secondary teachers have simply been told to 'build on' their pupils' primary science experiences. It should be recognised, however, that the notion of 'building on' is not nearly as straightforward as is sometimes implied. Much has yet to be done to deconstruct this idea and to reconstruct it in a form that is more explicitly supportive of curricular planning and presentation. Indeed, there may be mileage in jettisoning the phrase altogether. 'Building on' serves the situation poorly, being too passive with respect to primary science. Expressions such as 'taking account of', or even 'exploiting', pupils' prior experiences may be more productive.

It is also contended, though more tentatively, that there may be a case for teachers setting out from a 'similarity' perspective on continuity rather than a 'starting point/level' perspective. Initially, then, the emphasis might rest on making explicit, as far as proves possible, the links between the experiences that children encounter in secondary science and those already encountered in primary science. This can be justified on a number of counts. Current learning theories present a powerful rationale for such a process. The use of continuity links ('Remember that experiment you did in Year 9 ... ') is routine among secondary teachers as they revisit topics. Hence the approach goes with the grain of existing good practice. Finally, the Northern Ireland study would lend some support for this proposal. As indicated, there was an association between teachers holding a 'similarity' perspective of continuity and actually 'taking account', however rudimentarily, of primary science. This is not to imply, of course, that the former inevitably leads to the latter! There was evidence, too, that, when teachers have pertinent information they are willing and able to use it in this way. Thus, something as simple as, 'Those of you who went to BallyX Primary, do you remember making lighthouses ... ', was reported to have prompted a lively and productive discussion.

Of course, even this approach is demanding. It requires that secondary teachers possess the relevant information. There is a need, therefore, to develop efficient and effective means for disseminating information through local school networks. This suggests, minimally, an exchange of schemes of work (preferably in person, but perhaps on paper, or online) with proper account being taken of the time required to assimilate such material. Furthermore, it was noted that many in the Northern Ireland study found it difficult to identify the ideas that their pupils had acquired through primary science. There is a need, then, for teachers to become more adept at engaging children effectively in science-related talk. In this regard, Gunnell (1999) describes a very interesting innovation where a group of primary pupils discussed their work with secondary teachers at a 'Heads of Science Conference'. Significantly, perhaps, the paper describing the project is entitled 'Meeting the Children', but subtitled, 'I'm rattled – I didn't realise they could do that'! Finally, there is a need for teachers to take on board the implications of learning theories, including memory theories, for their work with their new pupils. Then that barrier to action, the 'done it but don't know it' phenomenon, may be recognised not necessarily as a failure of teaching, nor as a failure of learning, but as a staging post along the way to understanding.

The highlighting, on a whole class basis, of the relationship between primary and secondary science experiences will be of benefit to pupils. This much is implied in current learning theories. In the last analysis, however, continuity is achieved only in so far as it is achieved for the individual child. Inevitably pupils will enter secondary school with different levels of understanding derived in different curricular contexts. Ideally, then, the 'starting point' should be consistent with the current state of a child's knowledge. It must be said that such a conceptualisation of primary–secondary curricular continuity is very challenging. If progress in this direction is to be made, teachers will need the opportunity to enhance their skills in three vital areas; formative assessment; the preparation and use of transfer documentation; and differentiation. Furthermore, as Galton *et al.* (1999) have so pertinently pointed out, it is also important that 'traditional structures of schooling are altered in ways that allow for a greater degree of individual responsiveness on the part of teachers'. Resources are needed to support these processes; appropriate assessment instruments, well-designed means for recording learning; and curricular materials which offer a range of activities associated with specific scientific ideas. In this way, pupils who have already tackled one task in primary school could be offered alternative experiences that would reinforce their earlier work at an appropriate level and allow them to extend their knowledge and skill by applying them in new contexts.

It will be noted that, among all these suggestions, no clarion call has yet been issued for primary and secondary teachers to get together. This is quite deliberate. The Northern Ireland survey has shown how seldom contacts translate into continuity. Rather than exhort to contact, if exhortations are to be made, they should direct toward both contact and continuity. This is a small point, but important. That said, it is most desirable that primary teachers and secondary teachers do come together to discuss how best they can take account of each other's work. As Davidson and Moore (1996) contend, in this context, 'the key to enhancing children's learning is to put in place conditions which support and promote professional dialogue'.

Finally, there is a need for more 'subject-specific, action-explicit' accounts of how lofty principle translates into daily practice. Essentially, there would be value in a publication presenting a series of 'continuity models' generated through school-based or schools-based development work. Evaluation, perhaps with external support, is also important. It is necessary to know if, and in what way, a particular approach to promoting curricular continuity actually contributes to children's learning in science in the broadest sense.

Conclusion

Wynne Harlen (1996) has summarised the situation with respect to cross-phase curricular continuity as providing cause for both 'optimism' and 'pessimism'. This seems a fair assessment. Across the United Kingdom, evidence suggests that centrally devised curricula have had some, but by no means substantial, success in promoting planning for primary–secondary science continuity. In the majority of schools, it is still left to the pupils to establish the links between their previous experiences and their present experiences. It is still left to the pupils to accommodate to work that may be pitched too high or too low.

Is this an issue of importance? Certainly, some believe so. Indeed, the House of Commons Education Committee, after hearing testimony from a number of science educators, concluded:

> The issue of continuity and progression between Key Stages, especially between Key Stages 2 and 3, is among the most important to be tackled if substantial improvement in the educational system is to be achieved.
> (House of Commons Education Committee 1995: para 65)

It is also, however, an issue of considerable complexity. Those teachers who are prepared to take on this particular challenge, in however small a way, deserve regard. It is from them, primarily, that we will learn the way forward.

Questions

1   The House of Commons Educational Committee claims 'The issue of continuity and progression ... between Key Stage 2 and 3 is among the most important to be tackled if substantial improvement in the education system is to be achieved'. To what extent do you agree with this assertion?
2   It is contended in this chapter that there is a strong case for opening up a debate as to how best curricular continuity may be conceptualised. What do you think primary–secondary science curricular continuity entails? Is there also a place for what is sometimes termed 'planned discontinuity'?
3   Using specific examples from primary and secondary schemes of work, suggest how the links between the experiences that children encounter in secondary science and those encountered in primary science could be made explicit. How might this process enhance children's learning in science?

Further reading

Schagen, S. and Kerr, D. (1999) *Bridging the Gap? The National Curriculum and Progression from Primary to Secondary School*, Slough: NFER.

The NFER has a tradition of carrying out high-quality research on themes related to the primary–secondary interface and the publications which result from such studies always make interesting reading. This report examines issues of 'curriculum continuity' and 'individual progression' in the light of recent educational reform.

Nicholls, G. and Gardner, J. (1999) *Pupils in Transition. Moving between Key Stages*, London: Routledge.

It is pleasing to see a whole book devoted to primary–secondary issues. This text explores the concerns and roles of the major stakeholders in transition; the pupils and their parents, the primary school teachers and the secondary school teachers. Specific advice is offered on how to develop a transition audit, designed to help schools identify the strengths and weaknesses in their procedures.

Galton, M., Gray J. and Rudduck, J. (1999) *The Impact of School Transitions and Transfers on Pupil Progress and Attainment*, Nottingham: DFEE Publications.

Early in 1999, the DFEE commissioned a review of the effects on pupils' progress and attitudes to learning of two related experiences: the move from one school to another and the move from one year group to the next within a school. This important publication is the report of the study. It presents the research evidence for 'dips' in progress at these critical junctures and it identifies strategies for raising and maintaining standards across transition and transfer.

Finally, be on the look out for a book provisionally entitled *Moving from the Primary Classroom*, and due for publication by Routledge in 2001. The original volume, by Galton and Willcocks, made a considerable impact on our thinking about cross-phase issues.

15 Children's attitudes to science

Beyond the men in white coats

Pat Bricheno, Jane Johnston
and John Sears

Introduction

Attitudes are important in developing how we think and ultimately influencing the choices we make. If we want children to be good scientists and to choose to become scientists, then their attitudes and how these are formed are important. This chapter will examine what we mean by an 'attitude' and in particular what 'attitudes in science' means. It will consider how these attitudes are developed and will then look at some studies concerning attitude change and development. The key questions we wish to address are:

- what are attitudes relating to science?
- what influences their formation in the early years?
- what happens when pupils transfer to secondary school?
- how do attitudes influence uptake to A-levels?

Attitudes

The history of the meaning of the term 'attitudes' is long and complex and full of disagreement, and yet most people would agree that attitude is a fundamental concept in analysing human behaviour. Attitude is clearly a theoretical construct to help explain the covariation between stimuli and responses. Most theorists have assumed that attitudes are a form of learned disposition, 'the concrete representations of culture' (Allport 1935), although some psychologists have suggested that some attitudes may have a biological (indeed genetic) base (McGuire 1985, reported in Eagly and Chaiken 1993). We would suggest that a useful definition would be *a learned state that creates a disposition to respond in particular (consistent) ways to particular objects*. This learned state should further be acknowledged as an evaluative tendency that judges 'objects' in terms of favour or disfavour, such 'objects' being values, courses of action, persons or things.

Attitude has been explained as having affective, cognitive and conative (behavioural) strands for many years. Current understanding suggests that affective attitudes are the root of both cognitive and behavioural attitudes, so that how we behave is a result of how we think and an inter-relation of how we feel and think.

Feelings   ←   Thinking   →   Actions

(affective attitudes) → (cognitive attitudes)   (conative attitudes)

Attitudes in science

In science education, a major division has been drawn between scientific attitudes, necessary to undertake scientific inquiry, and attitudes towards science (Klopfer 1971; Gardner 1975; Johnston 1996).

Those attitudes necessary to undertake scientific inquiry can be said to follow a process which supports and reflects the scientific and teaching processes. Within the process is a set of attitudes connected with motivation or motivating attitudes (Johnston 1996) (these attitudes include initial scientific curiosity and a questioning approach to scientific exploration or investigation). While it is essential for future development in science that this motivation is intrinsic, initially it is part of the role of the teacher to motivate the pupil and develop the desire to know.

Once engaged on a piece of scientific inquiry, two further sets of attitudes, one generic and one specific, are important. The generic group derives from the need for individuals to work together and involve attitudes such as co-operation, tolerance and responsibility to others. There are also a set of generic practical attitudes. These include, perseverance, creativity in approach and thought, flexibility and sensitivity to others' ideas, to society and to the environment. It is lack, or perceived lack, of sensitivity which often gives science a bad name.

The specific set of attitudes is concerned with reflection, and it is these attitudes which support understanding in science. In order to reflect on scientific data it is essential to be open to alternative ideas, to look at data objectively, but to be tentative enough to consider alternative views.

Fraser (1981) identifies seven groups of attitudes which he measured in his Test of Science Related Attitudes (TOSRA). They are attitudes:

- towards the social implications of science
- towards the normality of scientists
- to scientific inquiry
- which are needed to be scientific
- towards the enjoyment of science lessons
- towards science as a leisure interest
- towards a career in science

The groups generally reflect the cognitive, behavioural and affective domains, although some groups may appear to fit into more than one category. There is some evidence that the separate groups are themselves highly correlated which would suggest that they may all be measures of one underlying set of values, or of a single attitude, but since they clearly describe different things in terms of meaning they do provide an indicator as to the set of beliefs and attitudes that people hold.

Education has generally focused on changing scientific attitudes which are rooted in behaviour and cognition (for example, Harlen 1977a, 1977b). Research, on the other hand, has concentrated on identifying aspects of affective attitudes (Fraser 1978) and the effects of affective attitudes on behaviour and cognition (Fraser 1982; Shrigley 1990).

What affects the development of attitudes?

Attitudes appear to develop through interactions and experiences throughout life, with family, teachers and peers and be influenced by unconscious interests, ideas, behaviours and prejudices. There is evidence that positive experiences, or critical incidents (LaLumia and Baglan 1981; Gray 1996), aid the development of positive science-related attitudes. School experiences in particular appear to have a profound influence on attitudes. Pictures of scientists drawn by young children to ascertain their views of science and scientists (Chambers 1983) show that pupils draw themselves, where their school science is experiential, or their teacher where the teaching is more demonstrative and didactic. The pictures have also indicated other influences such as cartoon images and vet programmes on the television.

QCA have recently re-emphasised the importance of values (QCA 1999a), after a period where school science was devoid of relevant context or opportunities for moral and ethical debate (Johnston 1995). This is the first attempt for many years to reintroduce attitude forming contexts in school science. This fits with the notion that the contextualization of science in school is also powerful in developing awareness of the social implications and hence attitudes to science. As Driver *et al.* have said, the 'ability to make sense of scientific controversies and disputes [can be seen as] an important facet of public understanding of science' (Driver *et al.* 1996: 134).

Within scientific interactions, at school or home, adult role models play an important part in developing attitudes. An adult who demonstrates enthusiasm for scientific inquiry and is seen to be actively engaged in learning alongside the developing child, will provide a positive role model and support the development of positive science-related attitudes. Adults who themselves see science in a negative light, or are apprehensive about scientific pursuits, are more likely to provide a negative role model. It is an acknowledgement of the influence of school and home on the development of science-related attitudes which has led to recognition of the need to develop the attitudes of teachers and training teachers (Johnston *et al.* 1998; Watters and Ginns, 1994) and parents (ASE 1992b), as well as children.

Attitudes and the early years

Learning in science can be seen as a complex inter-relationship between conceptual understanding, conative development and attitudes. For example, motivation and the desire to know will encourage conceptual development and reflective attitudes, such as objectivity and tentativeness, and these in turn will support the development of the skill of interpretation. In this way, attitudes can be said to be important to both cognitive and conative development.

Primary children involved in motivating and challenging school experiences have been observed to change results of scientific explorations if they do not concur with their conceptual understandings (Johnston 1996). Others have recorded results to conform or please rather than because they accept or understand them. Young children clearly require support to reflect and interpret data objectively and have their beliefs and understandings challenged without demotivation or alienation.

Views of science show that many young children have a stereotypical view of the white-coated male scientist who has something to do with chemicals and things (Johnston 1996). This view is not helpful. Some primary children have expressed a dislike for investigative science activities despite being observed to be motivated and enthusiastic. The main reason for this dislike is that science enquiry does not necessarily involve a correct answer and whilst the children enjoy the process of science, they desire to succeed and have correct answers which are 'safe and satisfying'.

Despite this, young children enjoy experiential scientific learning because of its practical nature. However, as children develop through the primary years they can become less enthusiastic about science. This is, in part, a consequence of a curriculum focused on knowledge rather than understanding and the perpetuation of the myth that science is a factual subject where 'correct' answers and the written word predominate. In the primary years the practical nature of science has been supported in part by national criteria and whilst the part played by attitudes in scientific development has been acknowledged (NCC 1988a), there has been little or no subsequent support for teachers. This is largely because the main focus has been raising standards of knowledge. It is unfortunate that primary teachers are not always supported in their view of the importance that experience and attitudes have on understanding. There is a clear need for a curriculum which recognises the part played by attitudes on learning and supports, understanding of how attitudes develop, and knowledge of how to incorporate affective development alongside the conative and cognitive.

Science attitude changes at KS 2–3 transition

The major disruption in pupils' educational, emotional and social development, following the transfer to secondary school, has been an issue of continued concern for at least the last three decades (for example, Galton and Willcocks 1983; Ruddock *et al.* 1996). Research into attitudes to science has continued over a similar period, and has generally found that, despite pupils' early enthusiasm for science (Ormerod and Duckworth 1975), attitudes become less positive at or after transfer to secondary school (for example, Hadden and Johnstone 1983; Keys 1987). However, most of the research has been cross-sectional and so cannot identify those individuals whose attitudes change on transfer.

Furthermore, there are few studies that have examined attitude change on transfer since the introduction of the National Curriculum. In theory, the National

Curriculum should enable pupils to perceive the curriculum as continuous and the sharp break at transfer should now be less marked. Has this proved to be the case in practice? To what extent does attitude to science now change on transfer and what factors are associated with such a change?

These questions form the basis of a new longitudinal study of individual changes in attitude at transfer (Bricheno 2001). A 20 per cent sample of pupils (n=3373), in their final year in seventy-six primary schools in Essex was surveyed in November 1995. The majority of these pupils were surveyed again in Year 7. The questionnaire focused on attitudes to school science lessons, enjoyment of school and frequency of classroom activities in science. Figure 15.1 shows the distribution of changes in attitude.

Clearly some pupils have become less positive and others more positive, but almost 80 per cent show little change in their attitude to science. This is good news for science teachers, and indicates that for the great majority of pupils secondary science is not regarded as a negative experience. However, there are large changes in attitude for the remaining 20 per cent of pupils, and analysis indicates that these changes in attitudes to science are associated with five significant variables, of which two will be considered here: pupils' enjoyment of school, and

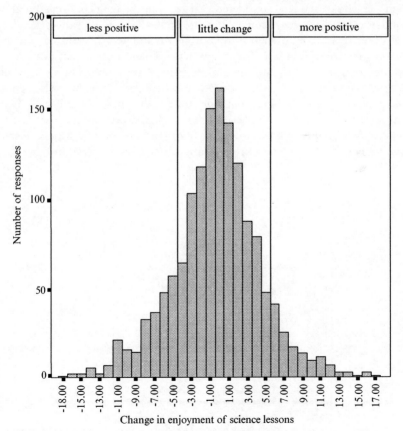

Figure 15.1 Changes in enjoyment of science on transfer

changes in collaborative learning. These variables may be important in allowing identification of practical measures to promote more positive attitudes on transfer.

The most significant variable associated with changing attitudes to science is the change in enjoyment of school. Generally, pupils whose attitude to school became less positive also became less positive about science.

Analysis of the many variables related to changes in enjoyment of school would doubtless indicate important influences on attitudes to both school and science. However, of those school characteristics investigated, the proportion of GCSE passes obtained by the secondary school was one of the most significant. The lower the proportion of GCSE passes the more the attitude to school, and to science, falls (Figure 15.2). There is evidence in the literature that GCSE examination results reflect the level of deprivation in an area (Gibson and Asthana 1998). Thus, a link between changing attitudes and socio-economic environment can be inferred, with attitudes to school and to science declining more in more deprived areas. This finding supports other research, which suggests that attitude to school is related to socio-economic status (for example, Nisbet and Entwistle 1969). In view of the link between *school* attitudes and *science* attitudes, it seems likely that there is also a link between social class and science attitude.

When the whole sample is considered year by year, the data confirms the findings of other researchers (for example, Hendley *et al.* 1995), in that there are clear sex differences in attitude to science in both Year 6 and Year 7, with boys having much more positive attitudes to science. When individual *changes* in attitude to science are compared no significant sex differences are found. However, when *changes* in attitudes to *school* on transfer are also included in the analysis, significant sex differences can be seen, but only for pupils whose attitude to school remains unchanged. For this sample, changes in girls' attitudes to school and to science are significantly related to the schools' uptake of free school meals, however, for boys there is no significant relationship. These findings indicate that

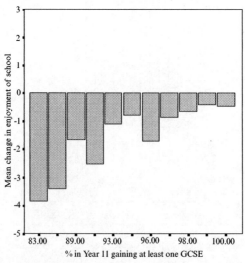

Figure 15.2 Relationship between schools' GCSE results and enjoyment of school

there may be important sex-related changes on transfer, but that such differences are modulated by changes in attitude to school and may therefore be linked to other factors such as socio-economic conditions.

The second significant finding of the present research is that pupils who experienced more collaborative working on transfer were likely to enjoy science more at secondary school. This relationship is represented in Figure 15.3, which plots changes in enjoyment of science against changes in the perceived amount of collaborative work. The *change* in the amount of collaborative work on transfer is significantly linked with changes in attitude to science whereas the *amount* of collaborative work at primary or secondary school alone is not. Thus, even where secondary schools place considerable emphasis on collaborative work, pupils may still *perceive* a reduction if their primary school had frequently adopted this teaching style. This is an important point and highlights the necessity for close links between primary and secondary schools. The need to keep up a dialogue to assist curriculum progression has frequently been stressed (for example, SCAA 1996), but the changes in pedagogic approaches are less often considered (Galton 1998).

Collaborative working, involving both discussion and active learning, is thought to improve motivation and encourage understanding in science (for example, Murphy 1994). Discussion is thought to assist the development of understanding, and active learning to encourage more positive attitudes (Woolnough 1994). The frequency of small group practical work generally increases on transfer and its positive effect on attitudes to science can be seen as support for Woolnough's view. An emphasis on the use of practical work and on working in small groups may improve attitudes to science, but unless there is an increase in the amount of active learning on transfer, it is unlikely to be an effective motivator.

Science has been credited with offering greater variety of teaching styles than other academic subjects, and pupils may base their opinion of secondary science on

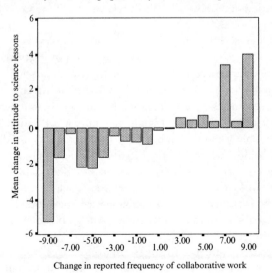

Figure 15.3 Relationship between enjoyment of science and the use of collaborative work

how much variation in style of teaching and activities is perceived, in comparison with primary school science (Cullingford 1991; Kinder *et al.* 1996). At transfer, secondary science has a huge advantage over primary science as it offers more specialist facilities and frequent opportunities for practical work. This advantage accounts for much of the positive comment made about secondary science, for example:

> I think science is better now because we get to do better experiments, in primary school we just did things like electric, but here we use acid and stuff. I used to hate science but now I love it.

But the amount of variation is also an important factor as shown by this comment:

> Science at secondary school is better than science at primary school. Because at secondary school we do things like acids, the body etc., whereas at the Junior we did experiments like grip on shoes. In other words science at secondary school varies but at Junior school it was the same thing every time.

Attitudes on transfer from GCSE to A-level

Much has been made of the drop in science students at A-level and entering university. Apart from the obvious demographic drop, the question seems to be: are pupil attitudes stopping them taking science post-16?

A survey of A-level Year 12 and 13 pupils from six different mixed comprehensive schools in the south of England (partially reported in Sears 1993, 1995) gathered pupils' attitudes to science using Fraser's TOSRA. The survey also included a set of questions (Woolnough 1991) relating to the reasons why pupils had made their A-level choices.

Pupils from a double-award background were significantly less positive in their attitudes to the social value of science and their perception of scientists as normal people. Moreover, they were negative towards their enjoyment of science lessons at GCSE and in the idea of having science as a hobby, and significantly more so than those students from a separate subject background. Some of these differences may be due to the fact that this double-award group generally was the first of its kind. This may have meant many pupils having negative feelings about their loss of choice. It is also probably true to say that in its first year of implementation, teachers will have been faced with very different situations which may have reduced their ability to make the subject as enjoyable as usual.

When looking only at students from a double-award background, the sex imbalance has not changed. Far more boys than girls still go on to A-level physical science courses, and the girls were far less positive than boys about their science. Overall, the most positive were boys from separate sciences, followed by boys from double-award courses, then girls from separate sciences and finally girls from double-award courses. So it seems that boys who specialise early in separate sciences have very positive views of science.

Most students gave as their main reason for choosing A-level subjects that they liked them, but significantly more boys than girls chose for career reasons. However, girls choosing science A-levels were far more likely to carry on to higher education in science than boys, suggesting a higher career commitment amongst the scientific girls. This extended to those doing mixed A-level courses, where a higher proportion of girls went on to do science courses in higher education.

Overall, the science A-level courses took more than their fair share of able students. This finding is also reported in the DfE (1994a) report. When looked at carefully it shows that pupils going on to study physical science A-level are above the average for all A-level students as judged by their GCSE scores. This may contribute to an almost universally held view that sciences are more difficult than other subjects. This was particularly strongly felt by the girls in the sample. On a reassuring note, the whole group were generally positive about their science teachers and the practical nature of science.

Cluster analysis showed that those who took science at A-level were largely above average, positive in all their attitudes on TOSRA, and with a predominance of able boys from a separate science background. There was a large group of non-scientists who were positive about the practical nature of science but who had not enjoyed GCSE, and a small group who were totally negative about science and had chosen arts A-levels (not surprisingly). The most interesting group, however, was one in which most pupils were doing non-science A-levels, or only biology. They nonetheless had a very positive attitude to nearly everything to do with science. The reason they appeared not to be taking science at A-level was due to their perception that science is very difficult.

A further survey followed a group from Year 11 through to Year 13 using similar questions and methods. The main results showed that boys and girls were significantly different in their responses. Boys were more positive about every scale except the normality of scientists. Both were positive about the nature of scientific enquiry and the value of science, but girls did not enjoy their science lessons. Neither group perceived science as a desirable leisure activity.

When the group was analysed by set (there were eight), the top set was overwhelmingly positive about everything except science as a leisure activity. Sets 7 and 8 were positive only about the social value of science and the value of scientific enquiry. They were neutral about scientific attitudes and negative about everything else. These three sets were significantly different from each other and the rest, but the middle sets (2–6) were not significantly different from each other.

Cluster analysis produced a very similar pattern to the initial survey. There was a very positive group who went on to do science and a small, generally negative group who for the most part left school and got jobs.

Discussion

There is clear evidence that a positive attitude to science is produced by active pupil involvement and group work. Thus the organisation of pedagogy in the primary science curriculum is critical in setting up initial attitudes to science. There is also clear evidence that attitude affects later choices.

There are two specific issues that school science departments could practically address in relation to transfer. Firstly, the general deprivation of the area in which the school is situated should be taken into account when planning science programmes of study, and since attitudes to science are more likely to decline in less socially advantaged areas, a more active and less teacher directed scheme of work might help to counteract this effect.

Secondly, it is also very important to maintain strong links between primary and secondary schools. At present, liaison tends to concentrate on pastoral matters and to a lesser extent on the curriculum content. The research shows us that attention should be focused on pedagogy so that pupils experience a positive change on transfer.

Further up the school, most pupils enjoy their science and in particular the practical nature of science. Most, however, see science as difficult and prefer to choose other subjects. At A-level the scientists represent a group of generally above-average pupils which may partly contribute to the notion of science being difficult. Contrary to popular reports in the media, most pupils see the social value of science. There seems to be no evidence of a 'turn away' from science at this age due to a sense of science being a 'bad' thing. It is more a case of other things being preferable.

The areas to give us most pause for thought would appear to be twofold. We have not managed to change the sex differences in attitudes to science. Generally, girls do not enjoy science as much as boys from an early age. Sex stereotyping by subject choice still prevails and seems to run deep within the culture. This cannot be a satisfactory result of science teaching, and must be addressed as a continuing major issue; awareness is not enough.

The second area relates to the effects of social class and economic deprivation. Few of our future scientists are coming from poor families, a situation that has no acceptable justification. We are not managing to persuade the lower achievers that science is worthwhile.

Questions

1   To what extent are the negative attitudes in lower sets and lower socio-economic groups due to teacher expectation?
2   To what extent are negative attitudes due to an inappropriate curriculum?
3   To what extent are negative attitudes due to inappropriate teaching methods?
4   What can schools and individual teachers do to support the development of positive attitudes?
5   What sort of curriculum support could develop positive attitudes?

Further reading

Levinson, R. (ed.) (1994) *Teaching Science*, London: Routledge.
   This book collects together some of the theories and ideas mentioned in the KS2–KS3 study and discusses practical routes to more effective science teaching.

Osborne, J., Driver, R. and Simon, S. (1996) *Attitudes to Science*, ASE.
   A review of research proposals for studies to inform policy relating to uptake to science.

Woolnough, B.E. (1991) *The Making of Engineers and Scientists*, Oxford: Oxford University Department of Education Studies.
This study gives the details of the source of some of the questionnaire tools used in the KS4–post-16 study. It is an interesting report on schools with a successful record of getting sixth formers to go on to study applied science at degree level.

16 Non-judgemental differentiation

Teaching and learning styles for
the future

*Jasmin Chapman, Paul Hamer
and John Sears*

Although 'differentiation' has been a buzzword of recent times, good teachers have
always tried to cater for the individual needs of their pupils. This chapter explores
what is meant by differentiation, and challenges the notion that ability is the
best determinant of our approach to differentiation. Rather, it argues for the idea
of 'non-judgemental differentiation' which looks to cater for the learning style of
each pupil. It then considers the implication of this approach on teaching style,
assessment and resource management.

What is differentiation?

> Differentiation is based on an understanding of individual difference, also the
> worth and value of each pupil's learning.
>
> (Barthorpe and Visser 1991: 1)

> Differentiation refers to all the processes involved in learning which deal with
> differences in learners and attempt to motivate and assess positively at all
> levels of achievement.
>
> (Versey *et al.* 1993: 3)

> ... differentiated practice represents a view of what 'good science teaching'
> might be – the provision of appropriate teaching/learning experiences for *all*
> pupils, not just those at the extremes.
>
> (SCAA 1994: 25)

As can be seen, differentiation has been defined by numerous authors in a
variety of ways. The essential message, however, is that *differentiation concerns how
we manage the learning of individual pupils in order to maximise the progress each makes.*
Discussion with numerous colleagues in schools, at conferences and in training
sessions, similarly reveals a broad variety of interpretations of the term 'differentiation'. Most of the definitions, however, polarise around one or other of two
National Curriculum Council (NCC) definitions:

the matching of work to the abilities of individual pupils so that they are stretched but still achieve success.

(NCC 1993: 102)

the process by which curricular objectives, teaching methods, resources and learning activities are planned to cater for the needs of individual pupils.

(NCC 1993: 83)

The first school of thought (differentiation by task demand) maintains that differentiation constitutes the provision of different work, often based around a core activity provided to the majority, to extend the 'most able' and support the 'least able'. Such an approach is based on the notion of entitlement to a core science, while still enabling the 'most able' to make further progress. This assumes teachers will have made an accurate assessment of the current levels of performance of pupils and will have a clear measure of the potential of such pupils. This will enable the teacher to set appropriate, challenging material. The second school of thought (differentiation by approach to learning) centres on the work of a number of researchers and writers (for example, Gardner, Jensen, Lazear, Rose, Smith) who have espoused an alternative approach reflecting recent developments in the understanding of brain function and learning. This school of thought maintains that differentiation should take account of a *number* of differences between learners (see Table 16.1 for examples), but especially those which define the most suitable learning approach for them. 'Non-judgemental differentiation' was the phrase coined by the Learners' Co-operative (*circa* 1996) to describe the philosophy underpinning this approach to differentiation.

Table 16.1 Differences between learners

Difference	Comment
Perception of information	visual/auditory/kinaesthetic preference
Processing of information	multiple intelligences profile, based on Gardner
Information storage in memory	iconic/symbolic/enactive, based on Bruner
Time referencing	past/now/future (see below)
Pace of work	fast/slow
Reading age	calculated using standard tests
Gender	national underachievement of boys
Personality type	extrovert or introvert
Response to learning task	holist or serialist (see below)
Logic	deductive/inductive
Developmental stage	based on Piaget or Erikson
Social class	N.B. changes in definition
Ethnic background	celebrate cultural diversity
Life experience and interests	models, ideas and experiences
Disposition to learning, or motivation	surface, achieving and deep

Jensen (1995) considers how learners view time as a major influence on how individuals learn. He identifies three categories of what he terms 'time referencing' as listed in the table above. 'Future'-referenced learners are strong visualisers who can plan ahead and who are motivated by goal and rewards. 'Now' learners have poor planning ability and often cannot see the consequences of their actions. 'Past' learners can use experience, for example by their reflection on what strategies have worked or not in the past. To facilitate 'time referencing', teachers can do two things: plan 'events' into the yearly schemes of work for future and past referencing, and systematically use language such as 'when we', 'now let's' and 'tomorrow we will'.

Bishop and Denley (1997) describe serialists as learners who need to see the 'picture build a piece at a time', while holists need to see 'the whole picture first in order to make sense of the parts'. Giving the big picture to a class creates no problems for serialists and is essential to holists.

Many attempts have been made to categorise the strategies that teachers use to achieve differentiation. Table 16.2 shows how some of these may be identified as belonging to the two approaches. In the context of our analysis, the commonly

Table 16.2 Approaches to differentiation

Differentiation by task demand	Differentiation by approach to learning
Core extension support.	Multiple intelligences determination of activity, i.e. pupils use a questionnaire to identify their intelligences profile and choose tasks matched to that intelligence (when working on strengths).
Must – Should – Could coverage of curriculum for different teaching groups; i.e. tasks are divided into the three categories and pupils start with 'Must' tasks. If they are successful they go on to 'Should' tasks. 'Could' tasks are seen as extension work.	Pupil choice of activity from alternatives in a more dependent group, or self-initiated and self-directed learning in a more independent group; for example, individualised materials provided after negotiation and (self) assessment.
Graded exercises (increasing demand in a sequence of short tasks), possibly structured using Bloom's Taxonomy (differentiation by cognitive demand).	Varying the degree of independence expected; for example, working on a task by independent study on the Internet.
Providing resources/activities covering the same content at different levels of difficulty/reading age/mathematical/scientific skill demand.	Pupils work in supportive pairs/small study groups – they identify weaknesses, break down the task and work on parts of the whole.
Setting or streaming to allow deployment of different tasks and resources.	Grouping by sex or learning style, or interest.

used categorisation 'differentiation by task' becomes a confusing description, as different tasks for different learners is a feature of both approaches. The issue here is whether the tasks differ in demand or style.

Although differentiation is a complex issue, much of the confusion over its definition can be resolved by understanding the two fundamental approaches shown above. One argues for a content structured approach and the other for a learning style structured approach. Both would claim to be developing the pupil to the greatest possible extent and both would subscribe to the view that:

> Effective differentiation [only] occurs when teachers:
> * plan for differentiation in their lesson preparation
> * use appropriate management and teaching strategies during the lesson
> * feed back information about achievement to advance individuals' learning in subsequent lessons.
>
> (Revell 1995: 18)

The influence of ability?

> Although teachers were reluctant to say that differentiation was mainly about ability grouping, many schools reported an increase in the proportion of pupils taught for at least some time in classes grouped by ability; this shift coincided with the period when differentiation had become a higher priority.
>
> (Weston *et al.* 1996: 1)

All forms of differentiation by task demand are based on an implicit notion of differences in ability among pupils. Ability is such a basic assumption in education that it is rarely challenged and barely considered. What do we mean when we say that a pupil has ability? Underlying the idea of ability is the common sense notion of general intelligence. In this understanding, someone who is good in one field would be expected to be good in many. Is a successful entrepreneur intelligent despite a complete lack of exam grades? The answer would sensibly seem to be 'yes', and the word 'intelligent' is certainly applied in such cases, and yet here we have someone who has not necessarily demonstrated excellence in a wide range of fields. This simple example shows that the word 'intelligence' is a disjunctive concept, that is, one with many meanings, all of which are acceptable but which are alternative and not easily compatible with each other.

Several workers have suggested alternatives to the notion of a single, fixed intelligence which has been pervasive since Binet and Simon's work at the turn of the century. Guilford (1967) proposed a matrix of thirty abilities, each of which could be exhibited with four kinds of content. Howard Gardner's seminal text *Frames of Mind* (1983), makes cogent argument for seven intelligences (see Table 16.3) (referred to as abilities by some writers), each rigorously scrutinised by a set of eight criteria. David Perkins proposes three intelligences, two of which can be consciously developed (Perkins 1995; Brown 1999). However, statistically there is always an underlying common factor in intelligence studies; the 'g' of general intelligence. So what is this, and can we get to know anything about it?

Entwistle (1998) gives an overview of the debate among psychologists regarding the notion of general intelligence and concludes that there is a hierarchy of intellectual abilities:

> Perhaps the best way to consider intelligence or creativity in relation to intellectual abilities is … [to suggest] that intelligence and creativity represent higher level skills … in which people are able to *combine* any or all of the lower level skills to achieve the required outcomes. It is in the *effective use* of available skills in combination to reach the desired outcomes that intelligence or creativity are seen in action.
>
> (Entwistle 1998: 159)

This way of understanding 'general' intelligence accounts for the diverse ways in

Table 16.3 Howard Gardner's seven intelligences

Description of intelligence/learner	Some activities for each intelligence
Body-physical learners usually have exceptional control of their movement. They enjoy activities involving touch and become restless if they have to sit still for long periods.	Make/sort flashcards, role-play, games, model building, hands on tasks such as practical, highlighting text, concept map by placing 'post-it' notes.
Intrapersonal learners often think about thinking and how to learn.	Keep a personal learning diary, link new learning to what they know, ask emotional questions.
Interpersonal learners relate well to others and mix easily.	Teach others, concept map by discussion, swap problems, share notes.
Linguistic learners enjoy listening, reading and are good at spelling. Some prefer to speak and others to write.	Make wordlist/ glossary, library search, use topic words as basis for a speech, make up word game.
Mathematical-logical learners like to be organised and often approach tasks in a structured way.	List concepts as numbered key points, use tables and graphs, use time-lines.
Musical learners tend to be good at recognising tunes, however they do not necessarily play an instrument.	Compose rap/ jingle, learn to a rhythm, use music during study.
Visual–spatial learners usually have a good sense of direction. They tend to enjoy activities like map reading and chess. They may have artistic talent.	Make cartoons or mind maps, iconise ideas, colour code notes, construct story board or slide show.

It is worth noting here that we have found it more constructive to discuss 'ways of learning' with pupils rather than 'types of learner'. This helps to avoid any permanent labelling of individuals which intelligent action can manifest itself, and suggests to the authors that measures which try to assess 'g' are less useful than measures which try to assess component skills when it comes to determining teaching strategies.

Also embedded in the notion of ability is the view that there is something inherent or innate, usually called potential, which underlies the pupil's performance. In this description, potential (and hence ability and intelligence) is assumed to have a normal distribution. This means it is popularly treated as a genetic trait that can be influenced by the environment; like height. So the argument would run that even if you give everyone an excellent diet, some people will have a maximum height level of 1.5m whilst others will have one of 1.8m. Similarly, even if you could give people perfect learning conditions, some will achieve 10 GCSE grade 'A's while others will achieve no GCSEs at all. This latter contention, when stated in the extreme, sounds suspect. The brain has ten to the power ten nerve cells, each capable of making at least a thousand interconnections. Indeed, even though there may be a limiting potential to brain function, it is our contention that most people rarely approach this and many fall far short. This would account for the way many great thinkers were dismissed at school (Einstein being perhaps the best-known) because people confused *current performance* with ability and potential.

Consequently, we would wish to challenge the notion of a general intelligence, genetically determined, as having much value in helping us educate pupils. Moreover, we wish to question the link between measured performance and potential as having been established except in the crudest of extremes (such as brain damage). Success in life outside school shows clearly that current performance is an unreliable predictor of intelligent behaviour.

Over and above the genetic argument is that of teacher expectation. Numerous studies (Rosenthal and Jacobson (1968) being seminal) have shown that teacher expectation can have a dramatic effect on attainment. Moreover, these studies show that it is the labelling of a child that is a major factor in determining outcomes. We also know that social class, sex and ethnicity are major determinants of attainment (Jackson 1964, 1982; Boaler 1997; OFSTED 1998c). Unless one wishes to argue for a genetic component to these as being overriding, the conclusion that circumstances and expectations control attainment is inevitable.

It is therefore the contention of the authors that the notion of ability as a major *determinant for differentiation* is misguided and carries the risk of being a self-fulfilling prophecy. Thus we conclude that types of differentiation by task demand, based on structured content of varying difficulty, are inappropriate to the needs of most pupils. We assert that a move towards differentiating by 'approach to learning' will improve performance and motivation, resulting in raised standards.

The challenge for teachers

> The mind is not a vessel to be filled but a fire to be lighted.
>
> (Plutarch)

The last two decades of research into the brain and learning, combined with the changing experiences of childhood brought about by technological and cultural changes mean that the old transmitter–receiver model of teaching is no longer appropriate:

> The research indicates that the transmission model is not very effective.
>
> (Jonathan Osborne, 22 October 1999, in an INSET session
> for teachers in Camden)

> The power and charisma of the media has changed student standards for communication. The congruency of actors and impact of multi-media electronic presentations spoil students for unrealistic standards ... Students bring the mindset of television to class each day. In comparison, students often see teachers as inadequate or boring. Thus, many students have less respect for their teachers, daydream more and participate less in class.
>
> (Jensen 1995: 3)

This view is shared by others, who feel that today's challenge is teaching 'the post-Nintendo generation, which is used to a multiplicity of information sources' (Cunningham *et al.* 1997: 11). However, old paradigms do not die so easily. The content-rich curriculum, continuing external pressures, existing classroom design and delayed availability of the newest technology, combined with 'change exhaustion', all contribute to inhibit the evolution of teachers' practice. Whatever their starting point, the key question for teachers to consider is whether their preferred teaching style matches the range of learning styles in their classes. If it does not, those learners who are not matched are less likely to be engaged, with consequent risks of poor performance and inappropriate behaviour.

Developing practice clearly has implications for classroom management, departmental practices and school policies. In the classroom, there are issues of how the room is arranged to allow appropriate seating, what resources are used, how resources are distributed, collected and stored and how time is balanced between teacher input and student centred activity. The level of planning involved in preparing differentiated lessons:

> takes an enormous amount of time and competes with a multitude of other commitments and demands ... individuals working in isolation, even with the very best of intentions, will make relatively little impact. [Differentiation] necessitates a concerted and departmental approach.
>
> (Hughes 1997: 56)

Furthermore, isolated efforts have implications for continuity within a department. What happens to pupils taught in a highly differentiated way one year who are subsequently taught as a whole class? The need to work together, discussing pedagogy, observing colleagues' lessons, planning in groups and possibly even looking at each other's mark books will have different implications in different departments. The acquisition of practice, whether from colleagues or from external sources, necessitates an action research culture within a department. There are likely to be implications for how department meeting time is used and this, in turn, may create a tension with the requirements of systems in the school, which will need to be resolved.

If effective differentiation is to take place, the teacher must have a clear idea of what the needs of individual pupils are. There is therefore an inescapable link between differentiation and (particularly formative and diagnostic) assessment. The type of assessment data collected and kept should be appropriate to the differentiation strategies subsequently applied. This clearly has implications for marking policy and for the way in which records are kept and passed on when pupils change teachers.

A way forward

The authors' own experience of attempting to develop *differentiation by approach to learning* offers a way forward which allows a judicious balance between teacher-centred episodes and student-centred episodes, which can change as a class acquires skills and develops increasing independence in learning. The application of a Six-stage Model of Learning (see Table 16.4) allowed us to respond to individual needs while still being required to teach a content rich curriculum. It also facilitated decisions such as:

- when to differentiate for approaches to learning
- which strategy/ies to use when differentiating
- when, and for whom, to use ICT

and integration of recommended good practice such as:

- development of key skills, particularly of improving own learning and performance, communication, working with others and problem solving
- using accelerated learning techniques such as cognitive maps
- incorporating creative activities
- providing opportunities to learn through discussion

The Six-stage Model also provides a user-friendly lexicon for dialogue and a framework for discussions with pupils about successful learning strategies and areas needing improvement.

> Encouraging multiple abilities becomes part of the larger effort to establish motivational equity – everyone striving for positive reasons open to all via their preferred style of expression.
>
> (Covington 1998: 267)

In addition to facilitating important decisions and allowing integration of good practice this approach includes many elements that promote pupils' intrinsic motivation, such as:

- it recognises their individuality (our pupils have greatly valued this);
- it gives ownership and responsibility to the learner thus building self esteem;
- it allows for reward to be related to readiness to learn.

The approach allows for the range of diversity in every class, provides equitable alternatives for any pupils with special needs, diversifies the resources used, encourages active engagement and promotes independence whilst providing a rationale for matching an activity to the learner(s). While it does not preclude the selective use of tasks of varying demand as a supplementary layer of differentiation, it becomes much more likely that pupils will appropriately self-select the level of difficulty they achieve.

This approach does have classroom and resource management implications. Extra resources are needed initially to model formats to facilitate multiple intelligence approaches. Subsequently, there is less demand than in differentiated worksheet-type approaches, although there is a greater variety of material needed for *making* notes. Time is needed for redrafting summaries/notes, but redrafting can be part of a review cycle, and time not used taking dictation or copying from

Table 16.4 A six-stage model of learning

Stage	Activities
1 Right Frame of Mind	Establishing prior knowledge (formative assessment), connecting the learning, giving the big picture and setting targets; getting learners relaxed, confident, motivated and unstressed
2 Getting the Facts	With more dependent pupils: multi-sensory input to accommodate learners' perception preferences; with more independent pupils: learners choose information sources and acquisition steps
3 Exploration	Individual/pair/small group activities differentiated by preferred processing mode (multiple intelligences); checking and correcting; MAKING notes in chosen form – meaningful reorganisation of information; formative assessment
4 Memorising	Review, using notes (= aide-memoire/revision port - folio) to transfer learning from short-term to long-term memory
5 Show You Know	Opportunities for learners to demonstrate new knowledge and understanding through group and class activities such as talks, tests and quizzes; further reflection; formative assessment
6 Evaluation of Learning	Learners reflect, and discuss with peers and teacher, 'What went well?' 'What could have gone better?' in terms of the learning – metacognitive reflection; diagnostic self-assessment

sources can allow not only this approach, but also more time for practical investigations and for developing understanding.

Tackling differentiation through approaches to learning seems, to us, to offer a pathway from the twentieth-century paradigm to a twenty-first-century paradigm.

Questions

1   How can you match specific learning needs with ICT-based information?
2   Contemplate the range of media that will be available in your classroom if pinboards, whiteboards and blackboards are supplemented with (not replaced by) screens and smartboards; if students are recording work (in whatever format) on index cards, A3 and A4 paper, in books, on audio tape or at monitors via pencil, pen, keyboard, mouse or microphone. What are the implications for resource management and assessment?
3   Consider any topic that you currently teach. Devise a variety of tasks for teaching the topic based on different learning styles founded in the seven multiple intelligences.
4   Is it important to teach pupils about the six stages of learning and about learning styles?

Further reading

Bellanca, J., Chapman, C. and Schwartz, E. (1994) *Multiple Assessments for Multiple Intelligences*, Illinois, IRI/Skylight Training and Publishing.

Any move towards multiple intelligence teaching in your classroom, department or school will necessarily throw up assessment issues. The book is designed to align assessment with classroom practices that promote the development of multiple intelligences. The book starts by discussing the assessment challenge, surveys strategies and tools for assessments and then goes into considerable detail regarding the assessment of each specific intelligence.

Biggs, J.B. and Moore, P.J. (1993) *Process of Learning*, Australia, Prentice Hall.

Written specifically for students in initial teacher education, this text sets out to link educational psychology and what happens in classrooms. The most theoretical of the texts we have included here, *Process of Learning*, underpins much of our own development work supporting student construction of knowledge and understanding, the contexts of learning, and the balance in the learner–teacher system.

DePorter, B. and Hernaki, M. (1992) *Quantum Learning*, London, Piatkus.

A rich source of ideas about accelerated learning techniques that can be integrated into the six-stage model described. This book is exemplary in that it uses the techniques to teach the techniques; the text is easy to read and the right-hand pages effectively provide a digest of the content. Together with the special pages at the start and end of each chapter this makes the book a reference that you will return to time and again.

Lazear, D. (1991) *Seven Ways of Knowing: Teaching for Multiple Intelligences*, Illinois, IRI/Skylight Training and Publishing.

The first of a series of (cross-curricular) books that Lazear has written on the seven intelligences, this book focuses on integrating the various intelligence capacities and skills into existing school curricula. The text moves from attainment of basic skills for each intelligence through tacit use, aware use and strategic use to reflective use of the intelligences and concludes with a description of the 'Multiple Intelligence School'. Lazear's second text, *Seven Ways of Teaching*, presents model lessons for each intelligence. His third book, *Seven Pathways of Learning*, is devoted to teaching students and parents about multiple intelligences.

Postlethwaite, K. (1993) *Differentiated Science Teaching*, Buckingham and Philadelphia: Open University Press.

This book contains a good overview of pupil differences and gives a fuller discussion of the problem of general intelligence and the use of mastery learning. Due to its date it mainly considers responses to pupil differences in terms of task demand. Nonetheless, it is a good starting point.

17 Are gender differences in achievement avoidable?

Patricia Murphy

Introduction

The issue of gender and science education has been debated for over three decades. In the 1970s and 1980s the main concern was with females' access, participation and achievement in science. In the 1990s the concern shifted to focus on male under-achievement and the general decline in interest in science amongst pupils post-16. A frequently cited quote in writings about science learning is that of Ausubel:

> 'If I had to reduce all of educational psychology to just one principle, I would say this: The most important single factor influencing learning is what the learner already knows. Ascertain this and teach him (*sic*) accordingly'
>
> (Ausubel 1968: iv)

While this principle remains an important one in any constructivist approach to teaching and learning it fails to take account of the relationship of the social world and the learner. As Rogoff puts it, learners 'are active participants in understanding their world, building on both genetic and sociocultural constraints and resources' (Rogoff 1990: 37). If we take seriously developments in understanding about learning, then we cannot understand individuals' thinking apart from the contexts in which it appears; contexts in which people's experiences and values are significantly shaped by their gender.

To consider the impact of gender on pupils' engagement and achievement in science, it is essential to understand how gender mediates pupils' thinking both within and without school and the relationship between these two sources of learning. The evidence referred to in the chapter is concerned in the main with group differences. While a focus on group differences fails to take account of the variation amongst girls and boys, it helps to illuminate the nature of gender mediation and its impact. The chapter addresses three questions:

- do gender differences in uptake and achievement in science and technology related courses exist?
- what are the sources of these differences and how do they mediate teaching and learning in schools?
- if there are existing and anticipated gender-related problems in science

education what are these, which pupils are likely to be affected by them and how can they be addressed?

Achievement trends

International and national surveys

Evidence of a gender problem in science education came from surveys that compared performance across nations or across regions within a nation. Between the 1970s and 1980s, two IEA studies (International Association for the Evaluation of Educational Achievement) established a gender gap in favour of boys in all branches of science and the gap was found to increase with age. The performance gap was greater in the tests of physical science. Boys also showed more positive attitudes towards science than girls and reported a higher level of interest in science related activities. The overall gap in science performance was attributed to girls' lower performance on items testing understanding rather than recall of science (Keeves 1986, 1992). The USA National Assessment and Educational Progress (NAEP) science surveys replicated the IEA pattern of performance (NAEP 1978). The British Columbia Science Surveys (BCSS) (Hobbs *et al.* 1979), however, found boys ahead of girls only on tests of physics and measurement skills.

The national surveys of science performance carried out in the 80s in England, Wales and Northern Ireland for pupils aged 11, 13 and 15 years old (Assessment of Performance Unit (APU)) also found that gender differences increased with age. These surveys, unlike others, included a broad range of test items which assessed scientific process skills and procedural understanding as well as concept application. The findings showed that across the ages girls' and boys' performance depended on the construct assessed, with girls outperforming boys on practical tests of making and interpreting observations while boys' superior performance was in the application of physical science concepts (DES 1988b, 1988c, 1989b). The attitude questionnaire showed girls' interests lying in biological and medical applications and boys' interests involving physics and technological applications.

The third International Mathematics and Science Study reported that for pupils aged 12–13 years and 14–15 years there were no statistically significant differences except in chemistry, and then only for 12–13-year-olds (Keys *et al.* 1996). A review of US studies of science performance (Willingham and Cole 1997) also suggests that a decrease in the performance gap between girls and boys has occurred over the last three decades. The gap that does exist increases as pupils go through school.

General Certificate of Secondary Education (GCSE): entry and performance in science

Another source of information is examination entry and performance at the end of compulsory schooling. Prior to the national curriculum, far fewer girls than boys were entered for physics, chemistry and science examinations at 16-plus, and far fewer boys were entered for biology. Boys outperformed girls in general science, chemistry and physics, and girls outperformed boys in biology. In 1993, girls outperformed boys in the GCSE single-award science, and performed equally well in double-award science. By 1997 there was a performance gap in favour of girls. More boys than girls continued to take single sciences across the three subjects. There were small performance differences in favour of girls in physics and chemistry, and a quite large gap in favour of boys in biology.

These overall sub-group comparisons need to be interpreted with care, particularly in the case of single sciences where the populations are selective and may reflect different ability spreads. The distribution of grades shows that boys and girls are represented across the full grade profile for these examinations. Gorard *et al.* (1999) report that there are no systematic differences at any age between the performance of boys and girls at the lowest level of any measure of attainment, the achievement gaps are at the highest level of attainment. A further factor is *how* grades are achieved in combined science when overall performance appears to be similar. Bell's analysis (1997) at question level revealed that boys were outperforming girls on questions requiring the application of physics concepts.

The problem of the incomparability of populations taking different examinations is further compounded by tiered entry. There is evidence from research in GCSE mathematics (Stobart *et al.* 1992) that more boys than girls are *not* entered for GCSE because pupil disaffection is increased in the lower tier. Disaffection is considered to be greater for boys than girls.

Fewer girls than boys were placed in the higher tier because of their perceived lack of confidence and an assumption that girls are more adversely affected by examinations than boys. In both cases, the teachers' judgements were based on affective rather than cognitive characteristics of pupils.

National Assessment in England

At age 10–11, girls are found to slightly outperform boys overall in science. However, fewer girls than boys achieve the higher level of attainment and more girls than boys achieve the average levels (QCA 1998b). At age 13–14, KS3 there were no overall differences in the performance of girls and boys (QCA 1998a). There are two tiers of entry for this Key Stage. In the 1996 KS3 tests, fewer girls than boys were entered for the higher tier (32 per cent compared with 37 per cent). On the higher tier paper, males outperformed females on the greater majority of question parts. Of the twenty question parts where a gender difference in performance was noted, sixteen were concerned with physics topics, three with chemistry/earth science, and only one with biology.

Since 1990, the rates of entry into physics and chemistry A-level examinations (age 18-plus) has declined significantly for both males and females in spite of a marked increase in female entrants to A-level. Research has shown that the entry patterns found at A-level are maintained into higher education. Smithers (1997) reported that in spite of the massive expansion in degree entry between 1986–95, chemistry and physics numbers have remained on a plateau of around 3000 in England. Head (1999) reported the dominance of men over women in university entrance in the physical sciences (81 per cent in physics, 62 per cent in chemistry), with the reverse being true in biology (55 per cent women). In engineering in 1997 there were six times as many male graduates as women. The figures show little change in entry across the various engineering disciplines in the last ten years.

Performance trends show no overall differences between girls and boys. Males and females are represented across the range of achievements in national tests and examinations. Any gender-related issues in science education cannot therefore be attributed to innate differences between sex groups. A review of a range of entry and achievement patterns suggests that girls and boys are equally able to undertake and achieve in science and technology courses. Significant gender differences in pupils' options reveal traditional 'masculine' and 'feminine' subject and occupational stereotypes. These differences continue in post compulsory education, in universities and in the workplace. What is more, these differences appear to withstand radical changes in curriculum and assessment policy and practice.

Gender differences in pupils' interests and expectations

The lack of evidence of cognitive differences between the sexes has led to an emphasis on psycho-social explanations for gender differences. In the early development of gender identities Duveen (2000) emphasises the transition from 'external identities as children are incorporated into the social world through the actions of others, to internalised identities as children become independent actors in the field of gender'. As a consequence, boys and girls engage in different hobbies and pastimes from an early age. They develop different ways of responding to the world and making sense of it. As Fivush (1998: 60) observes, 'gender thus moves beyond knowing which behaviours are deemed appropriate for females and males to become a self-regulating system'. Browne and Ross (1991) studied a large sample of pre-school children and observed that from a very young age children develop clear ideas about what 'girls' do and what 'boys' do. The activities girls were observed to take part in by choice were labelled as *creative* and included, drawing, creative activity, reading a book or talking to an adult. Boys, on the other hand, were observed to prefer *constructional* activities.

In another research study, Murphy (1997) noted that children's interests were either seen as unproblematic, and therefore not challenged, if they corresponded with pre-school activity, or were exploited to ensure engagement with particular learning goals. In other words gender differences are built on in schooling as the following quotes from day care staff indicate:

> Getting them [the boys] to settle down to a story was really quite a task. What I resort to is any book that has a tractor, a dumper in it, any sort of machinery. I don't have a problem settling the girls.

> Girls are much more interested in drawing and as a result quite often are more forward than boys when it comes to using pencils and scissors. Girls seem to enjoy the colours and the process of drawing. Boys just aren't interested.
>
> (Murphy 1997: 97, 98)

The self-regulating nature of gender development serves to shape pupils' views of their realms of competence in school which, in turn, affects their achievements in science. Across the hundreds of science tasks monitored by the APU, there were found to be systematic *content* effects; that is, it was not the task itself but what the task was about that influenced performance. For example, interpreting a table of information about flowering plants or about spare parts for cars. Across the ages, girls and boys as groups avoided certain contents irrespective of what construct was being assessed or their understanding of it. Typically, questions that involved content related to health, reproduction, nutrition and domestic situations showed girls performing at a higher level than boys. This performance difference arose because more girls than boys attempted the questions and reported that they felt confident in their ability to respond. In questions where the content was more overtly 'masculine' the converse occurred. 'Masculine' contents included cars, building sites, submarines, machinery, space travel and so on.

Interests and salience

The different experiences pupils acquire outside of school not only affect the skills and knowledge they develop but crucially, their understandings of the situations and problems in which to apply them. Activities which are gender-typed vary in their *goals* and *purposes*. Thus, if girls are engaging more in creative, socially orientated tasks and boys more in constructional technical tasks, then what they learn to attend to will vary. When asked to observe phenomena, objects or events without any cues as to what was salient, girls more than boys took note of colours, sounds, smells and texture. Boys took note of structural details. When boys were directed in tasks to observe sounds and so on, they were perfectly capable of so doing. However, without this direction students' differing views of salience remain unchallenged and the potential constraints on their learning continue.

Research by Murphy (1991) found that the setting of tasks in science were treated differently by girls and boys. Girls tended to consider contextual features as an integral part of the tasks they formulated unlike boys who tended to consider issues in isolation. One effect of this is that girls formulate more complex multi-variable investigations, which may be very difficult for them to address procedurally. Furthermore, their tasks are often not recognised by teachers, who judge them to be examples of girls' misunderstanding. Consequently girls are often required to pursue other pupils' tasks or accept a teacher-imposed one. In a situation where pupils aged 9–10 were investigating the rate of dissolving, a teacher used a worksheet which suggested the 'problem' was a father who could not get his sugar to dissolve in his tea. The actual task specified on the same worksheet was to: 'Find out how the time taken for sugar to dissolve depends on the temperature of the liquid.' The teacher had been at pains to represent science as relevant to children's daily lives in previous activities but had also, throughout his teaching, introduced pupils to the nature of scientific evidence and appropriate procedures to acquire it. In a mixed group of one girl and two boys, the children's different views of what the problem was emerged. For the boys, it was to carry out a science investigation; for the girl, it was to solve the father's dilemma. One boy suggested therefore that three temperature readings were essential, cold, warm and hot. For the girl, only warm and hot were necessary as she commented: 'Nobody drinks cold tea.' Neither the boys nor the teacher could understand the girl's refusal to undertake the third reading, as she was able to state the task as being to find out how temperature affects dissolving. Nor was the girl able to explain that the evidence she needed was for the father in the worksheet and *not* to establish a pattern in results which would allow her to describe a relationship between two variables. In the end, she was required to do what she saw as the boys' investigation.

Girl: Why should I have to do what the boy wants?
Teacher: But he's come up with a suggestion.
Girl: Yeah, a suggestion and you want me to do it. You think it's a good idea?
Teacher: I do think it's a good idea.
Girl: But if I don't, do I still have to do it?
Teacher: Is it going to tell you something? You give him a good reason why you shouldn't do it.
Girl: Right, the situation is that someone wants their sugar to dissolve quicker in their tea, right? So we, so nobody, but they still want warm tea or hot tea but they don't want exactly cold.
Teacher: You're too hung up on this rather than what it is you're trying to find out.

For the teacher and the boy, the everyday setting was irrelevant to the task. For the girl, the context was integral to the task. The problem she was trying to solve was the dilemma of the father's unsweetened tea, and as she said repeatedly, 'no one drinks cold tea'.

In school science, it is often assumed that students will focus on single variable effects and that once pupils can do this they will do it irrespective of contextual issues. There is considerable evidence that extraction is an approach to thinking that males employ more than females (Head 1996.) However, if extraction is a significant requirement for learning in science education, this needs to be made clear to pupils. Furthermore, more careful attention needs to be paid to how science is represented to pupils. Pupils could easily be shown how a relationship between temperature and rate of dissolving could be used to explain how best to dissolve sugar in tea. What is problematic is to represent science as *directly* engaged with solving everyday problems rather than offering explanations for them. Teaching pupils how science acts in the world needs to be part of the specified curriculum, particularly any future curriculum concerned with scientific literacy.

Gendered styles of learning

The more pupils engage in gendered activities, the more they develop gender-related ways of being in the world. Two generalised aspects of these gendered ways are pupils' learned styles of communication, both written and oral.

Research has linked pupils' gendered choices of reading to the styles of written response they develop. At age 15, over half the boys surveyed by the APU, compared to one-third of the girls, said they preferred reading books which gave accurate facts. Twice as many girls than boys liked to read 'to help understand their own and other people's personal problems'. A girl's preferred written style is described as extended, reflective composition, with boys' style being more often episodic, factual and focusing on commentative detail (Gorman *et al.* 1988).

Research in science suggests that a particular style of response is valued in subjects like physics and it is a style more consonant with boys' learned styles of writing (Elwood and Comber 1996). Furthermore, attributes of style come to be associated with cognitive abilities. Hence drawing on multiple perspectives more typical in a female response is interpreted by teachers as 'a lack of courage to discard irrelevant details'. Whereas male responses are described as more clinical, strongly arguing a point and are associated with risk-taking, flair and sparkle. One reason for the decrease in interest and participation of girls in science may be that their competence is questioned at the same time as their preferred and learned ways of responding to the world are devalued. Interventions which have made explicit the style of response expected, and extended the range valued, had a significant effect on females' level of achievement in physics at age 18 (Hildebrand 1996).

Gender differences in the ways in which adults talk with girls and boys have also been established in research. Girls are both talked to more than boys and seek exchange with adults more. Pre-school children's talk also reveals significant gender differences in girls' and boys' style of communication (Thompson 1994). Girls' preference for working collaboratively and through discussion with others was noted in the UK surveys of design and technology (Kimbell *et al.* 1991). Girls were observed displaying an ability to take on a wide range of issues in discussion and acting as facilitators to the boys' ideas, 'being able to give them lots of support and to point out the strengths and weaknesses of their ideas'.

Research looking at talk in science classrooms and design and technology workshops (Murphy 1999b) found that girls more than boys talked out loud about their work, and actively sought each other's views and gave each other support. Consequently, girls were more likely to develop shared reference to support their problem solving. Boys' lack of shared talk was not seen as problematic. Indeed, the successful pupil at secondary level appeared to be the one who worked independently and quickly. Boys who needed help typically avoided asking teachers and waited for support when their male counterparts had finished their work. This had significant negative effects on their progress.

Teacher expectations and gender

The expectations of teachers have been found to have a direct impact on pupils' beliefs about their competence. Girls continue to rate their achievements in science lower than boys. This is a cross cultural phenomenon. In the study into gender differences in examinations at 18-plus, physics teachers' assessment of female attitudes to the subject were much less positive than for males (Elwood and Comber 1996). The majority of teachers disagreed with suggestions that female students had the confidence to succeed at physics. Nor did teachers expect their female students to pursue a career that involved physics. Male students were, however, expected to continue with their studies beyond A-level.

Teachers' beliefs about pupils do influence their self-concepts in relation to subjects. Head (1996) describes the way males tend to attribute success to their own efforts and failure to external factors. Girls, however, do the converse. An extensive review of research studies (Howe 1999) concluded that boys dominated class interactions, and that boys were selected more often by teachers than girls in part because they attracted more attention. Boys also received more feedback from teachers both positive and negative. Girls received less negative feedback but what they received was focused on their work and influenced their expectations of themselves and their abilities negatively (Dweck *et al.* 1978). One issue that is rarely discussed is the effect of teachers' behaviours on boys' performance. If some boys hold an exaggerated view of their potential achievements, and if they have learnt to attribute failure to external factors, their ability to reflect on their own learning is restricted. Furthermore, if some male students struggle in science because of a mismatch between their beliefs about their ability and reality, then disaffection and demotivation may be a consequence.

Discussion

The debate about gender differences has clarified that innate cognitive differences between girls and boys are not the issue. However, girls' increased participation and success in science only obtains when access is required rather than a matter of choice. Furthermore, performance results analysed at question level continue to show significant differences between the achievements of girls and boys on aspects of science. A further area that needs consideration is tiered entry in national and exam entry. There is evidence that ceiling and floor effects on pupils' achievements arise because of teachers' perceptions of gender differences related to affective rather than cognitive factors.

Such effects matter because of the impact they have on pupils' views of themselves in relation to science. Teachers evaluating KS3 assessment observed that it functions as 'a disincentive to further learning' (ATL 1998: 28). Furthermore the preponderance of physical science tasks in the higher tier paper was seen to discriminate against girls (ATL 1999). Assessment in science influences the development of pupils' self-esteem. A self-protective reaction to its influence therefore, will lead pupils to turn away from science. If the subject, in its definition of achievement and ways of knowing, already marginalises some pupils, formal assessments introduced throughout schooling could accelerate and increase the disaffection.

When choices remain, there emerge traditional stereotypical patterns in course uptake. There is evidence of some change to this in girls' enhanced entry and performance at A-level. However, the decline in uptake post-16 in physics and chemistry is a matter for concern. Some argue that as there is no crisis in science and technology related career recruitment, this concern is misplaced. This begs the question of the purpose and goal of education post-16, and raises the related question of the reasons behind pupils' choices. The increased uptake of mixed A-levels to serve more wide-ranging career choices is one explanation. Another can be perceptions of subjects such as science post-16. Elwood and Comber (1996) reported that most teachers and students considered A-level physics difficult, and some teachers described it as boring 'an issue-less, non-discursive subject leading to sterile teaching and teachers'. In response to this there have been some major curriculum developments, such as the Institute of Physics A-level project and the SLIP curriculum project (Whitelegg and Parry 1999). There is evidence that such initiatives work if there are accompanying shifts in the teaching and learning strategies to ensure pupils' experiences are valued and alternative ways of working allowed. These alternative ways included co-operative group work, creative drawing and writing, roleplay, problem solving, brainstorming and modelling. The curriculum changes had also to be incorporated into the assessment procedures; i.e. assessment tasks set in real world contexts to match students' interests and a range of ways of showing learning allowed including the visual, student-designed investigations and process folios of students' changing ideas. All of these attributes can be related to developments in views about effective teaching and learning.

Such changes were implemented in the Australian State Victoria Certificate of Education physics curriculum and examination for 18-year-olds, and there was a 10 per cent increase in the pass level for all students. There were dramatic shifts in the number of females achieving 'A' grades, 44 per cent compared with 29 per cent for males. However, this was not the case for all girls. Both in enrolment and achievement levels, girls from low socio-economic areas were still disadvantaged (Hildebrand 1996). The extant social conditions that confront some pupils, particularly those from low socio-economic backgrounds, may reduce their ability to deal flexibly with gender stereotypes associated with roles and adult work. It is, therefore, crucial that in implementing interventions to enhance access and achievement, that differences within and between gender groups are considered.

Currently, any changes to reintroduce choice in the science curriculum for 14–16-year-olds will disadvantage pupils, girls more than boys, but also boys who already feel that science is too difficult or of less relevance to their lives. As the EOC noted, 'without a renewed emphasis on developing gender equality in schools, opening up choice increases stereotyping, reinstates a gendered curriculum and reduces the potential for equality in the work place' (EOC 1999: 217).

Replacing a pedagogy for 'boys' with a pedagogy and curriculum for 'some girls' is not the answer. Providing initial teachers and practising teachers with evidence of pupils' different reactions to the same science content, set in difference contexts, will raise their awareness of the issue and of the options and possibilities available in the science curriculum. This evidence is increasingly available (Sjøberg 1999). A more radical and enduring change would emerge if models of learning environments which enhance the interests of a range of pupils were developed and made available, including modifications of teaching material and strategies. It is not the choice of context that matters, but how that context is used to motivate and engage pupils and allow them to bridge between their past experiences and future learning in ways that make sense of them. Changes to learning environments make demands on pupils as well as teachers. As Perrenoud (1998) suggested, we need to counter pupils' habits by reconstructing teaching contacts if any pedagogic intervention is to succeed. Without such changes, our national curriculum and assessment system may increasingly meet the needs of only some pupils and continue to fail the most vulnerable.

Questions

1   How can the current initial teacher training curriculum be altered to equip teachers with the understanding and practice to work with gender effects in the classroom?
2   What changes to the organisation of science teaching would be necessary to achieve learning environments that cater for individual differences?

Further reading

Epstein, D., Elwood, J., Hey, V. and Maw, J. (1998) *'Failing Boys?' – Issues in Gender and Achievement*, Buckingham: Open University Press.

This book takes a general look at the issue of underachievement. It demonstrates the need to treat with gender at the school level using sensitive collection and analysis of local data.

Salisbury, J. and Riddell, S. (2000) *Gender, Policy and Educational Change: Shifting Agendas in the UK and Europe*, London: Routledge.

This is another useful general publication. It looks at gender equality policies to see the effect of changes in the UK and beyond.

Murphy, P. and Gipps, C. (1996) *Equity in the Classroom: Towards Effective Pedagogy for Girls and Boys*, London: Falmer.

This publication is more practice orientated and more specifically relevant to science teaching in the classroom. It includes overviews of issues, case studies of interventions and their evaluation and provides many insights from other subject areas such as mathematics, IT, language and so on.

Parker, L., Rennie, L. and Fraser, B. (1997) *Gender, Science and Mathematics: Shortening the Shadow*, Dordrecht: Kluwer Academic Publishers.

This publication is mainly about science and draws on international perspectives to provide a good overview of issues.

18 Ability grouping
What is the evidence?

Laura Sukhnandan

In recent years, there has been a great deal of discussion about the most effective and efficient ways to group pupils in order to raise levels of achievement. This chapter is based on a review of research which investigated the dominant forms of ability grouping in Britain: streaming, setting, within-class grouping, and mixed ability classes. The chapter attempts to identify the impact of these different types of ability grouping on pupils' experiences of learning at both a general level and in relation to science in particular. This will provide a context for understanding why growing numbers of secondary and primary schools have begun to increase their use of grouping pupils by ability (OFSTED 1998a, 1998b). This chapter will therefore:

- define the different types of ability grouping that have been prevalent in Britain;
- provide an overview of the general trends in the use of different types of ability grouping in relation to the teaching of science;
- review research which has investigated the impact of different types of ability grouping on pupil achievement and on teaching and learning processes;
- use the findings from previous research to provide a rationale for why schools are increasingly organising their pupils by ability.

Defining different types of ability grouping

In Britain there have been four dominant forms of ability grouping: streaming, setting, within-class grouping, and mixed ability grouping. The main aim of streaming is to reduce the heterogeneity of the learning group, which helps teachers to match educational experiences to pupils' ability levels more effectively and facilitate whole-class teaching. Like streaming, the main aim of setting is to reduce the heterogeneity within a class. However, unlike streaming, setting offers greater flexibility as pupils are allocated to sets on the basis of their performance in a particular subject, which means that they are not necessarily in the same set for every subject.

Within-class grouping involves dividing a class into small groups often in terms of ability but occasionally in relation to other factors such as gender and friendship (Lou *et al.* 1996). Within-class grouping enables teachers to provide different groups of pupils with teaching methods and a curriculum that are tailored specifically for their needs. Finally, mixed ability grouping is based on the belief that pupils' needs cannot be effectively catered for through different forms of homogeneous grouping and therefore require specifically tailored individualised teaching.

Trends in pupils organisation

At the primary level, mixed ability teaching has traditionally been the dominant form of pupil organisation. This was partly because it was the only form of grouping that was practical given the restricted size of many schools. From the late 1940s to mid-1960s, streaming was popular in the majority of large primary schools but, following the publication of the Plowden Report, there was a significant shift back to the use of mixed ability classes. A recent survey of primary pupil organisation found that 97 per cent of primary schools organised their pupils in mixed ability classes (Lee and Croll 1995). However, within these classes, within-class grouping was almost universally used some of the time and setting was occasionally used in the top junior years of large primary schools for reading and, less frequently, for mathematics (Harlen and Malcolm 1997).

A more recent study by OFSTED (1998c), which investigated the use of setting in primary schools, found evidence which showed that the use of setting had doubled from 2 per cent of all lessons observed in 1996–7 to 4 per cent of all lessons in 1997–8. The use of setting in some lessons was found in 70 per cent of junior schools and 40 per cent of 5–11 primary schools. The highest proportion of setted lessons was found in Years 5 and 6, with 77 per cent of these lessons in mathematics, 63 per cent in English and 10 per cent in science. Setting was rarely used in other year groups and in other subject areas.

At the secondary level, streaming was the norm until comprehensive reorganisation, when it was largely replaced by mixed ability grouping in the lower secondary years for all subjects, with the exception of mathematics and modern foreign languages, and setting in the upper years for some subjects. In a recent OFSTED Report (1998a), it was revealed that in Year 7 mixed ability grouping prevailed in all subjects with the exception of mathematics. However, in Years 8 and 9 setting became increasingly common and was found in roughly equal proportions with mixed ability grouping in science as well as in English, history and geography. By KS4, the report stated that 90 per cent of science classes were taught in sets with the remaining 10 per cent taught in mixed ability classes.

The effects of different forms of ability grouping

At the primary level, there has been a considerable amount of research that has investigated the impact of streaming in comparison with non-grouping which has inevitably covered all subject areas (Jackson 1964; Barker-Lunn 1970). The majority of research investigating the impact of both setting and within-class grouping has tended to focus on mathematics and reading (Slavin, 1987).

At the secondary level, while research has investigated the effects of streaming and setting in comparison with mixed ability teaching, some researchers have not made clear distinctions between the two forms of grouping pupils by ability (Slavin 1990). The majority of these studies have tended to focus on the impact of these forms of grouping on pupils in relation to mathematics and English (Fogelman *et al.* 1978; Boaler 1997). However, some studies have investigated the impact of streaming (Hacker *et al.* 1991, 1992; Newbold 1977) and setting (Hoffer 1992; Frost 1978) in relation to science. Due to the infrequent use of within-class grouping at the secondary level, there has been little research conducted into its effectiveness.

The focus of research studies, in terms of subject areas, reflects the fact that ability grouping is usually used in 'linear' subjects such as mathematics, sciences and modern foreign languages, because teachers generally believe that these subjects require pupils to work through a body of knowledge in a logical sequence and because the teacher, rather than curriculum materials, is often perceived as the central resource. It is therefore considered more suitable, in these subjects, to have classes containing pupils of similar ability who can work at a similar pace to one another (Reid *et al.* 1981).

The impact of ability grouping on achievement

In general, the findings of many studies as well as meta-analyses and reviews of work in this area reveal that streaming and setting compared with mixed ability grouping have no overall significant effect on pupil achievement, at either the primary or the secondary level or in relation to particular subject areas (Barker-Lunn 1970; Slavin 1987, 1990). Yet a number of studies have found that streaming and setting compared with mixed ability teaching have a positive to neutral effect on the achievement of high-ability pupils and a neutral to negative effect on the achievement of low ability pupils (Newbold 1977; Frost 1978). Nevertheless, evidence from meta-analyses in this field does not support this claim but suggests that different forms of ability grouping have no significant effect on pupil achievement regardless of pupil level of ability (Slavin 1987; Kulik and Kulik 1982).

In contrast to these general findings it is useful to recognise that some studies have found significant differences in terms of both overall achievement and for pupils of different ability levels. For example, Frost (1978) conducted a study which investigated the effects of setting compared with mixed ability grouping in science, on Year 8 pupils in one comprehensive. Three-quarters of the second year (which included pupils of all abilities) were divided into three classes (sets) on the basis of their previous year's performance in science, while the remaining one-quarter was left as a mixed ability group. The same group of teachers taught the classes in rotation, and mobility between the setted classes was on the basis of exceptional performance in end of term tests. At the end of the year, pupils' marks in all three sciences were combined and analysed. Frost found that, overall, pupils who were put into sets achieved more than those in the mixed ability class. Differences in levels of achievement were most marked among pupils of high ability with those in sets outperforming their counterparts in the mixed ability class, while differences among pupils of low ability were imperceptible.

In an attempt to understand the discrepancy between studies which show that streaming and setting, compared with mixed ability teaching, have no overall impact on pupil achievement but have a differential impact on pupils of different ability levels, Hoffer (1992) conducted a study into middle school ability and pupil achievement in science and mathematics. The study was based on 1900 middle school pupils as they progressed from 7th grade (Year 8) in 1987 to 9th grade (Year 10) in 1989. Data was collected on pupils' achievement tests in science and mathematics to compare the achievement of ability-grouped and non-grouped pupils, on average, and in relation to their levels of ability (high, middle and low). Hoffer found that, overall, grouping had no benefits in either science or mathematics. Interestingly, Hoffer suggested that this overall net effect of zero occurred because although pupils in high ability groups learned more than their non-grouped counterparts, those in low ability groups learned less than their non-grouped counterparts. Summarising, Hoffer stated:

> ability grouping in seventh- and eighth-grade mathematics and science is clearly not an optimal arrangement compared with the non-grouped alternative, for low-group students are significant losers.
>
> (Hoffer 1992: 221)

On the basis of these findings, Hoffer concluded that the differential effect of grouping on pupils of different ability levels possibly occurs as a result of the lower status that is often accorded to low ability groups.

However, as stated at the beginning of this section, research has generally failed to identify any conclusive benefits of streaming and setting compared with mixed ability teaching at either the primary or secondary level or in particular subject areas (Slavin 1987, 1990). In contrast to these findings, the limited evidence on within-class grouping compared with other forms of ability grouping, predominantly at the primary level, has found it to have a positive effect on pupil achievement both overall and for pupils of all ability levels (Slavin and Karweit 1985; Lou *et al.* 1996). For example, a meta-analysis of fifty-one studies by Lou *et al.* (1996) concluded that within-class grouping appeared to have a significantly greater effect in mathematics and science than in other subject areas. The researchers therefore suggested that the effectiveness of within-class grouping for different subjects may be due to differences in the extent to which subjects have a marked developmental sequence.

The main reason for the inconsistency in the findings of research on ability grouping can be attributed to two main factors: firstly, to the methodological limitations of many studies in this field, and secondly to the inability of researchers to isolate the effects of grouping from both pre-existing differences (such as the perceptions, attitudes, beliefs and expectations of teachers and pupils) as well as from the additional changes which grouping brings with it, such as variations in teaching methods and curriculum materials/content.

As a result, some researchers have moved beyond simple investigations into the relationship between systems of ability grouping and levels of achievement, to explore the mechanisms by which different types of grouping may affect achievement. Such research focused primarily on three main areas: the influence of institutional structures; the effect of the teacher; and the impact on pupils' experiences of schooling and learning. The findings of such research have generally been far more consistent than the findings of studies investigating the impact of ability grouping on pupil achievement.

The impact of ability grouping on teaching and learning

Firstly, with regard to the influence of institutional structures, it has been shown that the extent to which different forms of grouping pupils by ability can fulfil their main aim of reducing the heterogeneity within a class is dependent on:

- the diversity of a school's catchment area
- the process by which pupils are allocated to streams, sets and groups
- the extent to which different systems offer mobility

The findings from studies investigating these issues have revealed that pupil allocation to ability groups is often done on a subjective and inconsistent basis, which often reinforces divisions along lines of social class, season of birth and race (Barker-Lunn 1970; Ball 1981). In addition, few schools have appropriate systems in place which allow pupil mobility between different ability groups (Douglas 1964). It can consequently be argued that systems of grouping pupils by ability are rarely implemented in ways which enable this form of organisation to meet its main aims effectively.

Secondly, in relation to the effect of the teacher, a number of studies have shown that the effectiveness of different forms of ability grouping is dependent on the extent to which teachers are able and willing to adopt different teaching approaches when instructing classes of different ability levels (Kulik and Kulik 1982, 1987; Lou *et al.* 1996). The findings from such research suggests that where teachers are able to modify the curriculum programme, their level of instruction and the pace and pitch of their lessons in relation to the ability level of the class, different forms of ability grouping can have a positive effect on pupil achievement.

One example of a study, which investigated these issues, is that of Hacker *et al.* (1991, 1992). They conducted research into the influences of organisational change, from streaming to mixed ability classes, on classroom processes in science lessons. The study was based on three coeducational secondary schools, which planned to replace streaming with mixed ability classes, and on nine teachers who taught an integrated science curriculum to 14-year-olds. In the first phase of the study, when the schools still used streaming, teachers were observed during six science lessons with high-ability groups and during six science lessons with low-ability groups. Within each class, six pupils were randomly selected and their interactions were recorded during a particular time period.

The authors found no difference in the overall frequency of interactions when teachers moved from high- to low-ability classes, which suggests that teachers did not respond to the change in the ability level of classes simply by slowing down the pace of their delivery. However, the authors did find that teachers adopted quite different teaching strategies with classes of different abilities in science, as there were significant changes in the types of interactions that were taking place in high-ability classes compared with low-ability classes. In high-ability classes, pupils were more likely to initiate talk, work independently of the teacher and utilise multi-media materials. In addition, greater emphasis was placed on acquiring concepts, learning principles, and applying these constructs to problem-solving activities. In contrast, in low ability classes there was greater teacher direction and greater structuring of learning experiences particularly during practical work.

The second phase of the study was conducted one year after the three secondary schools replaced streaming with mixed ability classes. The same nine teachers were observed again, teaching the same curriculum to 14-year-old pupils. All of the teachers had been given in-service training emphasising the importance of using individualised teaching methods, especially structured worksheets. For each teacher, six mixed ability science lessons were observed. Within each lesson, two sets of data were collected; one set was based on the interaction of six pupils who would have been allocated to the high-ability class, and one set was based on the interactions of six pupils who would have been allocated to the low-ability class. The pupils chosen were matched for science reasoning ability with those that had been selected for study from the streamed classes.

Hacker *et al.* found that although all of the teachers claimed to have adopted individualised approaches, less than ten per cent of the class time observed was actually characterised by 'true' individualised teaching. They concluded that organisational change was confounded with a retention of teaching style that was more appropriate to the teaching of pupils grouped by ability. Consequently, mixed ability science classes appeared to be treated as though they were low ability streams, as teachers tended to teach to the middle of the class, and true individualised teaching was a rare occurrence, which inevitably had adverse effects on pupils of high ability. They stated:

> if changes in opportunities to practise intellectual skills in the classroom are reflected in changes in achievement, the changes in classroom behaviours reported here (for high ability pupils) may well provide the key to understanding concerns with declining science achievement levels of able children in heterogeneous groupings.
>
> (Hacker *et al.* 1992: 122)

The effectiveness of grouping pupils by ability has not only been found to be related to different teaching methods, but has also been associated with factors such as teacher allocation and teacher attitudes and perceptions. For example, teachers who are most experienced and more highly qualified are more likely to be allocated to teach pupils of high ability (Ball 1981; Boaler 1997). Furthermore, teachers also tend to have more positive, interactions with, attitudes towards, perceptions and expectations of, high-ability pupils compared to pupils of low ability, which can increase high-ability pupils' levels of motivation and achievement. This then reinforces teachers' perceptions, leading to the creation of a vicious circle; an effect which happens in reverse for low ability pupils (Harlen and Malcolm 1997).

Thirdly, it has been argued in regard to the impact of pupils' experiences of schooling and learning that streaming and setting compared with within-class grouping and mixed ability grouping have a detrimental effect on the attitudes and self-esteem of pupils of middle and low ability, which can be associated with a decrease in achievement (Barker-Lunn 1970; Boaler 1997). In contrast to these findings, a recent OFSTED Report (1998c) investigating the impact of setting at the primary level noted that pupils in low sets were not characterised by low self-esteem, poor behaviour and negative attitudes towards learning. Nevertheless, it has been suggested that grouping pupils by ability can deprive low-ability pupils of peer support and positive role models, while mixed ability grouping fosters social integration (Findley and Bryan 1975; Reid et al. 1981). However, research in this area remains inconclusive.

Furthermore, it has been argued that low-ability pupils who are grouped by ability as opposed to those in mixed ability groups are less likely to participate in school activities, exhibit lower expectations, experience more disciplinary problems and have higher levels of absenteeism and non-completion (Barker-Lunn 1970; Findley and Bryan 1975). In addition, numerous studies have found that grouping pupils by ability reinforces segregation of pupils in terms of social class, gender and race (Boaler 1997; OFSTED 1998c). As a result, low-ability classes/groups tend to contain a disproportionately large number of pupils from working-class backgrounds, boys and pupils from ethnic minority groups.

Understanding changes in the use of pupil organisation

Evidence to date suggests that increasing numbers of schools are moving towards greater use of grouping pupils by ability. Given that the research evidence in this area is inconsistent and therefore far from conclusive it is interesting to investigate possible explanations for this development.

Two main causal factors have been suggested (Sukhnandan and Lee, 1998). Firstly, there is the introduction of the national curriculum and its assessments which are based on a highly structured and tiered format, which many teachers believe is not compatible with mixed ability teaching. Secondly, there is the move towards a market-led education system which emphasises parental choice and school league tables, forcing schools into competition with one another.

These policy initiatives have arguably pushed schools to focus on cost-effective ways to facilitate the teaching of the national curriculum, to attract the parents of pupils who are likely to do well in national curriculum assessments and to implement strategies to improve pupils' levels of achievement as measured by the tests. In order to address these issues schools have inevitably moved towards the introduction or extension of grouping pupils by ability, a shift which has been fuelled by education commentators and politicians who have claimed that a return to setting will help to raise standards.

A study conducted by OFSTED (1998c) which focused on the use of setting in primary schools endorsed the government's view that setting is worth considering. The report stated that mixed ability teaching created a lot of pressure on teachers to meet the needs of all pupils and as a consequence often led to teachers teaching to the middle of the class. In contrast, the report noted, setting allowed the teacher to utilise whole-class teaching methods and thus to teach the entire group for a much greater proportion of the time. It therefore concluded that as long as teachers understood the potential of setting pupils by ability and modified their teaching techniques accordingly it could be beneficial:

> Obviously setting, of itself, will not compensate for poor teaching, but it may help to reduce the pressures that tend to erode teachers' confidence and weakened teaching in mixed ability classes.
>
> (OFSTED 1998c: 2)

These findings on the use of setting at the primary level substantiate those of a previous OFSTED (1993) report that investigated the response of 205 secondary schools to the science national curriculum during 1992–3. The report stated that in mixed ability classes, work was rarely well-matched to the full range of ability. As a result, in Year 7 able pupils were underachieving while in Year 9 less able pupils were often confronted with work that was too difficult. At KS3, standards and teaching were strongest in high-ability sets where work was generally appropriately challenging and brisk. In contrast, standards and teaching were less satisfactory in low-ability sets, where it was felt too little was expected. A similar pattern was also found in relation to KS4: 'standards were at their best in upper ability groups while there was a high proportion of lessons involving work of an unsatisfactory standard in low ability and mixed ability groups' (OFSTED 1993: 10).

Conclusion

This chapter reveals that the only consistent finding to have emerged from previous research investigating the impact of different forms of ability grouping on pupil achievement is that there are no consistent findings. However, from the findings of previous work in this area it is possible to argue that streaming and setting compared with mixed ability teaching have no significant effect on pupil achievement, either overall or for pupils of different ability levels. This finding remains consistent for pupils at primary and secondary levels and across all subject areas. In contrast, the findings from the limited research conducted into the effects of within-class grouping, predominately at the primary level, suggest that it has a beneficial impact on pupils of all abilities especially in subjects such as mathematics and science.

Research investigating the mechanisms by which different types of pupil organisation may affect pupil achievement have focused on three main areas:

1   institutional structures, where findings reveal that the extent to which a system of grouping can effectively be implemented is dependent on a range of factors such as catchment area, and the process by which pupils are allocated to groups, and is therefore variable;

2   teaching processes, where studies suggest that the success of different forms of pupil organisation relates to the extent to which teachers are able to adapt their teaching methods to match the ability level/range of the class as well as

to the process by which teachers are allocated to different classes and the personal orientation of teachers towards pupils of different abilities;

3   pupils' experiences of schooling and learning, where research reveals that grouping pupils by ability can have a detrimental effect on low and middle ability pupils' attitudes towards school which can have a negative impact on their levels of motivation and achievement, and where ability grouping has been found to reinforce the segregation of pupils in terms of class, gender, race and season of birth.

Questions

1   What is the relationship between different forms of ability grouping and the teaching and learning of science? Any such research would represent a significant contribution to the study of ability grouping, which has suffered from a range of methodological limitations.

2   What is the impact of different forms of pupil organisation in relation to various topic areas and tasks within the science curriculum?

3   What is the impact of different forms of pupil organisation in relation to different groups of pupils in terms of their academic and social characteristics? (It would also be useful if researchers in this field conducted investigations into the use of different combinations of pupil grouping for different situations as well as into the possible use of alternative forms of pupil grouping.)

Further reading

Harlen, W. and Malcolm, H. (1997) *Setting and Streaming: a Research Review (Using Research Series 18)*, Edinburgh: SCRE.

This is a best-evidence synthesis of studies, meta-analyses and reviews on ability grouping at the primary and secondary level. It found no evidence that streaming or setting compared with non-grouping raised the achievement of pupils at either the primary or secondary level, in any subject or for pupils of any particular ability. However, within-class grouping, at the primary level was found to increase the achievement of all pupils in mathematics.

Kulik, C-L.C. and Kulik, J.A. (1982) 'Research synthesis on ability grouping', *Educational Leadership* 39(8): 619–21.

This is a meta-analysis of 109 studies on the effects of ability grouping on pupil achievement. It found that streaming had a small, positive effect on the overall achievement of pupils. In addition, within-class grouping increased pupils' overall achievement levels regardless of pupils' levels of ability.

Slavin, R.E. (1987) 'Ability grouping and achievement in elementary schools: a best evidence synthesis', *Review of Educational Research* 57(3): 293–336.

This is a best-evidence synthesis (which combines features of meta-analytic and narrative reviews) of twenty-nine studies on the effects of different forms of ability grouping on the achievement of elementary pupils. Slavin found that streaming compared within non-streaming had no effect on pupil achievement, regardless of pupil level of ability, in reading or mathematics. The findings on setting for reading and mathematics were inconclusive.

However, within-class grouping compared with whole-class teaching was found to have a positive effect on pupil achievement in the upper primary level.

Slavin, R.E. (1990) 'Achievement effects of ability grouping in secondary schools: a best evidence synthesis', *Review of Educational Research* 60(3): 471–99.

This is a best-evidence synthesis of twenty-nine studies on the effects of streaming compared to non-grouping on the achievement of secondary school pupils. Slavin found that there were no significant effects of ability grouping on pupil achievement. There were also no consistent patterns in terms of pupils' ability levels, the number of ability groups to which pupils were assigned, subject areas, study location or date of study.

19 A challenging curriculum for the more able pupil

Pat O'Brien

Introduction

It is raining outside. The Y5 class is engaged on a task to build an electric circuit using wires, bulb and battery. There are questions to answer about what happens when the wire is connected or disconnected, drawings to make of the circuit. One girl is sitting alone looking out of the window – bored. She has, typically, finished all the tasks well before the rest of the class. An extra task is needed to occupy her. The teacher has identified the girl as a more able pupil, so he sits with her talking about the circuit and then asks her to imagine she is so small she can see inside the wire: 'Describe what you would see.'

The pupil went to a corner with a piece of paper. She drew and wrote. Eventually she came up to the teacher and recounted the following explanation: 'I think there are "sparky bits" coming from the battery along the wire to the bulb. In the bulb these "sparky bits" have a fight with something and light comes out. This makes them very tired and so they have to return to the battery to become "sparky" again.'

This pupil has given an interesting model of electric flow that does not use conventional language but does demonstrate some awareness of current, electrons, resistance, energy differences and the need for complete circuits. It will be another two to three years before she is taught the paradigm model. The aspects of 'more ableness' are clearly developed in this pupil, and it is clear the curriculum is failing to challenge her. In short, she is floating but not swimming, and the challenge for teachers is to identify these pupils and give them access to a challenging curriculum that allows them to make progress.

This pupil is like many more able pupils, showing the potential to be a higher achiever. This could be in any of the following areas:

- general intellectual ability
- specific academic aptitude
- creative or productive thinking
- leadership ability
- visual and performing arts
- psychomotor ability

(Marland 1971)

Often their style of learning does not fit neatly with any single curriculum structure we might employ to teach the group. In fact, the more able pupil is sometimes one who severely tests the system. To illustrate the case, consider two troublesome and difficult girls who were on the point of exclusion. In lessons they asked challenging questions, often impolitely, were frequently frustrated by the low expectations and were non-compliant when it came to learning. Identified as being more able in science, they were entered in a research project competition where they were academically challenged. The change in behaviour was dramatic; both achieved very good GCSE results and one embarked upon an A-level science course. This is not an isolated example, and there is much evidence (OFSTED 1997) that many English schools find it difficult to provide for the more able. Reports by Her Majesty's Chief Inspector of Schools have frequently referred to the lack of adequate and appropriate provision for the more able pupils

More able pupils are a group of pupils with a particular educational need. They desire a curriculum that challenges them at their level of achievement with teaching that acknowledges a desire for challenging questions with a high degree of creativity. OFSTED's criticism of teaching in science indicates that teachers do not often provide challenge in the classroom for the more able. The challenges that are provided by teachers are without careful planning and are frequently in a crisis management style. In some cases use is made of extension material which offers differentiation, but by the more able pupils doing *more* work rather than *different* work. This leads to some inappropriate activity for them, and indicates a lack of careful identification of the needs of these pupils.

There are difficult questions to be asked about provision for more able pupils in science, and hard decisions to be made about the way we organise the curriculum. Creativity is the very essence, the joy, of doing science. For the more able, AT1 does not fully address creativity because of its reliance upon developing expertise in the process skills and techniques of science. A recent research project noted that some Year 5–6 pupils commented on finding school science too structured, leading them to become bored with science. It was also found that this trait was higher in Year 10–11 (O'Brien 1997). Creativity, the time for exploration and a time for thinking experiments, appears to be something missing for these pupils.

What do we mean by 'more able'?

What do we mean by 'more able', and how does that relate to 'gifted', 'talented' or 'academic high achiever'? What are the characteristics that allow us to identify these pupils? Do we talk about a national group or the school's local 'more able' pupils and what is a manageable proportion?

When a school writes a policy on dealing with more able pupils, it should define the terms it is using so that there is a shared language and definition that will guide the identification process. Some of the terms that could be used to define ableness are:

- *More able* pupils are those with high potential ability in certain specific areas that can be developed by effective teaching. This definition identifies a role for the teacher in dealing with the more able pupil.

- *Talented* pupils are those who have a specific ability that makes them exceptionally good at music, languages, mathematics, sport or art. This can seemingly appear as a natural talent.
- *Gifted* pupils are those who score highly on cognitive ability tests, 120-plus and/or the top 4–5 per cent.
- *Academically high achievers* are pupils who score highly on academic tests. Care needs to be taken with this term, as not all 'more able' pupils perform well in measured academic tests since they can be selective about their areas for effort, or they can show behaviour problems, or can suffer from a cloaking disability such as dyslexia
- *Exceptionally able* pupils are those who score off the cognitive ability scale, the top 0.001 per cent. These pupils require a special type of education and frequently go to special schools.

If we consider the school population as a normal distribution, then the national 'more able' group could be considered as those beyond one standard deviation above the mean. This would identify a top 16 per cent of the total national school population, while a school adopting the same principle would identify their top 16 per cent as their more able. The implication of this principle is that every school would have a requirement for a curriculum for their more able pupils.

How do we recognise the more able pupil?

Identification of the more able is not a science, it is an art of mixing quantitative and qualitative procedures. Using tests can give standardised scores helping to place pupils in a rank order against their peers. These will not give a clear picture of ability since most tests are set in a narrow spectrum. The use of specific tests like science reasoning can give a direct indication of the pupil's response to science abilities; others can relate to ableness such as higher level thinking or problem solving. Tests take no account of the teacher's personal professional judgements in the classroom, and notice should be taken of opinions from a number of sources. To help identify the style of ableness, specific criteria lists can be helpful particularly if the teacher is unsure what to look for (Freeman 1998). When evaluating the department's ability to identify more able pupils one would expect to see a mixture of the following:

Tests

- baseline entry
- Key Stage tests
- Cognitive Ability Tests
- reading tests
- module tests

Response

- response to higher level tasks

- response to problem solving
- response to thinking tasks

Opinion

- teacher nomination
- parental nomination
- self-nomination
- peer nomination

Diagnostic assessment

- pupils work in class
- use of criteria lists (NACE)
- portfolio records of progression

The use of such lists can help departments to set up criteria in the identification of the more able pupil in class. To aid teachers in the identification of more able pupils the National Association for Able Children in Education (NACE) have identified some of the more obvious characteristics that can be observed (O'Brien 1999). Able children may show:

- a progression of process skills used for planning explorations or investigations which appear to be roughly equivalent to those expected for the next key stage pupils. This includes a good awareness of modelling and using models to explain events beyond cause and effect. These will be seen as very creative ideas and descriptions but not always using exact language.
- use of language which may be precise and concise using concepts to describe events and phenomena. They recognise words as concepts and develop ideas using those concepts. They have a 'wacky' sense of humour and play with words and language in novel situations. It is useful to help pupils discover the origins of the words to help develop their skills in using language.
- accuracy and precision in practical work, often showing an obsession with variables and their relationships. They use graphs with confidence and derive relationships from those graphs. There is a consideration of error and its effect upon the results. As they get older, they begin to recognise and experiment with mathematical applications to explain changes.
- a withdrawn approach to solving problems and they will 'butterfly' between tasks, but this does not mean a lack of concentration but more a higher order skill of reflecting by changing the nature of the task. This can lead to some frustration because there will be, from the teacher, a requirement for perseverance on a task, and this constant flitting from task to task will create a perception of apathy, naughtiness or poor behaviour. This can lead to confrontation and aggression.
- a good personal understanding of their own learning style and the way they think. This high degree of metacognition enables them to reflect upon their experiences and evaluate those experiences as important to their learning.

What type of activity should be in the curriculum?

The more able are frequently quick to pick up knowledge, but do not always have good memories unless the knowledge has importance or fascination for them. They can frequently reason well and solve problems but are not always well-developed in their thinking skills.

More able pupils are very aware of their own personal thinking styles and the best approach to use to help them learn more effectively. They use this awareness to maximise their learning strategies by using a number of techniques like mnemonics relating to text, words or numbers, or other thinking strategies such as mind mapping to organise their knowledge, or brainstorming to search for plausible ideas. This awareness, however, does not always allow the more able pupil to be more effective. They have a need to be taught how to think, and this will require both intervention to enhance general thinking, targeting in subject-specific thinking (such as inference and evaluating strengths of argument) and learning to transfer thinking skills across the curriculum (McGuinness 1999).

Thinking is a skill and has as much need to be taught as any other skill. There are grounds to believe that in any given subject a pupil will learn to develop his or her thinking skills, but frequently these are so specific and embedded in a context that the pupil does not learn to transfer the skills. As with any other operating skill, there is a need for targeted work on pure thinking skills. Pupils have the potential to learn, but do not always receive the right conditions to learn the skills of effective thinking. More able pupils are not necessarily good thinkers; some may develop a thinking style oriented towards considering certainties as answers rather than considering probabilities. This may make them impulsive thinkers who react quickly with definite answers or become reluctant when uncertain.

Sometimes the style of teaching can encourage this unsatisfactory thinking approach. There is a danger of putting more emphasis on cleverness than upon wisdom; a situation in which the learner learns to use verbal fluency to construct an answer and yet not display rational use of knowledge (Lewin 1987). Lewin identifies this as the intelligence trap. A pupil knows an answer, but not how to use it.

There must be a conscious effort on behalf of the school to develop thinking skills early, and this requires an active inclusion of thinking as a topic on equal parity with literacy and numeracy. This will require schools to identify active thinking courses within the curriculum. There are a number available as whole school models, such as the Somerset Thinking Skills Course, Teaching for Multiple Intelligences, Fisher's *Teaching Thinking* (1998) and a subject-specific course, Cognitive Acceleration in Science Education (Adey *et al.* 1989). In all of the above courses, the focused sessions teach the pupils all or some of the following thinking strategies:

- *Focus and clarify the problem*, examining the problem, being clear about what constitutes the distractions and what is the precise nature of the problem.
- *Speculate about the problem*, examining ideas that could be applied to the problem by hypothesising about what we know, what that means and what might happen if we change the variables or conditions.

- *Rehearse ideas*, practising solutions to gather more information about the degree of precision and possible sources of error.
- *Look wider*, questioning and checking the solution. Why is it working? Are we still on target or is there another solution?
- *Am I saying what I mean?* Examine the language of answering and say it precisely but with interest by explaining ideas using different forms of communication.
- *What is this the same as?* Look for groups to help develop shortcuts in thinking about solutions to similar types of problems rather than considering all problems to be unique. With this skill goes the ability to recognise when a problem is unique.
- *Stick to the knitting*, remaining on task with the problem and learning to recognise when the pathway is irrelevant or a tangent. This skill is about sifting the knowledge to bring to bear that information which will help to solve the problem.
- *Be broad but selective*, researching more than one source and being able to think about the chain of reasoning to develop a logical progression in the solution.
- *Know one's strengths and weakness*, learning to recognise where we need to seek some help from someone else. Learn to work in a co-operative group.
- *Set your target*, being purposeful, knowing your direction, considering your personal targets and linking them with those set by others so there is compromise and harmony, not clash and discord.

Much has been made of enhancing thinking skills by using CASE (Cognitive Acceleration through Science Education) or any other tool that assists the development of higher order thinking skills. However, for the more able it is better to adjust the overall curriculum since all the important aspects can be developed together and contribute to the development of the pupil, by being part of the day-to-day work and not additional activities. Burden (1998) identifies three types of activity that need to be in that curriculum:

- higher order thinking skills such as generalising and evaluating
- direct activities relating to text for developing higher order study skills
- in-depth study topics which emphasise a 'real product' outcome

Enrichment and extension should develop out of the taught curriculum and be linked with a range of extra-curricular activities such as reading about science, viewing science programmes, science clubs and science challenges. This was developed by the Berkshire Science Advisory Team (O'Brien 1997) as the following model (see Figure 19.1)

This model has been expanded by NACE (O'Brien 1998a, 1998b) and illustrates that in designing a curriculum for the more able, teachers need to consider thinking skills development through language, concept and process, context and management of the learning environment (Table 19.1).

In the design of the topics, the range of activities is important. The more able

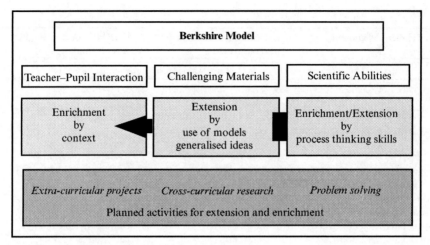

Figure 19.1 The Berkshire Model

pupils begin to show high levels of interest when they are asked to apply their knowledge and use that to analyse, evaluate and develop new ideas. For that reason, it is important that activity design should seek to develop the following progression of levels of knowledge and understanding for all pupils, but with the more able in mind the activity would start at application (Table 19.2).

In the use of language, much can be done to present a higher level of challenge. Clive Sutton (1992) has looked at the interplay of language and meaning in science and found it can help develop a consideration of the relationship of word structure to a description of meaning. Words can be seen as fossils of past ideas and this can be adapted to an activity, 'Fossil Hunting', in which the pupil searches out the origin of the word; for example:

> Dissolve: combination of the Latin *dis*, meaning 'apart', and *solvere*, meaning 'release' or 'loosen'. So a pupil meeting any word having one of these word bits can begin to make a guess at the meaning behind the word.

Other techniques develop higher order study skills in which pupils link ideas in a text. Pupils are given a short passage to read. They circle key words and underline ideas and using arrows they link ideas and key words. They then take these and rewrite the material in their own words. This teaches the pupil to identify the important ideas and then to summarise them.

In the everyday work of the classroom, the style of questioning needs careful attention to further extend the pupil. Teachers are very good at asking recall or observation style questions. They are generally good at asking questions requiring predictive answers. There are some who are good at asking pupils to question the purpose and relationship of what they are doing to the solution of the problem they are attempting by asking them to reason out direct relationships. The most

Table 19.1   A map of science progression for the more able from nursery to Key Stage 4

Enrichment by context	Extension by use of models/ generalised ideas	Enrichment/extension by process thinking skills
Under the above headings progression is from Nursery at bottom of the table to Key Stage 4		
Sc0 – Nature/Culture	*Sc2,3,4 – Knowledge and Content*	*Sc1 – Process Skills*
Key Stage 3/4 Applications:		
	Classification	Hypothesise/prediction
	Genetics and heredity	Relationship – variables
Unfamiliar contexts involve	Cell specialisation	ICT research/modelling
a mixture of probability	Natural element cycles	Precise and appropriate
economics, ethics or social	Atomic events	result collection
dilemmas, technology	Model development	Variables/probability
issues, environmental issues,	Particulate models	Concept of relative rates
philosophy and culture of	Energy transfer	Patterns/relationships
science through history	Concentration/collisions	Quantitative relationships
Extra-curricular use of CREST	Charge flow	Conclusions showing
	Analogues	abstract and mathematical
	Mathematical modelling	relationships to models
	Astrophysics	Evaluation of conclusion
Key Stage 1/2 Applications:		
	Cells as living things	
In unfamiliar contexts	Plants as primary food	Question/hypothesis
Technology	Reproduction	Prediction variables – linked
Environmental	Variety of living things	Variables – multiple
Historical	Classification by properties	
	Chemical changes	
	Physical changes using	ICT – data-logging
	particles	ICT – spreadsheet records
	Separation principles	ICT – simulations
Extra-curricular use of	Mass and weight	Precision in collecting
BAYS	Forces balanced/unbalanced	multiple results over time
	Light travels	Relationship in results
	Solar system	Conclusions – reasoning
Nursery Applications:		
Everyday experiences	Things move	Multiple and accurate
Areas outside school or home	Living *v.* non-living	Observations
	Materials and properties	Measuring
Extra-curricular use of visits	The environment	Clear logical questions
		Language

Table 19.2 Using Bloom's taxonomy

	Style of work appropriate for this domain
Knowledge	What do you know about …? Know the following words …
Knowing	Collect more ideas and facts about … Complete the following …
Comprehension	How does … happen? What is the difference between …?
Show knowledge	Describe … What would you do to …? How accurate … ?
Application	What can you do if … ? Explain using diagrams how …
Make use of	If you change …. what will happen?
Analysis	Make a crossword on … Explain how … affects ….
Break down, relate	Decide which is best and why.
Synthesis	Write a biography of … Describe the ideal …
Creative; What if	What would happen if there was a complete reversal of … ?
Evaluation	What have you learnt well? What was difficult to learn?
Personal reflection	If … happens what would be the comments of …? Imagine you are … what would be your response to …

Source: using Bloom's taxonomy (Bloom 1976)

successful teachers push the questioning even further by asking pupils to consider the correlational relationships and to apply those to problems. The most successful sequence to challenge the more able can be typified as:

- observation: 'What do you see?' 'Look carefully and describe how it happens.'
- prediction: 'What will happen if ?' 'What's the next thing to happen when?'
- causal reasoning: 'This happens because … happened.' 'If you do this then … will happen.'
- correlational reasoning: 'It could be … are connected and so … will happen and … will change by …' 'These two factors could be connected.'
- application: 'If we consider this problem …' 'What do you think will be the important thing to do to make … happen?'
- synthesis: 'What would you want to investigate to explore this problem?'
- evaluation: 'What would be the consequence of that research?' 'Would you get the same result or are there other conditions which would affect the event?'

Some schools have found they can design a curriculum for the more able by accelerating their learning. One approach is to take the material from the next key stage but there are difficulties with this approach. Departments have to keep careful records of a pupil's exposure to the curriculum. Teachers have to keep careful records of progress and match that to appropriate starting points. Many schools find this a difficult approach because of the problems of tracking. Acceleration can be helped by using textbooks from the next Key Stage to extend the content. The difficulty is that a pupil's factual knowledge can be developed without sufficient development of the key ideas in a *range* of contexts.

Other schools have concentrated upon further development of scientific models in a wide range of different contexts. Placing an idea in an unfamiliar context such as an historical, social, technological or economic one can enrich the problem by offering further demand to the pupil. The pupil should be asked to model what they think is happening, and then compare their ideas with paradigm models. Another way is to present pupils with the evidence and ask them to evaluate a solution using only the evidence available. Then, using present-day information, evaluate the changes in the scientific thinking. This can be done with such historic ideas as the Phlogiston Theory, evidence for particles, or Aristotle's ladder of classification. Other schools have coupled focused classroom teaching with more independent learning styles involving extensive library and ICT searches linked with focused writing tasks and more complex problem solving as part of science investigation activities, many of these using Science and Technology in Society (SATIS) (ASE 1996) materials.

The use of interactive approaches using ICT can allow pupils to develop micro-environments, enabling them to explore their own ideas by hypothesising and experimenting. This requires carefully chosen software such as simulations on video or CD-ROMs that allow or give immediate feedback such as *Thinker Tools* for teaching the laws of force and motion. They should promote discussion and reflection. The use of video-conferencing through the Internet extends the class-room allowing the pupil the opportunity to share ideas from a wider range of sources. The danger of the Internet is that the range of information is very high and not always good or accurate. For this reason the range of material available needs to be checked and evaluated by the pupil and then re-told in their words in relation to the particular context in which they are working.

Conclusion

Teachers need to take account of the most able pupils in their classes. Above all, they should motivate and enthuse pupils through the use of extra-curricular clubs that promote different thinking to school science and rewards success. These clubs need to be of an exploratory nature, such as British Association Youth Section (BAYS) or Creativity in Science and Technology (CREST), rather than revision clubs. The danger is of overload, and pupils have a right to enjoy their childhood without extensive cramming to secure goals in excess of those for the average pupil.

Questions

1   More able pupils are used to success. There is some unsubstantiated evidence that a large number of these students see failure as a drastic event. Should we

build in some failure to enable them to develop strategies for dealing with that eventuality?

2   If the most likely choices for schools in dealing with the more able are, to accelerate the learning of the pupils by putting into a higher year group, or to maintain the year set and use fine differentiation, consider what the implications are for the monitoring of the curriculum.

3   Consider the benefits for the pupils if the school adopted a vertical grouping for project days on a termly basis. Is it realistic to suspend the timetable for short periods of time to allow pupils the opportunity to explore more creative avenues of science through visits or the use of PhD students in school?

Further reading

Freeman, J. (1998) *Educating the Very Able: Current International Research: OFSTED Reviews of Research*, London: The Stationery Office.

A good synopsis of the range of provision some education institutions have adopted both in England and internationally. Some very good advice and ideas; good source for strategic thinking.

McGuinness, C. (1999) *From Thinking Skills to Thinking Classrooms*, London: DfEE.

Research Results of a DFEE research project on the development and use of thinking skills provision in schools. A good source of information on the range of techniques available. It includes a good discussion of the value of ICT to developing thinking skills. Indicates that thinking needs to be developed at all ability levels.

Teare, B. (1997) *Effective Provision for Able and Talented Children*, Stafford: Network Educational Press.

Barry Teare presents a comprehensive list of types of generic strategies for providing for the more able pupil. Many of these ideas have been adopted by teachers of all subjects in all key stages to develop teaching strategies for dealing with classes which include more able pupils. A good source of differentiation material.

20 Science for all

The challenge of inclusion

*Sheila Peterson, Judy Williams
and Pete Sorensen*

Introduction

The new National Curriculum for Science includes:

> a detailed, overarching statement which makes clear the principles schools
> must follow in their teaching right across the curriculum, to ensure that all
> pupils have the chance to succeed, whatever their individual needs and the
> potential barriers to their learning may be.
>
> (DfEE, QCA 1999c: 3).

The statement highlights three main principles for inclusion which must be paid
due regard when planning and teaching: setting suitable learning challenges;
responding to pupils' diverse learning needs; and overcoming potential barriers to
learning and assessment for individuals and groups of pupils (QCA 1999c).

In this chapter we will consider the implications of these principles and the
challenges which arise in seeking to make the science curriculum accessible to all
children. However, we consider that the key issues are generic ones and in seeking
to achieve them we believe that there is one factor that is of primary importance:
the attitude of the teacher. It is 'teachers' openness to find out about children as
people and individuals [which] provides an important key to inclusion' (Nutbrown
1998: 169). Thus we make no apologies for making the main focus of the chapter
the generic issues in relation to inclusion, while drawing on science-specific case
studies to illustrate the key points. The case studies presented are drawn from work
we have been involved with over a period of years.

It is vital for teachers to have an open mind, a flexible approach, a belief in
human rights, patience and a sense of humour if inclusion is to succeed. However,
such attributes are, of course, no different from those expected of all good teachers.
In this sense we will argue that successful inclusive practices are no more than a
description of good teaching practices. Further, inclusion is a basic human right as
reflected in UN Convention Articles which, for example, assert the rights of children with disabilities to 'enjoy a decent life' and state that 'education should be
directed to the child's personality, talents and mental and physical abilities' with
all children having the right 'to be educated to their potential within their own
communities' (United Nations 1989: Articles 23 and 29) Such ideas are reaffirmed

in the Salamanca Statement (UNESCO 1994), and this has been reflected in government policy statements such as *Excellence For All Children* (DfEE 1997).

There are many definitions of inclusive education, but for the purposes of this chapter we will simply define an inclusive school as 'one accepting of all children' (Thomas 1997: 103) with the added proviso that such a school will inevitably need to be open to change.

Background

A study of the history of educational provision for those with special educational needs (SEN) highlights the necessity for change. Many of those children educated in segregated provision are now adults very much wanting and demanding the inclusivity, not only of education, but also of society. This can be seen in the work of a plethora of organisations including the Alliance for Inclusive Education, the Centre for Studies on Inclusive Education and the Council for Disabled Children.

The 1944 Education Act was the beginning of any formal education for children based on categorising children in terms of a handicap, dealt with by specialists in a specialist institution away from schools. In short, children were identified by their medical condition. It was much later that the Chronically Sick and Disabled Persons Act (1970) transferred the responsibility for children termed 'severely subnormal' from the health authority to the education authority, requiring that educational establishments should be made accessible to disabled persons. However, this had a very limited effect on many schools, and it is only since the Disability Discrimination Act (1995) that there has been much sign of action. This Act has implications for the inclusion of disabled people into all of society and is slowly having an effect, although there is still a long way to go.

The Warnock Report (1978) identified three areas of need which must be satisfied for successful integration of pupils within schools. Firstly, there are *functional* ones, with joint participation in education programmes. Secondly, there are *locational* ones, where units are on the same site as mainstream schools. Finally, there are *social* ones, where children have opportunities to socialise in the playground, assemblies or lunchtimes. However, the practice did not meet the theory. The 1981 Education Act (DES 1981) led to some advancements, with its focus on special needs and the development of the concept of a 'continuum of need'. However, the identification and assessment of SEN caused problems. Decisions made on the basis of the predominant handicap often meant that children were found in schools that were completely unsuitable to their needs. As Cornwall (1996) suggests, the most suitable environment is one in which all children can flourish and not one which is specifically for one type of child and therefore excludes another type.

The 1988 Education Reform Act (DES 1988a) provided important support with its emphasis on an 'entitlement' curriculum. No special provision was made for different educational needs, but there was seen to be a need for a more broad and balanced curriculum with rigour applied to planning and a more interactive style of teaching. The introduction of new technologies was seen to have the potential for transforming the curriculum for pupils with a range of disabilities and learning difficulties. At the same time, the National Curriculum could have resulted in those children with special needs being disapplied from the curriculum. However, for those teaching in special schools it provided an opportunity to offer more breadth and balance to learning experiences. Differentiation became the key word in planning for children with educational needs. Ironically, there were some children for whom the NC was to offer a more restrictive education, depending on the assessment of their needs. However, the Fish Committee (ILEA 1985: para. 1.1.22), looking at special needs provision in London, agreed to the following: 'disabilities and significant difficulties do not diminish the right to equal access to, and participation in, society'.

Not all legislation in this period was supportive of the move to more integrative practices. The 1986 Education Act (DES 1986) saw the introduction of Local Management of Schools. In some areas this has inhibited the process of inclusive education. While the act sought to encourage more involvement with the community, together with greater accountability, it also made schools more competitive. In particular, financial considerations have produced some dire consequences in providing for children with SEN. In particular, LMS and the pressures it brings to schools have decreased the capability of mainstream schools to respond to pupils with SEN (Evans and Lunt 1993). Other legislation has supported the principle of inclusion without giving any real means for implementation. Thus the Children Act (1989) acknowledged a strong inclusive principle, but at the same time failed to explain to local education authorities how they were to provide the services for children with disabilities.

The 1993 Education Act created the Code of Practice, which recognised the need to educate all children as far as possible in mainstream schools. The Act also gave parents the right to choose to have their child educated in a mainstream school. This gave important support to those parents seeking to obtain places in mainstream schools, but there are many examples of the abuse of their rights in this regard. The problems with implementing the Code of Practice have been recognised and revisions are currently being made.

Implications

It is obvious from the developments outlined above that the issues need to be addressed by all teachers in the profession. The statement that 'each year a child may appear in our classrooms the likes of whom we have never seen before, and will demand of their teachers new and innovative ways of teaching' (Carpenter *et al.* 1996: 13) has already been the experience of many teachers. Clearly, we need to have strategies in place which enable us to respond to the needs of such individuals.

In looking at what has been happening in many schools Clough (1998: 75) has noted that 'much of our practical experience to date has been of integration which encompasses the expectation that a pupil will change or be supported to fit into the school'. He goes on to contrast this practice of integration with a description of inclusion:

Inclusion is active; inclusion is a process in which the school changes to suit the pupil, a process whereby schools and teachers are challenged to develop creative and co-operative solutions to differences they might previously have shelved.

(Clough 1998: 75)

How, then, can we develop inclusive practices? Given the diverse nature of needs, there is no simple formula. The analysis presented in the remainder of the chapter focuses mainly on issues which arise in relation to physical disability. However, the underlying principles are applicable to all pupils with SEN.

Our experience has led us to conclude that including pupils with physical disabilities in mainstream schools has three important components:

1   a readiness to operate within a social model, not an individual model, of disability.
2   an understanding of the individual nature of physical disability which is reflected in planning and management procedures.
3   a commitment to the process of enabling inclusion and accommodating difference which is reflected in whole school policy and individual classroom practice.

In the remainder of the chapter we will examine good practice in the light of these components.

A social model of disability

Focusing upon the physical condition can easily lead us to take as our starting point the traditional individual model of disability whereby the pupil is seen as faulty and in need of repair and the focus of professionals is to effect a cure. This model suggests that *we must change the individual to fit into the existing structures*.

A social model of disability, while recognising that a person with an impairment might have some limitations or restrictions placed upon them, emphasises that they are disabled by the society and environment in which they live where little or no provision is made to accommodate difference (Cornwall 1996). In this model it is recognised *that we must change the structures to accommodate the individual*. It is no longer a medical issue but becomes one of civil rights. This social model of disability enables us to see how disability is socially created and reinforced by everything we do. The buildings we build, the way we organise our transportation, the way in which we propagate ideas of what is or is not desirable in our society, together with a host of other factors, all contribute to this state of affairs.

Society has a history of negative images of disability which permeate our literature and can be present in our current curriculum (Rieser 1995). In addition, the things we say, the language we choose, and our feelings and behaviour will impact upon the level of disability experienced by pupils with physical disabilities within our classrooms and schools. Empathy not sympathy, plus a sound knowledge of individual ability, enables high expectation in the classroom. Being aware of cultural disadvantages and adopting a social model of disability is recognition of the fact that the pupil with physical disabilities will have difficulties arising from both internal and external factors. It is through combining this ideological starting point with an informed profile of the individual that we are able to see how we can more effectively make changes to reduce the impact of the disability.

Planning and management: whole school issues

Preparation for placement

The work on inclusion in science cannot be carried out in isolation:

> Including students with pd in the science curriculum is not the issue – there needs to be a whole school policy of inclusive education.
>
> (Byers 1998: 40)

> Careful planning for inclusion on a whole school basis is crucial. The SENCO is pivotal in this process and should be involved in the planning stages at the level of the school management team where budget holders from the school and the Local Education Authority can contribute. The funding issue is also of key importance as it has been found that 'positive attitudes to Inclusive Education are directly linked to resources attached to policies'.
>
> (Clough 1998: 75)

As part of the planning process it is important to undertake a placement assessment procedure which assesses accessibility and plans adaptations to the building which are possible. Accessibility is a central issue and within new school buildings this will be accommodated by the DDA (1995) but independent access to old buildings remains a process of imaginative adaptations or timetable options. Alternative access to areas that involve lengthy detours can exacerbate mobility difficulties. Science labs dedicated to specific aspects of the subject matter make switching rooms to enable access difficult. Curricula arranged in modular units in alternating locations can play havoc with plans to make environments accessible. If accessibility is too limited, then an effective placement procedure will necessitate looking at alternative schools.

The placement assessment procedure is an ideal opportunity to draw upon parental expertise using their holistic knowledge to identify needs, plan adjustments and alterations, and to identify strengths and weakness for teachers and support staff. This also serves to bring parents into an arena of collaboration.

Planning for the identification or equipment needs/modifications and who will take responsibility for these and the time scale is important and needs to happen twelve months in advance to enable budget planning. Pupils may have a care component in their support requirements and the LSA skills to support this must be reflected in the job descriptions with the necessary appointments and training in place ahead of time.

First steps

As part of the process of including several wheelchair users from the local special school, the science teacher visited the school to assess access and equipment needs with regard to practical science. He met with the LEA advisor and curriculum co-ordinator at the special school and agreed the modifications needed to allow access to his science classroom. In practice these proved to be relatively simple alterations to furniture and room layout, leading to several excited students able to engage fully in practical science for the first time.

Communication and training

The role of the SENCO is crucial. Pupils with physical disabilities need a SENCO to organise and manage the agencies involved and plan the process of transition, as well as the continuing inclusion process (see Roafe (1998) for an analysis of effective models of the way the SENCO can work with other agencies). The development of a system of communication, which enables the external agencies and the internal players, teachers and LSAs, to work collaboratively with parents and pupils is essential. Individual education plans should reflect the multi-disciplinary input, providing a working document to guide classroom practice.

Tanya

Tanya was a wheelchair user, with cerebral palsy affecting all four limbs and limited hand function. As such, Tanya presented mainstream teachers with huge anxieties. How could they possibly meet her needs? Couldn't someone else somewhere else be doing a better job? However, an IEP with clear targets covering all subjects and physical and independence goals, which had been created by the whole team taking joint responsibility for Tanya's placement, served to enable teachers to put their fears to one side and enjoy the contribution that Tanya made to their lessons. This planning allowed her to access practical science through LSA support in the classroom. It also allowed Tanya to achieve levels in science which were simply not possible in her special school. The care taken with planning had allowed Tanya's strong personality and commitment to flourish.

Curriculum planning

Understanding the issues: two curricula

Pupils with physical disabilities reflect the range of individuals existing within the population as a whole and, like any pupil, their needs and the severity of their condition can be seen on a continuum ranging from mild to severe. The whole child approach enables us to first appreciate their similarities with all other pupils. All pupils need access to the whole curriculum and the full range of educational opportunities, work best in environments where they feel valued and achieve when the expectations are realistic and high.

Although it is important that we see the pupil first and the disability second, it is also important that we understand the difference. All pupils with physical disabilities have two curricula to address: the National Curriculum and an ongoing physical curriculum. In the latter the pupil has to constantly address the development and maintenance of physical skills; learning as a skill movement which others have acquired through maturation. This physical curriculum is identified and supported by a multi-disciplinary team of professionals across Health and Education. It may involve actively learning movement by younger pupils, or the focus might be upon maintaining functional movement.

Addressing the physical is often a prerequisite to accessing learning. As a consequence, teachers will need to be willing to accommodate equipment within their classrooms which supports this physical curriculum. Adapted chairs support posture and promote more fluid hand function. Standing frames enable pupils to weight-bear regularly, which could be an essential contribution to the development of joints and bones. They also provide an upright higher position which can reflect on self esteem. Central positions which have uncluttered access have a more positive message than cumbersome arrangements close to the doorway. Sitting in the classroom and maintaining functional posture may require a constant expenditure of energy which will have a knock on effect upon concentration. Appreciating this will enable teachers to organise classrooms and to adjust expectations appropriately.

John, Paul and Alice

John, Paul and Alice were all wheelchair users who had spent their primary years at a special school. While they remained on the special school roll, they were now based at a mainstream secondary school and had joined a new form, attending most lessons with the mainstream group. As part of their vocational course at the school, a group of students at the school sought to plan the layout of the science lab to accommodate three wheelchairs within the body of the room. Fixed bench arrangements meant that a compromise had to be reached which left the three on one side of the room, though others from the form were able to work with them. When the school received the go ahead for its long awaited new lab, planning ensured that future wheelchair users could be positioned throughout the lab.

Flexible pathways

Normal routes where pupils access a whole course, followed by some form of accreditation, might need to be re-thought or broadened. We might need to have a flexible perspective of the curriculum on offer and our traditional ways of organising it. An increased range of accreditation would provide opportunities for a wider population.

It might be relevant to create curriculum pathways which enable pupils to select from the whole course on offer on the basis of what meets their individual requirements. In other words a flexible approach to the curriculum is required, based on individual needs. This might mean that the pupil accesses only part of the course or a relevant module. It could also mean that they might access the same module twice.

Mark

Mark's main access to learning was through listening, as his motor difficulties were so extensive that even his functional vision was dependent upon his ability to maintain sitting in a still position on that day. Academically Mark could be placed towards the higher level of his GCSE class. Mark chose science as part of a reduced curriculum that allowed for reinforcement lessons to be timetabled to ensure that Mark had heard everything. Notes were recorded by Mark onto a tape recorder or through voice activated software in a specially adapted space in the learning support area. In practical lessons Mark instructed his LSA on procedures. He is now entered for GCSE with every expectation of high achievement.

Heidi

Heidi, a bubbly, curly-haired adolescent, with limited fine motor skills and with communication needs, required support to enable her to access the science curriculum. This was achieved through the use of a voice output device and symbolic representations of language (see Blamires (1999) for further advancements in the technology to support communication needs), together with the collaborative work of mainstream Science specialists and special school staff with experience of communication systems. Heidi's lack of muscular control meant that she needed one-to-one support in carrying out science investigations. However, she was able to perform many experiments through supporting her upper arms and ensuring that non-breakable or clamped apparatus was substituted where possible. In other cases where fine manipulations were required, she gave instructions to her teacher. Heidi took the single science GCSE course in double science time, enabling her to have the extra time she needed to complete her work. By the end of Year 10 she had surprised all, including herself, with her achievements. At her annual review meeting she was asked what had been the best thing about doing science and replied 'finding out that I'm not stupid'.

This case study further illustrates the need to adopt flexible approaches in our planning and teaching. Individual curriculum planning of this nature, might help to combat what has been referred to as 'internal exclusion' (Feiler and Gibson 1999) whereby pupils are excluded within the school as a result of streaming or groupings of pupils or as a result of Government initiatives such as the Literacy and the Numeracy Strategies (DfEE 1998a, 1998b). However, sometimes the transition to more inclusive practices may mean that a group who have previously been in a special school start off in a separate, or 'base' group. In such cases there needs to be a staged process of developing access to science.

Group MSP (a Year 8 group of pupils with moderate to severe physical disabilities and associated learning difficulties)

Through liaison with mainstream staff over science room availability a small group of students, all of whom had the majority of their learning experiences in a unit based in a mainstream school, had some of their science lessons in the science laboratory. The students were able to have access to some science apparatus for the first time and were more focused on the science work. The excitement of being able to use Bunsen burners was barely contained!

The group above already had a separate identity from previous practice. They could be seen as having moved from 'external' to 'internal' exclusion, with a target of full inclusion once all felt properly prepared for the changes needed.

Policy and practice: enabling inclusion through accommodating difference

Impact of the physical disability on access to the curriculum

Physical disability might impact upon a pupil's access to learning due to some or all of the following considerations:

- time; everything undertaken may take additional time
- poor self-esteem
- level of independence
- mobility
- fatigue
- poor fine motor skills and the need to develop alternative recording systems or styles
- perceptual difficulties
- difficulties with controlling saliva
- communication difficulties
- difficulties with eating and drinking
- memory

- visual and hearing complications
- pain which might be ongoing in joints and muscles or sporadic
- broken sleep patterns
- constipation

Within the framework of the planning and management issues outlined above, such individual needs must be taken into account when seeking to include pupils in the classroom.

Differentiation

The advent of modern technology has provided opportunities for students with learning disabilities to access the curriculum, from the use of eyelashes to choose radio stations to word processing using a spell check. However, it needs to be recognised that 'the application of Enabling Technology for Inclusion requires more professional skills amongst all staff, not less, and ongoing professional development' (Blamires 1999).

Difficulties may fall within the range of learning needs experienced by other pupils within that group and these can be catered for by differentiated materials in the same way as for all other pupils (see Chapter 16 for ideas). All pupils with physical disabilities need more time and benefit from learning experiences which are less prescriptive, include a variety of tasks and outcomes and provide an element of choice. At the same time, most pupils with physical disabilities tend to have more days away from school than the average person and this will necessitate some system being developed to ensure continuity of learning.

In certain cases, the teacher may just be required to differentiate the curriculum to compensate for fine motor difficulties. If writing is a laborious, energy consuming activity it will be difficult for pupils to focus on learning. Teachers could eliminate copying as a task, reduce the volume of work for that pupil by focusing on the key concepts of the lesson, reduce written components of the lesson, use photocopies, or pre-prepared diagrams, or cut and paste for diagrams and labels.

Tests administered orally may move too fast so the pupil could attempt every other question and multiply the score by two. Setting out a numerical calculation in science may take so much time the pupil never gets the opportunity to undertake the activity. Teachers could instruct the LSA to do a part of the task for the pupil, either the first part, 'back chaining', or by finishing off work at a pre-arranged stage.

It is also important to develop alternative ways of recording. However, getting someone to scribe on your behalf needs practice to work effectively, and using a laptop with appropriate supportive software is often helpful. Work to be used by the pupil can be prepared in advance as a short cut.

If the pupil has a specific difficulty with perception, this will be identified by the occupational therapist and the differentiation might require us to alter the way we present materials, such as clear, enlarged materials, contrasting colours to ensure information is not lost against a busy background, presentation of materials on an angled surface, and support for layout with lined or squared paper to help prompt posture. It may require the planning of individual activities to develop perceptual ability and this might need to be time-tabled into the day.

Robert

Robert, a very bright pupil with athetoid cerebral palsy, was able to instruct his LSA very effectively using his verbal skills. Robert's observant LSA devised a Science experiment kit consisting of a Bunsen burner, a stand, a square of gauze, and a test tube holder, firmly screwed down on to a square of heat resistant material. The Bunsen burner was mounted on a movable arm which swung out for lighting and then swung back when needed. The whole kit could be clamped to the work surface at Robert's desk. Robert could access whole parts of experiments independently, which had an enormous impact upon his self-esteem. During the summer Robert worked successfully on his own personal goal of 'learning to pour from a jug'.

In certain cases specific disabilities may require us to accept that some aspects of the work are impossible to achieve and it is important that the teacher understands that this is a direct result of the condition and is not attributed to personal traits, such as laziness. There has been a wealth of research to illustrate the effects of labelling on achievement and behaviour.

The example above shows that differentiation of equipment might be all that is required to make an activity accessible; an additional length of hosing, tap extension handles, non-slip mats, clamps, clips, frames to support pouring, or tubing slipped over objects to enable a person to grip handles more easily. Such modifications need not be very expensive.

Extra-curricular activities

School trips provide a good opportunity to promote inclusive practice.

School trips constitute an area in which pupils with disabilities are frequently excluded. Teachers who are aware of this might think ahead and design trips which are accessible and which do not compromise the value of the activity for all.

The future

If our education system is to reflect the diversity of our culture, then our schools will have to become more inclusive. Currently too many of our learning structures remain narrow and exclusive. If we had an education system geared to meeting the diversity of pupil's learning needs, the inclusion of those with special educational needs becomes just one part of this diversity, and so does not have to be separately justified (Wedell 1995). Inclusive societies are built by people who have had the

---

Group LPS (a Year 9 group of pupils with a range of severe physical disabilities and associated learning difficulties)

Students with a range of learning difficulties, including a number of wheelchair users, attending a mainstream school were included in a trip to the Science Museum in London. Accessibility to the building and toilets were the main issues of concern, all of which proved to be satisfactory. Higher levels of staffing were necessary for a variety of reasons. The opportunity of a hands on approach to science in a safe, stimulating learning environment provided many different experiences for all of the students. The trip also provided the opportunity for social interaction with the chance for some students to show off their differing abilities.

---

opportunity to live and work in inclusive schools; where they have observed the challenges; where they might have had the opportunity to be a part of some of the solutions and where they have had first-hand experience of the contribution that all people can make.

Footnote

To support the move to inclusive practices, every school in England has been sent a document called 'Index for Inclusion' (CSIE 2000), containing a series of questions and activities challenging inequality in three key areas: culture, policies and practice. The Index can be used systematically or to focus on particular areas of concern and is to guide schools through a two to five-year programme of self-analysis and review. Schools which have piloted the Index have changed and adapted policies and practice as a direct response to issues raised. New Special Needs and Disability Rights Bills are also being developed, strengthening parents' rights to choose a mainstream education for their child. There is a long way to go before we achieve the ideals of the Salamanca Statement (UNESCO 1994) and some resistance remains. However, Curriculum 2000 at least provides a basis for advancement towards the goal of an inclusive education system providing equality of opportunity for all our pupils. We must now embrace the challenge.

Questions

1   Is your Science Department/area accessible to pupils with physical disabilities? If not, what could be done to change this?
2   Does the organisation of the science curriculum allow pupils with special needs to be catered for? Have the Schemes of Work been written to account for and draw on diversity? If not, how could they be developed to meet the targets of the new NC?
3   Concerns about Health and Safety have acted as a barrier to including some pupils with special needs in science. How can these be overcome?

4   How does the Science Department liaise with the SENCO in planning for special needs in science? Is LSA and other support provision managed to allow the department to respond to the diversity of its students? Are there opportunities for planning with LSAs?

Further information

The Special Needs Xplanatory (www.canterbury.ac.uk/xplanatory/xplan.htm).

This site provides links to suppliers of a whole range of products designed to support inclusion.

The ACE Centre Advisory Trust, 92, Windmill Road, Oxford, OX3 7DR.

This provides support for the assessment of students with communication difficulties and advises on approaches to improving their communication skills using the latest technological and other approaches. Website address: www.ace-cent.dircon.co.uk.

The Association for Science Education.

The ASE has recently developed a plan of action to support SEN (Sandford Smith 1999). A resources list, together with training opportunities and a chat room relating to SEN, can be accessed at their website address: http://www.ase.org.uk.

21 Information and communications technology in science education

A long gestation

Phil Poole

Introduction

After some twenty years of deployment in schools, computers still do not play a significant role in the teaching strategies employed by the majority of science teachers. This statement is, of course, also true of most other curriculum subjects as we enter the new millennium. Cox and Johnson (1993: 15) concluded from their ImpacT research that 'the majority of school pupils are not yet provided with opportunities to take full advantage of the potential of the full range of software, a substantial amount of which is currently available in the school or the LEA'. The Stevenson Report (1998: 6) concluded that 'the state of ICT in our schools is primitive and not improving'.

What makes the situation in science education more remarkable is the extent to which, at a national level, science teachers have been at the forefront of developing particular aspects of ICT during this time. Why, then, is the use of ICT in current practice so sparse in most departments?

Firstly, it is expensive. A PC in every laboratory still demands resources that are out of the reach of normal departmental allocations. Computers compete for priority with recent textbooks. Schools have focused on developing network technology rooms at the expense of distributed PCs in departments. Long-term planning for curriculum use is an impediment to most teachers and constrains teachers' spontaneity to respond to opportunities that arise. Secondly, most science teachers are not well trained in the use of ICT at a professional level. The current technology did not exist when they were trained, staff development has been sparse and access to hardware and peripherals is generally difficult. Thirdly, most teachers remain unconvinced about the effectiveness of ICT in improving the performance of pupils.

Capstick and Poole (1995: 3) registered a number of features observable in an audit of schools commissioned by NCET, namely:

- Relatively few teachers have completely integrated the use of computers into their normal programmes of work
- Confidence in the learning potential of computers is largely an act of faith
- Schools have insufficient time and support to plan for computer use
- Teachers need curriculum materials backed by a clear rationale for the use of IT

- Few teachers realise how IT can improve access to the curriculum for pupils with special educational needs.

Imperatives from the National Curriculum have also had little permanent impact over the decade. The first version of the NC in 1989 had a whole Attainment Target dedicated to ICT. This was adventurous given the state of classroom practice at the time. However in the revision (1995) the ICT component was reduced to a very bland statement:

> Pupils should be given opportunities, where appropriate, in their study of science to develop and apply their information technology (IT) capability in their study of science.
>
> (DfE 1995a: 1)

Little progress was made during the subsequent years. The pressure to deliver a still crowded curriculum and the lack of a clear incentive from the statutory order led many science departments to make a token gesture towards ICT. However, the 1999 Order contains a firmer statement about the contribution that ICT should make to the overall experience of pupils. In particular it highlights its role in Sc1 Scientific Enquiry in 'obtaining and presenting evidence' and in the 'breadth of study'.

A rationale for inclusion of ICT in science education

The profession should increasingly include practitioners with a range of ICT experience in their own scientific work. If they feel that school science should reflect the practice of the scientific community, then introducing pupils to ICT as a natural part of their experience of science is an imperative. So how do scientists currently make use of ICT in their work?

- they collect information automatically;
- they handle data from experiments;
- they model ideas;
- they search for information;
- they present information and data;
- they collaborate with other scientists.

It should, therefore, be possible to see these uses reflected in professional practice in science education. The exemplars discussed later show a promising spread of activity that covers many of these areas.

Effectiveness of ICT as a teaching and learning strategy

Firm evidence of the effect of ICT on pupils' performance has been difficult to find. There is plenty of anecdotal evidence and case studies abound, but there is little hard empirical data. One piece of action research conducted at Cornwallis School in Kent used funding from the TTA to conduct and report on work in the department. The school was investing heavily in ICT resources (in science, they created ICT-rich laboratories using laptops in about 40 per cent of lessons) and attempted to measure any gains that occurred. Musker reported that:

> There was an increase in the academic performance in the enriched ICT group. Furthermore the group's proficiency and confidence in the use of ICT increased. The students also thought ICT in the classroom stimulated learning.
>
> (Musker 1997: 3)

Is ICT worth the investment in time and resources?

ICT enables a teacher to support learning as much as to deliver knowledge. This brings many benefits to both pupils and staff. Where such use can provide resources for learning which are more effective, richer and available out of contact hours, students will have greater control over timing and pace, and there will be more likelihood of resources suiting the style and stage of each student's learning. Of equal importance, teachers can expect to gain time for more individual attention to students and also to devote more effort to some other aspect of the teaching and learning process, or to make space for research or administration.

Potential benefits to teachers include:

- enabling pupils access to rich resources;
- more up-to-date information;
- providing differentiation strategies;
- more motivated pupils;
- better levels of performance;
- time saved in preparing, marking and administering;
- more time for individual attention to students;
- better inspection ratings;
- career advancement.

Potential benefits to institutions include:

- higher grades;
- better inspection ratings;
- progressive image with parents and pupils;
- potential benefits to pupils;
- better understanding;
- extra learning resources;
- more access to information;
- more choice of learning styles;
- more control;
- better communications;
- better feedback;
- more individual attention;
- mistakes made in private;

- more patient non-judgemental testing;
- more flexibility and sensitivity;
- more drill and practice;
- more enjoyment;
- ablility to work at their own pace;
- faster work.

Supporting differentiation

Properly integrated into the curriculum, ICT can help with specific learning problems. The Additional Information in the NC order indicates that when implementing the statutory inclusion statement, to provide effective learning opportunities, ICT can offer support to overcome potential barriers to learning in science. It can overcome difficulties with mobility or manipulative skills so that pupils can participate as fully and as safely as possible in experimental work or by using specialist items, including ICT.

Word processors have been particularly successful with pupils with specific writing difficulties. They offer science teachers a number of different opportunities to develop a pupil's basic skills. Drafting and re-drafting can be motivating at all levels, giving the chance to develop one's ideas without the chore of total rewriting. Word-bank programmes such as Wordbar can support spelling, vocabulary and specific problems such as dyslexia. A formative assessment opportunity can be far more motivating for pupils when pupils can submit their work as a file on which they get back the corrections.

In certain situations, ICT can probably be more effective than any other medium, for example:

- dynamic graph drawing;
- exploring models which are under student control;
- providing simulations as alternatives to practical work;
- drill and practice to replace material often covered too rapidly in class;
- to illustrate a lesson to improve visual communication.

Extending classroom practice

Can current practice reflect the aspirations of science teachers to reflect the world of scientific activity outside of the classroom? Can we justify the expense of running a computer in the laboratory if it means less resources for other teaching strategies? Reviewed below are some of main areas of practice which have impacted on schools where ICT has found a permanent place in departmental practice.

Collecting information automatically

One of the useful automatic functions that computers perform is measuring changes in the environment using electronic sensors. Scientists use automated equipment such as mass spectrometers, gas chromatographs and a range of environmental sensors. This is usually called sensing or datalogging. Computers offer teachers and pupils the opportunity to gather data which can then be processed to produce graphs and tables directly in the datalogging software or exported to a spreadsheet.

It is possible to arrange sensors to monitor changes in the environment and to feed the signals into a computer. For example, pupils could graph the changes in oxygen levels and temperature when pond weed is left on the surface of a container for a few days (long time intervals) or timing the acceleration of a falling object due to gravity (short time intervals).

To undertake sensing in the laboratory, classroom or in the field, teachers need access to:

- electronic sensors capable of being linked into an interface;
- an interface or buffer box which links to the computer;
- suitable software to aid analysis of the data that is collected.

Remote loggers are devices which can operate without always being connected up to a computer. Typical systems have names such as DL PLUS, EMU, and Datameter. These are available in most secondary science departments.

Sensing can change pupils' attitudes to practical science, often thought of as 'more trouble than it's worth'. Sensing can offer even the lowest attaining pupils an opportunity to achieve. On a user-friendly display, pupils can see instantly the results of their experiment evolving in real time.

The ease of collecting subsequent readings from a re-run of an experiment encourages pupils to appreciate experimental errors. For example, an 'acceleration due to gravity' reading will rarely produce 9.81 ms^{-2}, but ten readings will illustrate the spread of readings and an average is likely to be usefully close to the accepted value.

Pupils are far more motivated to change variables and see the results; they are far more likely to make predictions if the data gathering is painless. Sensing makes asking 'what if?' questions more likely and possible for the pupils, for example: 'If I doubled the amount of insulation, would it take twice as long to cool down?'

Electronic sensing equipment can assist in the capture of experimental results. The technology is not an alternative to learning how to measure variables with conventional instruments, but it can make it possible to record data that is difficult and/or expensive. It is most effective where it allows teachers and pupils to record data from experiments where the phenomena happen very slowly, very quickly or are generally hard to measure, such as the growth of a plant, the extension of a paper tissue, or the acceleration of an object due to gravity.

Handling data from experiments

The software provided with sensing equipment not only collects but also organises the data in tables, graphs and charts, taking the effort out of the presentation of results. The instant feedback allows pupils to discuss the results between themselves and with the teacher without a de-motivating wait imposed by traditional paper methods of displaying data. The demands to evaluate and conclude in Sc1 stretch the most able, and these are usually areas where achievement is lowest. Strategies which allow all pupils to interact more effectively with the data will enhance their chances of achieving higher grades.

In addition to proprietary software, spreadsheets can offer access and support in presenting and interpreting experimental data for a wide range of pupil capability. Powerful spreadsheet programs, such as Microsoft Excel, make decisions about the scales on axes, and even offer different types of graph. This transcends the more normal progress, provided by the teacher, from entering data on provided axes to deciding on their own axis scales and exploring different types of graphs in the context of different data. Access to ICT has meant that often primary school children have used spreadsheet applications without necessarily going through all these preliminary stages. However, without a sound understanding of the basic principles the power of spreadsheets in an experimental context will be lost. This means that the use of ICT for graphing needs to be part of a well co-ordinated programme for teaching graphical skills. The key issue is the pupil's ability to handle and interpret the data.

Modelling

Computer models are an important feature of scientific activity to which pupils should be introduced. Pupils will need to be introduced to simple models, which they test by changing a variable to see the effects on dependent variables. At a later stage they can be taught to construct their own simple models.

It is possible to investigate the impact of changing variables in a simulation of a phenomenon which is too fast or too slow to investigate in the school laboratory. For example, see the effect of withdrawing particular foods from the model of a balanced diet. Simulations are a subset of modelling activity. Pupils can investigate the effect of changing variables in a system or process, which would otherwise be difficult, dangerous, or take too long. For example, as a manager of a wildlife reserve the user can see the ecological consequences of certain decisions.

Simulations are just one aspect of modelling. Computer models can represent real or imagined situations. They are governed by rules and managed by the computer. They allow us to ask 'what would happen if …?' questions and to see what happens when changes are made. Modelling can use specific software, such as a custom written simulation, or generic software such as a spreadsheet can be made to represent the situation through a set of mathematical relationships, for example, investigating the flight of a ball by changing a variable such as the angle of the throw.

Pupils are natural modellers of situations as, through play, they begin to make sense of their world. A computer can be used to broaden this experience. Modelling helps pupils to see the relationship between cause and effect and encourages logical, sequential and creative thought. Activities based on modelling are often of a collaborative nature. In exploring and explaining their thoughts with the rest of the group, pupils will analyse what they are doing and consolidate their learning. Solving simple problems through early modelling develops the ability pupils will need later to visualise and solve abstract problems. The Crocodile Clips electrical circuit simulation has been very successful in enabling pupils to test if circuits will light a bulb successfully. If mistakes are made which destroy the bulb, the software illustrates the problem and pupils can try to understand patterns such as matching the voltage of the circuit to the construction of the circuit and the operating voltage of the bulb.

Searching for information

Teaching for, or using databases, is one of the more difficult aspects of ICT in science. Compiling and creating school databases can be undertaken as a class activity but this is time-consuming and needs organisation. Commercial data sets can be purchased to provide data files associated with particular areas of the curriculum. These can provide large quantities of data which would be difficult to create in a school environment. Some require specific software but more recently publishers are tending to supply data for generic Windows packages such as Microsoft Access and Microsoft Excel.

A computer can search through vast quantities of information, rapidly finding specific items, or a group of items that match an enquiry. Computers offer the pupil an opportunity for investigation and discovery of information from sources far beyond the scale available in the normal school library. Pupils not only develop their subject knowledge but also the skills needed to deal with the speed and flexibility of information retrieval available electronically.

The popularity of CD-ROM databases and access to the Internet has opened up database use in the classroom. CD-ROMs are also used as a source of information in many classrooms. Multimedia CD-ROMs enable pupils to browse through enormous quantities of information, including text, images, movies and sounds. The Internet creates a completely new opportunity for investigating and researching, but brings with it an even more acute need for research skills.

Pupils can explore information to seek patterns or individual answers to their searching. They might just be looking for an answer to a simple question such as 'when did …?', or they could be building a presentation on a specific subject that could include text, images and sounds. For example pupils could extract data from the Chemistry Set CD-ROM prior to looking for periodic patterns; they could search on-line or off line data bases for information on chemical hazards or use Encarta to search for information on a scientist.

Presenting information and data

Word processors and DTP offer science teachers a number of different opportunities to develop pupils' basic skills in the presentation of information. Teachers often offer a chain of instructions to pupils for practical work, which are rarely internalised. Actively thinking through a sequence can imprint it deeper on the understanding. Pupils, working in pairs, can use the 'drag and drop' feature of Microsoft Word to organise the sequence of events within an experiment. This saves time on copying and allows time for thinking and discussion.

Pupils can use DTP:

- to present their research findings to peers;
- as an assessable outcome of scientific enquiry;
- as a vehicle for extracting/organising information related to text (DARTS);
- to gather a variety of data: spreadsheets, graphs, pictures, text and organise into a coherent presentation. For example, can renewable energy sources provide an alternative to nuclear power?
- to summarise an investigation. Pupils could draw together descriptions of the process of the investigation, data in the form of tables and graphs, and graphic diagrams.

Collaborating with other scientists

The Internet can offer pupils the opportunity to:

- search on-line data bases for information on chemical hazards;
- talk to scientists via chat pages;
- visit museums and research facilities around the world;
- follow the progress of a space mission;
- communicate/share results of investigations between schools.

New technology

The pace of technological change in ICT is opening up opportunities that were inconceivable only a few years ago. Software is now far easier to learn to use. The Windows user interface provides a common platform between applications. Microsoft Office applications offer new capability for linking spreadsheet, database and presentation files to the Internet. Data can be displayed and edited on-line, offering pupils the opportunity to collect and contribute data at a global level.

The convergence of television resources and computers will allow teachers to preview and select digital educational programmes as part of their lesson planning without the need to record them against future potential use. Datalogging, using increasingly powerful dedicated processors linked directly to sensors, will increasingly replace the PC and interface systems of today. Laptops, Palmtops and programmable calculators are capable of performing operations that a few years ago required a desktop PC; for example, motion sensors can now be operated by programmable calculators.

The success of subject specific resources such as 'The Chemistry Set' and 'Crocodile Clips' are encouraging suppliers to develop other areas of science using a similar pedagogy which is more open and investigative rather than simply archiving items of knowledge. Dynamic modelling of molecules in chemistry and simulations in physics, for example Newton's Laws of Motion, are permanently transforming teaching resources.

The Internet is offering a number of key opportunities to transform pupils' experience of science. Home–school links are being established through the development of school Intranets available to pupils (and parents) at home. These may well be supported by major commercial suppliers, such as TES and BBC initiatives to support homework, revision and information for parents.

Access to members of the scientific community and its most recent data are available on line, such as Earthquake of the Day! The latest pictures of planetary probes, new chemical structures and health and safety information are only some of the powerful, up-to-date resources available on the Internet at no direct cost.

Staff development

Undoubtedly well-established practice at a national level shows enough promise to justify all teachers being aware of the possibilities and being able to make informed decisions about when, or when not, to use ICT. In 1999, the New Opportunities Funded (NOF) Training in ICT for subject teachers began. This Government initiative promises to deliver a high level of capability for the workforce to enable them to exploit the technology being developed as part of the National Grid for Learning (NGfL).

All science teachers will become familiar with the latest resources offered by the Internet. They will experience the range of activities available with a variety of ICT tools and be able to reflect on the pedagogy of using ICT in the classroom, such as Roger Frost's materials on datalogging. Scientific journals are coming on-line, and the NGfL aims to provide incentives for publishers to make more content available. In addition, commercial providers are increasingly offering enhancements to printed resources through access to Internet resources.

Conclusion

If the technological pull and the push from a number of central initiatives are successful, how will science teachers be using ICT? They will use it to:

- support pupils' research as part of scientific enquiry to access the world of scientific activity;
- collect data in experiments where speed, repetition or time make it difficult to use traditional methods;
- allow pupils to present data and ideas using a variety of ICT software;
- provide a range of learning resources via customised intranet/internet sites for home–school use;
- support access to the curriculum for pupils with special educational needs;
- access curriculum resources via the Internet and present these to pupils using a variety of methods including multimedia presentations;
- create differentiated worksheets to provide the stimulus for a wide range of activities.

The reality may be that schools and departments which embrace the new technology will move even further forward than they are at present and will amass more and more of it to provide higher quality resources and usually higher standards of achievement. We saw a similar scenario in the 1960s and 1970s in those schools that embraced teaching initiatives such as Nuffield Science. Schools embracing the new information age in its pedagogy are likely to surge ahead while others are left at the post using the same techniques they have for the last twenty years.

Questions

1   Has your experience with ICT in science education convinced you of the effectiveness of the technology to enrich the experience that pupils have?
2   What are the barriers to successful integration of ICT within schemes of work?
3   How will you maintain your awareness of new developments in ICT in science education?

Resources

http://vtc.ngfl.gov.uk/resource/cits/science/index.html.

This NGfL web site allows access to resources produced by the BECTa to support many aspects of ICT with many useful examples of exercises that teachers can create.

http://www.shu.ac.uk/schools/sci/sol/contents.htm.

This site is run by Sheffield Hallam University in conjunction with the ASE, and provides access to a broad range of information to support science teaching.

http://www.rogerfrost.com/.

Roger Frost has consistently produced a range of informative publications which not only give an overview of ICT in science but also provide detailed information on how to practically handle equipment. Many of his resources are freely available on the Internet through this web site.

Frost, R. (1999) *The IT in Secondary Science*, Hatfield: ASE; Frost, R. (1999) *The IT in Primary Science*, Hatfield: ASE.

These are excellent resources for teachers which are currently being revised on an annual basis. They contain a compendium of ideas for using computers in science, including worked examples, a topic guide to the science curriculum, worksheets and recommended resources and suppliers.

Frost, R. (1996) *The IT in Science Book of Data Logging and Control*, Hatfield: ASE.

Another extremely useful compendium of ideas from the same author, this time focused on the use of computer sensors with pupils aged 11–18.

Poole, P. (ed.) (1999) *Talking About ICT in Subject Teaching (Secondary)* and *Talking About ICT in Subject Teaching (Primary)*, Canterbury Christ Church University College.

This pair of books has been extremely well received. They cover the generic issues in the use of ICT, together with subject specific sections, matched to the standards expected of all teachers following completion of their NOF training in the use of ICT.

Bibliography

AAAS (1993) *Benchmarks for Science Literacy*, Oxford: American Association for the Advancement of Science/Oxford University Press.

Adey, P., Shayer, M. and Yates, C. (1989) *Thinking Science: The Curriculum Materials of the Cognitive Acceleration through Science Education (CASE) Project*, London: Nelson.

Aggleton, P. (1995) *Health Promotion and Young People*, London: Institute of Education Health and Education Research Unit.

Ahmed, J., Gulam, W.A. and Hapeshi, D. (1998) 'Brickbats, survival and resistance', *Multicultural Teaching* 16(3): 7–14.

Aikenhead, G.S. (1997) 'Toward a First Nations Cross-Cultural Science and Technology Curriculum', *Science Education* 81: 217–38.

Albone, E., Collins, N. and Hill, T. (eds) (1995) *Scientific Research in Schools: A Compendium of Practical Experience*, Bristol: Clifton Scientific Trust.

Aldrich, R. (1988) 'The National Curriculum: An Historical Perspective', in Lawton, D. and Chitty, C. (eds) (1988) *The National Curriculum*, London: The Institute of Education, Bedford Way Papers No. 33.

Alkin, M.C. and Kosecoff, J.P. (1974) *Evaluation and Decision-making: The Title VII Experience. CSE Monograph Series in Evaluation*, Los Angeles: Centre for the Study of Evaluation.

Allport, G.W. (1935) 'Attitudes', in Murchison, C. (ed.) (1935) *Handbook of Social Psychology*, Worcester, MA: Clark University Press.

Alters, B.J. (1997) ' Whose nature of science?', *Journal of Research in Science Teaching* 34(1): 39–55.

APU (1983) *A Review of Monitoring in Mathematics 1978–1982, Part 1*, DES.

—— (1985) *New Perspectives on the Mathematics Curriculum*, DES.

—— (1988) *Science at Age 15. A Review of APU Survey Findings 1980–84*, London: HMSO.

AQA (1999) GCE: *Science for Public Understanding*, Draft 15 October, 1999, Advanced subsidiary, AQA (NEAB).

Armstrong, H.E. (1884) *On the Teaching of Natural Sciences as Part of the Ordinary School Course, and on the Method of Teaching Chemistry in the Introductory Course in Science Classes in Schools and Colleges*, International Conference on Education, London.

ASE (1986) *Science and Technology in Society (SATIS)*, Hatfield: ASE.

—— (1992a) *Change in our Future: A Challenge for Science Education*, Hatfield: ASE.

—— (1992b), *The Whole Curriculum in Primary Schools – Maintaining Quality in the Teaching of Primary Science*, Hatfield: ASE.

—— (1995) *Open Science: A Discussion Document*, Hatfield: ASE.

—— (1996) *Science Resources for Key Stage 2: SATIS 8–14*, Hatfield: ASE.

Askew, M. and William, D. (1995) *Recent Research in Mathematics Education 5–16. OFSTED Reviews of Research*, London: HMSO.

Atkinson, M. and Elliott, L (2000) in *Guardian*, February 11, p. 6.

ATL (1998) *An Evaluation of the 1998 Key Stage 3 tests in English, Mathematics and Science*, London: Association of Teachers and Lecturers.

—— (1999) *An Evaluation of the 1999 Key Stage 3 Tests in English, Mathematics and Science*, London: Association of Teachers and Lecturers.

Ausubel, D.P. (1968) *Educational Psychology: A Cognitive View*, New York: Holt, Rinehart and Winston.

Ball, S.J. (1981) *Beachside Comprehensive: A Case-study of Secondary Schooling*, Cambridge: Cambridge University Press.

Barker-Lunn, J.C. (1970) *Streaming in the Primary School: a Longitudinal Study of Children in Streamed and Non-streamed Junior Schools*, Slough: NFER.

Barthorpe, T. and Visser, J. (1991) *Differentiation, Your Responsibility*, NARE Publications sub-committee.

Barton, A.C. (1998) 'Teaching science with homeless children: pedagogy, representation, and identity', *Journal of Research in Science Teaching* 35: 379–94.

Barton, R. and Rogers, L. (1991) 'The computer as an aid to practical science: studying motion with a computer', *Journal of Computer Assisted Learning* 7: 104–12.

Basini, A. (1996) 'The National Curriculum: Foundation Subjects', in Docking, J. (ed.), *National School Policy: Major Issues in Education Policy for Schools in England and Wales, 1979 Onwards*, London: David Fulton.

Bell, J. (1997) 'Sex Differences in Performance in Double Award Science GCSE', paper presented at BERA Belfast, August.

Bentley, T. (1998) *Learning Beyond the Classroom: Education for a Changing World*, London: Routledge.

Benyon, L. (1984) 'Investigation of the problems of continuity in the curriculum of primary and secondary schools', in *Curriculum* 5(1): 5–9.

Bibby, C. (1971) *T.H. Huxley on Education*, Cambridge: Cambridge University Press.

Bishop, K. and Denley, P. (1997) *Effective Learning in Science*, Stafford: Network Educational Press.

—— (1997), *Effective Learning in Science*, Stafford: Network Educational Press Ltd.

Black, H. (1986) 'Assessment for learning', in Nuttall, D.L. (ed.), *Assessing Educational Achievement*, London: Falmer Press.

Black, H.D. and Dockrell, W.B. (1980) *Diagnostic Assessment: A Teachers' Handbook*, Edinburgh: Scottish Council for Research in Education.

Black, P. (1995) '1987–1995 – the struggle to formulate a National Curriculum for science in England and Wales', *Studies in Science Education* 26: 159–88.

—— (1998) *Testing: Friend or Foe? Theory and Practice of Assessment and Testing*, London: Falmer.

Black, P. and Atkin, J.M. (eds) (1996) *Changing the Subject: Innovation in Science, Mathematics and Technology*, London: Routledge.

Black, P. and Wiliam, D. (1998a) 'Assessment and Classroom Learning', in *Assessment in Education* 5(1): 7–74.

—— (1998b) *Inside the Black Box: Raising Standards through Classroom Assessment*, London: King's College London.

Blamires, M. (1999) *Enabling Technology for Inclusion*, London: Paul Chapman Publishing.

Block, J.H., Efthim, H.E. and Burns, R. B. (1989) *Building Effective Mastery Learning in Schools*, New York: Longman.

Bloom, B.S. (ed.) (1956) *Taxonomy of Educational Objectives. Handbook I: Cognitive Domain*, London: Longman.

—— (1976) *Human Characteristics and School Learning*, New York: McGraw Hill.

Blunkett D. (1999) 'Achieving Excellence Through the National Curriculum' letter in QCA (1999a) *The Review of the National Curriculum in England The Secretary of State's Proposals*, London: DfEE.

Boaler, J. (1997) 'Setting, social class and survival of the quickest', *British Educational Research Journal* 23(5): 575–95.

Booth, T. and Ainscow, M. (1998) *From Them to Us*, London: Routledge.

Bricheno, P.A. (2001) Ph.D. thesis, University of Greenwich, in preparation.

Brown, A. (1987) 'Metacognition, executive control and other mysterious mechanisms' in Weinert, F.E. and Kluwe, R.H. (eds), *Metacognition, Motivation and Understanding*, Hillsdale, NJ: Lawrence Erlbaum.

Brown, M. (1999) *Thinking to Learn*, Oldcross Learning Services.

Browne, N. and Ross, C. (1991) 'Girls' stuff, boys' stuff: young children talking and playing', in Browne, N. (ed.), *Science and Technology in the Early Years*, Buckingham: Open University Press.

Bruner, J.S. (1986) *Actual Minds, Possible Worlds*, Cambridge, MA: Harvard University Press.

Burden, R. (1998) 'How can we best help children to become effective thinkers and learners? The case for and against thinking skills programmes', in Burden, R. and Williams, D. (eds), *Thinking Through the Curriculum*, London: Routledge.

Buss, K. (1999) 'Reviews – breakthrough', *British Society for the History of Science Education Forum* 27: 16. (*Breakthrough* publications are available from PREtext Publishing, Boston House, Wantage OX12 9FF.)

Butler, R. (1988) 'Enhancing and undermining intrinsic motivation: the effects of task-involving and ego-involving evaluation on interest and performance', *British Journal of Educational Psychology* 58: 1–14.

Byers, R (1998) 'Personal and social development for pupils with learning difficulties', in Tilstone, C., Florian, L. and Rose, R. (eds), *Promoting Inclusive Practice*, London: Routledge.

Capstick, N. and Poole, P. (1995) *Managing IT: A Planning Tool for Senior Managers*, NCET.

Carey, S. (1985) *Conceptual Change in Childhood*, Cambridge, MA: MIT Press.

Carpenter,B., Ashdown, R. and Bovair, K. (1996) *Enabling Access*, London: David Fulton.

Carvel, J. (1999) 'OFSTED chief must do better', *Guardian*, 15 June, p. 6 (an article responding to the report of the House of Commons Select Committee on Education inquiry into the work of OFSTED).

Cassidy, S. (1999) 'Science sacrificed on altar of literacy', *Times Educational Supplement*.

Cawthron, E.R. and Rowell, J.A. (1978) 'Epistemology and science education', *Studies in Science Education* 5: 31–59.

Centre for Studies on Inclusive Education (2000) *Index For Inclusion: Developing Learning and Participation in Schools*, CSIE with University of Manchester and Canterbury Christ Church University College.

Chalmers, A. (1990) *Science and its Fabrication*, Milton Keynes: Open University Press.

Chambers D.W. (1983) 'Stereotypical images of the scientist', *Science Education* 62(2): 225–65.

Chapman, B. (1976) 'The integration of science or the disintegration of science education?', *SSR* 58(202): 134–46.

Chapman, J. and Hamer, P. (eds) (1996) *The Differentiation Manual*, The Learners' Co-operative.

Chronically Sick and Disabled Persons Act (1970) London: HMSO.

Cicco, E., Farmer, M. and Hargrave, J. (1998) *Using the Internet in Secondary Schools*, London: Kogan Page.

Claxton, G. (1991) *Educating the Enquiring Mind: The Challenge for School Science*, Hemel Hempstead: Harvester Wheatsheaf.

CLIS (1987) *Children's Learning in Science Project*, Leeds: Centre for Studies in Science and Mathematics Education, University of Leeds.

Clough, P. (1998) *Managing Inclusive Education*, London: Paul Chapman Publishing.

Cobern, W.W. (1996) 'Constructivism and non-western science education research', *International Journal of Science Education* 18: 295–310.

Coles, A. and Turner, S.A. (1995) *Diet and Health in School Age Children*, London: Health Education Authority.

Coles, M. (1997) 'Science education: vocational and general approaches', *School Science Review* 79(286): 27–32.

—— (1998) 'Science for employment and higher education', *International Journal of Science Education* 20(5): 609–21.

Coles, M. and Matthews A. (1996) *Fitness for Purpose: A Means of Comparing Qualifications*, London: Schools' Curriculum and Assessment Authority and the National Council for Vocational Qualifications.

Commission of the European Communities (1995) *Teaching and Learning: Towards the Learning Society, White Paper on Education and Training*, Brussels, 29 November COM(95) 590.

Cornwall, J. (1996) *Choice Opportunity and Learning*, London: David Fulton.

Covington, M.V. (1998) *The Will To Learn: A Guide for Motivating Young People*, Cambridge: Cambridge University Press.

Cox, M. and Johnson, D. (1993) *The ImpacT Report: An Evaluation of the Impact of Information Technology on Children's Achievements in Primary and Secondary Schools*, DfEE and Kings College London.

Crebbin, C. (1989) 'Piecemeal Responses or a Co-ordinated Curriculum?' *Primary Science Review* 10 (Summer).

Crooks, T.J. (1988) 'The impact of classroom evaluation practices on students' *Review of Educational Research* 58(4): 438–81.

Croxford, L. (1997) 'Participation in science subjects: the effect of the Scottish curriculum framework', *Research Papers in Education* 12: 69–89.

CSTI (1993) *Mapping the Science, Technology and Mathematics Domain*, Council for Science and Technology Institutes.

Cullingford, C. (1991) *The Inner World of the School: Children's Ideas about Schools*, London: Cassell.

Cunningham, A. and Williams, P. (1993) 'De-centring the "big picture": The Origins of Modern Science and the modern origins of science', *British Journal for the History of Science* 26: 407–32.

Cunningham, M.F., Kent, F.H. and Muir, D. (1997) *Schools in Cyberspace: A Practical Guide to Using the Internet in Schools*, London: Hodder and Stoughton.

Davidson, B. and Moore, J. (1996) 'Across the primary–secondary divide', in Hart, S. (ed.), *Differentiation and the Secondary Curriculum, Debates and Dilemmas*, London: Routledge.

Davidson, G., Stevens, B. and Williams, A. (1998) 'Numeracy through geography teaching', *Geography* 23(4).

Davies, F. and Greene, T. (1984) *Reading for Learning in the Sciences*, Harlow: Oliver and Boyd.

Davies, J., Prendergast, S., Prout, A. and Tuckett, D. (1982) *Health Knowledge of Schoolchildren, Their Parents and Teachers*, Final Report of the Schools Council Health Education Project, Cambridge: Health Education Studies Unit.

Davis, B. (ed.) (1988) *The GASP Teacher's Handbook*, London: Hutchison.

Davis, S. (1999) 'Reengineering the classroom', in Bowring-Carr, C. and West-Burnham, J. (eds), *Managing Learning for Achievement: Strategies for Raising Achievement through Effective Learning*, London: Financial Times Pitman Publishing.

de Boo, M. (1999) *Enquiring Children, Challenging Teaching*, Buckingham: Open University Press.

Dearing, R. (1996) *16–19 qualifications: final report*, London: HMSO.

Department of Education Northern Ireland (1988) *Education in Northern Ireland: Proposals for Reform*, Bangor: DENI.

Department of Employment (1995) *The Disability Discrimination Act*, London: HMSO.

Department of Health (1989) *The Diets of British School Children: Sub-committee on Nutritional Surveillance. Committee on Medical Aspects of Food Policy*, Report on Health and Social Subjects No. 36, London: HMSO.

—— (1992) *The Health of the Nation*, London: HMSO.

—— (1996) *Guidelines on Educational Materials Concerned with Nutrition*, London: Department of Health.

Derricott, R. (1985) 'Establishing curricular continuity', in Derricott, R. (ed.), *Curriculum Continuity: Primary to Secondary*, Windsor: NFER-Nelson.

DES (1967) *Children and their Primary Schools*, the Plowden Report, London: HMSO.

—— (1978a) *Special Educational Needs: The Report of the Committee of Enquiry into the Education of Handicapped Children and Young People*, the Warnock Report, London: HMSO.

—— (1978b) *Primary Education in England*, London: HMSO.

—— (1979) *Aspects of Secondary Education*, London: HMSO.

—— (1981) *Education Act 1981*, London: HMSO.

—— (1985) *Science 5–16: A Statement of Policy*, London: HMSO.

—— (1986) *Education Act*, London: HMSO.

—— (1987) *The National Curriculum 5–16: A Consultative Document*, London: HMSO.

—— (1988a) *Education Reform Act*, London: HMSO.

—— (1988b) *Science at Age 11: A Review of APU Survey Findings*, London: HMSO.

—— (1988c) *Science at Age 15: A Review of APU Survey Findings*, London, HMSO.

—— (1988d) *Task Group on Assessment and Testing: A Report*, London: Department of Education and Science and the Welsh Office.

—— (1988e) *Task Group on Assessment and Testing: Three Supplementary Reports*, London: Department of Education and Science and the Welsh Office.

—— (1989a) *The National Curriculum: Science*, London: HMSO.

—— (1989b) *Science at Age 13: A Review of APU Survey Findings*, London: HMSO.

—— (1989c) *National Curriculum: From Policy to Practice*, London: HMSO.

—— (1989d) *Science in the National Curriculum*, London: HMSO.

—— (1991) *The National Curriculum: Science* London: HMSO.

DfE (1991) *Education and Training for the Twenty-first Century*, London: HMSO.

—— (1994a) *Science and Maths: A Consultation Paper on the Supply and Demand of Newly Qualified Young People*, London: HMSO.

—— (1994b) *Code of Practice on the Identification and Assessment of Special Educational Needs*, London: DfEE.

—— (1995a) *Science in the National Curriculum*, London: HMSO.

—— (1995b) *Mathematics in the National Curriculum*, London: HMSO.

—— (1997) *Excellence for All Children: Meeting Special Educational Needs*, London: HMSO.

DfEE (1998a) *The National Literacy Strategy*, London: DfEE.

—— (1998b) *Teaching: High Status, High Standards. Requirements for Courses of Initial Teacher Training*, Department for Education and Employment Circular 4/98. London: DfEE (http://www.teach-tta.gov.uk/library/nsqts.pdf).

—— (1999a) *Learning to Succeed*, London: HMSO.

—— (1999b) *National Numeracy Strategy*, London: DfEE.

—— (1999c) *The National Curriculum for England: Science*, London: DfEE/QCA.

—— (1999d) *National Curriculum in England. (a) Science (b) Citizenship*, London: Qualifications and Curriculum Authority (http://www.dfee.gov.uk/nc/index.html).

—— (1999e) *The National Curriculum: Handbook for Secondary Teachers in England Key Stages 3 and 4*, London: DfEE/QCA.

Donnelly, J.F. and Jenkins, E.W. (1999) *Science Teaching in Secondary Schools under the National Curriculum*, Leeds: Centre for Studies in Science and Mathematics Education, Centre for Policy Studies, University of Leeds.

Donnelly, J.F., Buchan, A.S., Jenkins, E.W. and Welford, A.G. (1993) *Investigations in Science Education Policy: Sc1 in the National Curriculum for England and Wales*, Leeds: Centre for Policy Studies in Education, University of Leeds.

—— (1994) *Investigations in Science Education Policy. Sc1 in the National Curriculum for England and Wales*, Leeds: University of Leeds.

Donnelly, J.F., Buchan, A.S., Jenkins, E.W., Laws, P. and Welford, A.G. (1996) *Investigations by Order: Policy, Curriculum and Science Teachers' Work under the Education Reform Act*, Nafferton: Studies in Science Education..

Douglas, J.W.B. (1964) *The Home and the School: A Study of Ability and Attainment in the Primary School*, London: MacGibbon & Kes.

Driver, R. (1976) *Science – a Journey in Thought in the Streamed Science: The training of Teachers*, Study Series no. 8, ASE.

—— (1983) *The Pupil as Scientist*, Milton Keynes: Open University Press.

Driver, R., Leach, J., Millar, R. and Scott, P. (1993) *Students' Understanding of the Nature of Science: Working Papers 1–11*, Leeds: Centre for Studies in Science and Mathematics Education.

—— (1996) *Young People's Images of Science*, Buckingham: Open University Press.

Driver, R., Squires, A., Rushworth, P. and Wood-Robinson, V. (1994) *Making Sense of Secondary Science*, London: Routledge.

Duschl, R.A. (1985) 'Science education and philosophy of science: twenty-five years of mutually exclusive development', *School Science and Mathematics* 87(7): 541–55.

Duveen, G. (2000) 'Representations, identities, resistance', in Deaux, K. and Philogene, G. (eds), *Social Representations: Introductions and Explorations*, Oxford: Blackwell.

Dweck, C.S., Davidson, W., Nelson, S. and Enna, B. (1978) 'Sex differences in learned helplessness: the contingencies of evaluative feedback in the classroom', *Development Psychology* 14: 268–76.

Eagly, A. and Chaiken, S. (1993) *The Psychology of Attitudes*, Fort Worth, TX: Harcourt Brace College Publishers.

Elwood, J. and Comber, C. (1996) *Gender Differences in Examinations at 18+ Final Report*, London: University of London Institute of Education.

Entwistle, N. (1998) *Styles of Learning and Teaching: An Integrated Outline of Educational Psychology for Students, Teachers and Lecturers*, London: David Fulton.

Equal Opportunities Commission (1999) 'Gender issues in vocational education and training and workplace achievement of 14–19-year olds: an EOC perspective', *Curriculum Journal* 10(2): 209–29.

European Union (1995) *White Paper on Education and Training, Teaching and Learning: Towards the Learning Society*, Brussels: European Union.

Evans, J. and Lunt, I. (1993) *British Journal of Special Education* 20(2): 59–62.

Fairbrother, B., Black, P. and Gill, P. (1993) *Teachers Assessing Pupils: Lessons from Science Classrooms*, Hatfield: ASE, King's College.

Feasey, R. (1999) *Primary Science and Literacy Links*, Hatfield: ASE.

Feiler, A. and Gibson, H. (1999) 'Threats to the inclusive movement', *British Journal of Special Education* 26(3): 147–52.

Feyerabend, P. (1988/1991) *Against Method*, London: Verso.

Findley, W.G. and Bryan, M.M. (1975) *The Pros and Cons of Ability Grouping*, Bloomington, IN: Phi Delta Kappa Educational Foundation.

Fisher, R. (1998) *Teaching Thinking*, London: Cassell.

Fitz-Gibbon, C. (1994) *Candidates' Performance in Public Examinations in Mathematics and Science*, London: SCAA.

Fivush, R. (1998) 'Interest, Gender and Personal Narrative: How Children Construct Self-Understanding', in Hoffman, L., Krapp, A., Penninger, A.K. and Baument, J. (eds), *Interest and Learning*, Kiel: University of Kiel.

Fogelman, K., Essen, J. and Tibbenham, A. (1978) 'Ability-grouping in secondary schools and attainment', *Educational Studies* 4(3): 201–12.

Follett, B. (1997) 'From animal behaviour to DNA and back again: in praise of molecular biology', *School Science Review* 78(284): 15–22.

Fraser, B.J. (1977) 'Selection and validation of attitude scales for curriculum evaluation', *Science Education* 61: 317–30.

—— (1978) 'Development of a test of science related attitudes', *Science Education* 62(4): 509–15.

—— (1981) *Test of science related attitudes: handbook*, Victoria, Australia: Council for Educational Research.

—— (1982) 'How Strongly are Attitude and Achievement Related', *School Science Review* 63(224): 557–59.

Freeman, J. (1998) *Educating the Very Able: Current International Research*, London: OFSTED.

Frith, D.S. (1984) *A Teachers' Guide to Assessment*, London: Stanley Thornes.

Frost, A.W. (1978) 'Mixed ability versus streaming in science: a controlled experiment', Science Education Notes, *School Science Review* 60(211): 346–8.

Frost, J. (1997) *Creativity in Primary Science*, Buckingham: Open University Press.

—— (ed.) (1995) *Teaching Science*, London: Woburn Press.

Further Education Unit (1994) *GNVQs 1993–94: a National Survey Report*, London: FEU, Institute of Education and Nuffield Foundation.

Gadd, K. and Sandford-Smith, D. (1999) 'Post-16 qualifications update', *Past Sixteen Science Issues*, October: 12–13.

Galton, M. (1998) Keynote address presented to a conference at the University of Cambridge School of Education: 'Improving the Transition from Primary to Secondary School'.

Galton, M. and Willcocks, J. (eds) (1983) *Moving from the Primary Classroom*, London: Routledge and Kegan Paul.

Galton, M., Gray, J. and Rudduck, J. (1999) *The Impact of School Transitions and Transfers on Pupil Progress and Attainment*, Nottingham: DFEE Publications.

Gardner, H. (1983) *Frames of Mind*, New York: Basic Books.

Gardner, P.L. (1975) 'Attitudes to Science', *Science Education* 2: 1–41.

Gibbons, M., Limoges, C., Nowotny, H., Schwartzman, S., Scott, P. and Trow, M. (1995) *The New Production of Knowledge*, London: Sage.

Gibson, A. and Asthana, S. (1998) 'Schools, pupils and examination results: contextualising school "performance"', *British Educational Research Journal* 24(3): 269–82.

Gill, P. (1995) 'Whither quantification? The place of mathematics in the learning of science', *School Science Review* 77(297): 103–6.

—— (1999) 'The National Curriculum for science as a resource for teaching mathematics', *Mathematics Teaching* 166: 32–3.

Gillborn, D. and Gipps. C. (1996) *Recent Research on the Achievements of Ethnic Minority Pupils*, London: HMSO.

Gipps, C. (1994a) *Beyond Testing: Towards a Theory of Educational Assessment*, London: Falmer.

—— (1994b) 'Developments in educational assessment: what makes a good test?', *Assessment in Education Principles, Policy and Practice* 1(3): 283–91.

Glaser, R. (1963) 'Instructional technology and the measurement of learning outcomes: some questions', *American Psychologist* 18: 519–21.

Goldstein, G. (1997) *Information Technology in English Schools: A commentary on Inspection Findings 1995–96*, London: OFSTED with NCET.

Goldsworthy, A., Watson, J.R. and Wood-Robinson, V. (1998) 'Sometimes its not fair!', *Primary Science Review* May–June: 15–17.

—— (1999) *Investigations: Getting to Grips with Graphs*, Hatfield: Association for Science Education.

—— (forthcoming) *Investigations: Developing Understanding*, Hatfield: ASE.

Gorard, S., Salisbury, J. and Rees, G. (1999) 'Reappraising the apparent underachievement of boys at school', *Gender and Education* 11(3).

Gorman, T.P., White, J., Brook, G., Maclure, M. and Kispal, A. (1988) *Language Performance in Schools: Review of APU Language Monitoring 1979–1983*, London: HMSO.

Gott, R. and Murphy, P. (1987) *Assessing Investigations at Ages 13 and 15, Science Report for Teachers 9*, London: DES.

Gott R. and Duggan S. (1995) *Investigative Work in the Science Curriculum*, Milton Keynes: Open University Press.

—— (1996) Practical work: its role in understanding of evidence in science, *International Journal of Science Education* 18(7): 791–806.

Gott, R., Duggan, S. and Johnson, P. (1999) 'What do practising applied scientists do and what are the implications for science education?', *Research in Science and Technological Education* 17(1): 97–107.

Gott, R., Duggan, S. and Jones, M. (1998) *Evidence in Science for Intermediate GNVQ Students*, unpublished teaching materials.

Gott, R., Foulds, K. and Johnson, P. (1997) *Science Investigations Book 1*, London: Collins Educational.

Gott, R., Foulds, K. and Jones, M. (1998) *Science Investigations Book 2*, London: Collins Educational.

Gott, R., Foulds, K. and Roberts, R. (1999) *Science Investigations Book 3*, London: Collins Educational.

Gray, A. (1996) 'The role of critical incidents in changing attitudes to science', paper presented to the British Educational Research Conference.

Guilford, J.P. (1967) *The Nature of Human Intelligence*, New York: McGraw-Hill.

Gunnell, B. (1999) 'Meeting the children', *Education in Science* 181: 10–11.
Guzzetti, B.J. and Williams, W.O. (1996) 'Gender, text and discussion: examining intellectual safety in the science classroom', *Journal of Research in Science Teaching* 33: 5–20.
Hacker, R.G., Rowe, M.J. and Evans, R.D. (1991) 'The influences of ability groupings for secondary science lessons upon classroom processes. Part 1: homogeneous groupings', Science Education Notes, *School Science Review* 73(262): 125–9.
—— (1992) 'The influences of ability groupings for secondary science lessons upon classroom processes. Part 2: heterogeneous groupings', Science Education Notes, *School Science Review* 73(264): 119–22.
Hadden, R.A. and Johnstone, A.H. (1983) 'Secondary school pupils' attitudes to science: the year of erosion', *European Journal of Science Education* 5: 309–18.
Hadow, A. (1931) *Report on Primary Education*, London: Board of Education.
Hall, W.C. (1969) 'General science to O-level', *School Science Review* 51(175): 433–7.
Harding, S. and McGregor, E. (1995) *The Gender Dimension of Science and Technology*, Paris: UNESCO.
Harlen, W. (1977a) *Match and Mismatch: Raising Questions*, Edinburgh: Oliver and Boyd.
—— (1977b) *Match and Mismatch: Finding Answers*, Edinburgh: Oliver and Boyd.
—— (1997) *The Teaching of Science in Primary Schools*, 2nd edn, London: David Fulton.
—— (1998) 'The last ten years; the next ten years', in Sherrington, R. (ed.) *ASE Guide to Primary Science Education*, Cheltenham: Stanley Thornes.
—— (1999a) *Effective Teaching of Science: A Review of Research*, Edinburgh: Scottish Council for Research in Education.
—— (1999b) 'Raising standards of achievement in science', *Research in Education* 64 (Spring).
Harlen, W., and Jelly, S. (1989) *Developing Science in the Primary Classroom*, Edinburgh: Oliver and Boyd.
Harlen, W. and Malcolm, H. (1997) *Setting and Streaming: a Research Review* (Using Research Series 18), Edinburgh: SCRE.
Harlen, W., Holroyd, C. and Byrne, M. (1995) *Confidence and Understanding in the Teaching of Science and Technology in Primary Schools*, Edinburgh: SCRE.
Hayes, P. (1998) 'Assessment in the classroom', in Ratcliffe, M. (ed.), *ASE Guide to Secondary Science*, Cheltenham: Stanley Thornes.
Head, J. (1996) 'Gender identity and cognitive style', in Murphy, P. and Gipps, C. (eds), *Equity in the Classroom: Towards Effective Pedagogy for Girls and Boys*, London: Falmer Press/UNESCO.
—— (1999) *Understanding the Boys: Issues of Behaviour and Achievement*, London: Falmer Press.
Health Education Authority (1989) *Health for Life 1: A Teacher's Planning Guide to Health Education in the Primary School*, Health Education Authority Primary School Project, London: Nelson.
—— (1993a)*Today's Young Adults – 16–19-year-olds look at Diet, Alcohol, Smoking, Drugs and Sexual Behaviour*, London: Health Education Authority.
—— (1993b)*Tomorrow's Young Adults*, London: Health Education Authority.
Hedger, K. and Jesson, D. (1999) *The Numbers Game: Using Assessment Data in Secondary Schools*, York: University of York Centre for Performance Evaluation and Resource Management.
Hendley, D., Parkinson, J., Stables, A. and Tanner, H. (1995) 'Gender differences in pupil attitudes to the National Curriculum Foundation subjects of English, mathematics, science and technology in Key Stage 3 in South Wales', *Educational Studies* 21(1): 85–97.
Hildebrand, G.M. (1996) 'Assessment interacts with gender', in Murphy, P. and Gipps, C. (eds), *Equity in the Classroom: Towards Effective Pedagogy for Girls and Boys*, London: Falmer Press/ UNESCO Publishing.
Hirst, P. (1974) *Knowledge and the Curriculum*, London: Routledge and Kegan Paul.
Hirst, P.H., and Peters, R.S. (1970) *The Logic of Education*, London: Routledge and Kegan Paul.
HMSO (1960) *Ministry of Education Pamphlet No.38, Science in Secondary Schools*, London: HMSO.
—— (1975) *Curricular differences for boys and girls*, London: HMSO.
Hobbs, E.D., Bolt, W.B., Erickson, G., Quelch, T.P. and Sieban, B.A. (1979) *British Columbia Science Assessment 1978, General Report 1*, Victoria, British Columbia: Ministry of Education.
Hobden, J. and Reiss, M. (1999) ' The primary teacher as scientist project', *Primary Science Review* 56: 2–3.
Hochbaum, G.M. (1979) 'Nutrition behaviour and education', in Levy, R. (ed.), *Nutrition, Lipids and Coronary Heart Disease*, New York: Raven Press.
Hodgson, B. and Scanlon, E. (1985) *Approaching Primary Science: A Reader*, London: Paul Chapman.
Hoffer, T.B. (1992) 'Middle school ability grouping and student achievement in science and mathematics', *Educational Evaluation and Policy Analysis* 14(3): 205–27.
Hollins, M. and Whitby, V. (1998) *Progression in Primary Science: A Guide to the Nature and Practice of Science in Key Stages 1 and 2*, London: David Fulton Publishers in Association with Roehampton Institute.

Honey, J. (ed.) (1990) *Investigating the Nature of Science*, Harlow: Longman/Nuffield–Chelsea Curriculum Trust.

House of Commons Education Committee (1995) *Fourth Report: Science and Technology in Schools*, London: HMSO.

Howe, C. (1999) *Gender and Classroom Interaction: A Research Review*, Edinburgh: Scottish Council for Research in Education, Education and Industry Department.

Hughes, M. (1997) *Lessons are for Learning*, Network Educational Press Ltd.

Ingle, R. and Jennings, A. (1981) *Science in Schools: Which Way Now?*, London: Institute of Education, University of London.

Inner London Education Authority (1985) *Equal Opportunities for All*, the Fish Report, London: ILEA.

Institute of Biology (1998) 'Biologists look forward to a more scientifically literate world: National Curriculum review', *School Science Review* 80(291): 25–8.

—— (1999) *Genetically Modified Food: Factsheet*, London: Institute of Biology.

Irwin, A. and Wynne, B. (eds) (1996) *Misunderstanding Science? The Public Reconstruction of Science and Technology*, Cambridge: Cambridge University Press.

Isaacs, N. (1958) *Scientific Trends in Young Children*, London: National Froebel Foundation.

Jackson, B. (1964) *Streaming: An Education System in Miniature*, London: Routledge and Kegan Paul.

Jackson, D.F., Doster, E.C., Meadows, L. and Wood, T. (1995) 'Hearts and minds in the science classroom: the education of a confirmed evolutionist', *Journal of Research in Science Teaching* 32: 585–611.

Jarman, R. (1990) 'Primary science: secondary science continuity: a new ERA?' *School Science Review* 71(257): 19–29.

—— (1993) 'Real experiments with bunsen burners: pupils' perceptions of the similarities and differences between primary science and secondary science', *School Science Review* 74(268): 19–29.

—— (1995). 'Science is a green field site: a study of primary science/secondary science continuity in Northern Ireland', *Educational Research* 37(2): 141–57.

—— (1997) 'Fine in theory: a study of primary: secondary continuity in science, prior and subsequent to the introduction of the Northern Ireland Curriculum', *Educational Research* 39(3): 291–310.

—— (1998) 'A study of primary–secondary curricular continuity in science', The Queen's University, Belfast: unpublished Ph.D. thesis.

Jenkins, E.W. (1979) *From Armstrong to Nuffield*, London: John Murray.

—— (1996), 'The "nature of science" as a curriculum component', *Journal of Curriculum Studies*, 28, 2: 137–150.

Jennings, A. (1992) *National Curriculum Science: So Near and yet So Far*, London: The London File, Institute of Education, University of London.

Jensen, E. (1995) *Super Teaching*, London: Turning Point Publishing.

Johnston, J. (1995) 'Morals and ethics in science; where have they gone?', *Education in Science* 163: 20–1.

—— (1996) *Early Explorations in Science*, Buckingham: Open University Press.

Johnston, J., Ahtee, M. and Hayes, M. (1998) 'Elementary teachers' perceptions of science and science teaching: comparison between Finland and England', in Kaartinen, S. (ed.), *Matemaattisten Aineiden Opetus ja Oppimen*, Oulu: Oulu University.

Keeves, J.P. (1986) 'Science education: the contribution of IEA research to a world perspective', in Postlethwaite, N.T. (ed.), *International Educational Research, Papers in Honor of Torsten Husén*, Oxford: Pergamon Press.

—— (1992) *Learning Science in a Changing World, Cross-National Studies of Science Achievement, 1970 to 1984*, Netherlands: International Association for the Evaluation of Educational Achievement (IEA).

Kelly, A.V. (1990) *The National Curriculum: A Critical Review*, London: Paul Chapman Publishing.

Keys, W. (1987) *Aspects of Science Education in English schools*, Windsor: NFER Nelson.

Keys, W., Harris, S. and Fernandes, C. (1996) *Third International Mathematics and Science Study. First National Report Part 1*, Slough: NFER.

Kimbell, R., Stables, K., Wheeler, T., Wosniak, A. and Kelly, V. (1991) *The Assessment of Performance in Design and Technology*, London: School Examinations and Assessment Authority.

Kinder, K., Wakefield, A. and Wilkins, A. (1996) *Talking Back: Pupil views on Disaffection*, Slough: NFER.

Klopfer, L.E. (1971) in Bloom, B.S., Hastings, J.T. and Madaus G.F. (eds), *Handbook on Summative and Formative Evaluation of Student Learning*, New York: McGraw-Hill.

Kulik, C-L.C. and Kulik, J.A. (1982) 'Research synthesis on ability grouping', *Educational Leadership* 39(8): 619–21.

Kulik, J.A. and Kulik, C-L.C. (1987) 'Effects of ability grouping on student achievement', *Equity and Excellence* 23(1–2): 22–30.

LaLumia, J. and Baglan, T. (1981) 'Choice of strategies for attitude change: an exploratory analysis', *Psychological Reports* 48: 793–4.

Layton, D. (1973) 'Secondary school curriculum and science education', *Physics Education* 8(1): 19–23.

Layton, D., Jenkins, E., Macgill, S. and Davey, A. (1993) *Inarticulate Science? Perspectives on the Public Understanding of Science and Some Implications for Science Education*, Driffield: Studies in Education.

Learning Through Science (1982) *Learning Through Science: Formulating a School Policy*, London: Macdonald Educational.

Lee, J. and Croll, P. (1995) 'Streaming and subject specialism at Key Stage 2: a survey in two local authorities', *Educational Studies* 21(2): 155–65.

Lenton, G. and Stevens, B. (1999) 'Numeracy in science', *School Science Review* 80(293): 59–64.

Lenton, G., Stevens, B. and Illes, R. (in press) 'Numeracy in science: pupils' understanding of graphs in science', *School Science Review* 82(299): 15–23.

Lewin, R. (1987) *A Practical Problem Solver's Handbook for Teachers and Students*, Reading: Royal County of Berkshire.

Lewis, M. and Parkin, T. (1998) *Science and Literacy: A Guide for Primary Teachers*, Nuffield Primary Science, Nuffield Exeter Extending Literacy, London: Collins.

Lewis, M. and Wray, D. (1996) *Writing Frames: Scaffolding Children's Non-Fiction Writing in a Range of Genres*, Reading: University of Reading, Reading and Language Information Centre.

—— (1998) *Writing across the Curriculum: Frames to Support Learning*, Reading: University of Reading, Reading and Language Information Centre.

Lipman, M. (1988) *Philosophy Goes to School*, Philadelphia: Temple University Press.

Local Government Act (1988) *Section 28*, London: HMSO.

Lock, R. (1990) 'Open-ended problem-solving investigations: what do we mean and how can we use them?', *School Science Review* 71(256): 63–72.

Lou, Y., Abrami, P.C., Spence, J.C., Poulson, C., Chambers, B. and d'APollonia, S. (1996) 'Within-class grouping: a meta-analysis', *Review of Educational Research* 66(4): 423–58.

Lucas, A. (1987) 'Public knowledge of biology', *Journal of Biological Education* 21(1): 41–5.

Macaskill, C. and Ogborn, J. (1996) 'Science and technology', *School Science Review* 77(281): 55–61.

Macfarlane, E. (1992) *Double award GCSE balanced science: its contribution to A-level success*, Report to the Royal Society, London.

Malcolm, H. and Simpson, M. (1997) *Implementing 5–14 in primary and secondary schools: steady development?*, Edinburgh: SOEID.

Marland, S.P. (1971) *Education of the gifted and talented, volume I: a report to the congress of the United States by the US commissioner of education*, Washington DC: US Government Printing Office.

Mason, G. (1998) *Change and diversity: the challenges facing chemistry higher education*, London: Royal Society of Chemistry and the Council for Industry and Higher Education.

Matthews, M. (1994) *Science Teaching: The Role of History and Philosophy of Science*, New York: Routledge.

Mauthner, M., Mayall, B. and Turner, S. (1993) *Food and primary children*, London: Institute of Education, University of London (SSCR and Science Education Department).

McGrath, C. (1999) 'Programme for international student assessment PISA', *Education in Science* 181: 26–7.

McGuinness, C. (1999) *From thinking skills to thinking classrooms*, London: DfEE Research.

Mercer, N. (1991) *Learning Through Talk*, Milton Keynes: Open University.

Millar, R. (ed.) (1989) *Doing Science: Images of Science in Science Education*, Lewes: Falmer Press.

—— (1996) ' Towards a science for public understanding', *School Science Review* 77(280): 7–18.

Millar, R. and Driver, R. (1987) 'Beyond process', *Studies in Science Education* 14: 33–62.

Millar, R. and Osborne, J. (eds) (1998) *Beyond 2000: Science Education for the Future: A Report with Ten Recommendations*, London: King's College London, School of Education.

Millar, R., Lubben, F., Gott, R. and Duggan, S. (1994) 'Investigating the school science laboratory: conceptual and procedural knowledge and their influence on performance', *Research Papers in Education* 9(2): 207–48.

Moon, B. and Brighouse, T. (1990) 'Introduction', in Brighouse, T. and Moon, B. (eds), *Managing the National Curriculum: Some Critical Perspective*, Harlow: Longman.

Murphy, P. (1991) 'Gender differences in pupils' reactions to practical work', in Woolnough, B. (ed.), *Practical Science*, Milton Keynes: Open University Press.

—— (1994) 'Gender differences in pupils' reactions to practical work', in Levinson, R. (ed.), *Teaching Science*, London: Routledge.

—— (1997) 'Gender differences: messages for science learning', in Harnqvist, K. and Bergen, A. (eds), *Growing up with science: developing early understanding of science*, London: Jessica Kingsley.

—— (1999a) 'Teaching and learning in primary science: present and future issues', paper presented at BERA Conference, Science in the Primary School: Evidence for Change?, Liverpool Hope University College, 9 October.

—— (1999b) 'Supporting collaborative learning: a gender dimension', in Murphy, P. (ed.), *Learners, Learning and Assessment*, London: Paul Chapman Publishing and Open University.

Murphy, P. and Gott, R. (1984) *APU Science Reports for Teachers, 2: Science: the Assessment Framework for Science at Ages 13 and 15*, London: Department of Education and Science.

Murray, P. and Penman, J. (1996) *Let Our Children Be*, Sheffield: Parents with Attitude.

Musker, R. (1997) 'Using computers to improve performance in science', in *Teaching as a Research-based Profession: The Teacher Research Grant Scheme*, London: TTA.

National Assessment of Educational Progress (1978) *Science Achievement in the Schools: A Summary of Results from the 1976–77 National Assessment of Science*, Washington, DC: Education Commission of the States.

NCC (1988a) *Science Non-Statutory Guidance*, York: NCC.

—— (1988b) *Curriculum Guidance 3: The Whole Curriculum*, York: NCC.

—— (1989) *Science: National Curriculum*, York: NCC.

—— (1990) *Curriculum Guidance 5: Health education*, York: NCC.

—— (1993) *Teaching Science At Key Stages 3 and 4*, York: NCC.

Needham, R. (1987) 'Teaching strategies for developing and understanding science', in *Children's Learning in Science Project: CLIS in the Classroom*, Leeds: Centre for Studies in Science and Mathematics Education, University of Leeds.

Newbold, D. (1977) *Ability Grouping: The Banbury Enquiry*, Windsor: NFER.

Newton, P., Driver, R. and Osborne, J. (1999) 'The place of argumentation in the pedagogy of school science', *International Journal of Science Education* 21(5): 553–76.

Nisbet, J.D. and Entwistle, N.J. (1969) *The Transition to Secondary Education*, London: University of London Press.

Nott, M. (1994) 'Practical approaches to teaching and learning about the nature of science', in Wellington, J. (ed.), *Secondary Science. Contemporary Issues and Practical Approaches*, London: Routledge.

Nott, M and Wellington, J. (1996) ' Probing teachers' views of the nature of science: How should we be doing it and where should we be looking?', in Welford, G., Osborne, J. and Scott, P. (eds), *Research in Science Education in Europe: Current Themes and Issues*, London: Falmer Press.

—— (1999) 'The state we're in: issues in Key Stage 3 and Key Stage 4 science', *School Science Review* 81(294): 13–8.

Nuffield Junior Science Project (1967) *Teachers Guide 2*, London: Collins.

Nutbrown, C. (1998) 'Managing to include? rights, responsibilities and respect'. in Clough, P. (ed.), *Managing Inclusive Education: From Policy to Practice*, London: Paul Chapman Publishing.

O'Brien, P. (1997) *More Able Pupils in Science Project: Part of the Berkshire Improvements in Standards Initiative. A Report on Issues for action*, Reading: Berkshire Education Quality Assurance.

—— (1998a) *Teaching Scientifically Able Pupils in the Primary School*, Oxford: NACE/GlaxoWellcome.

—— (1998b) *Teaching Scientifically Able Pupils in the Secondary School*, Oxford: NACE/GlaxoWellcome.

—— (1999) 'How do we identify the more able pupil in science?', *Educating Able Children* 3: 14–18.

O'Connell, L., Shannon, B. and Sims, L. (1981) 'Assessing nutrition-related attitudes and beliefs of teachers', *Journal of Nutrition Education* 13(1, Supplement): 81–5.

O'Donnell, T. and Gray, G. (1994) *The Health Promoting College*, London: Health Education Authority.

OFSTED (1993) *Science. Key Stages 1, 2, 3 and 4. Fourth Year, 1992–93*, London: HMSO.

—— (1996) *Subjects and Standards: Issues for School Development arising from OFSTED Inspection Findings 1994–5, Key Stages 3 and 4 and Post-16*, London: HMSO.

—— (1997) *The Annual Report of Her Majesty's Chief Inspector of Schools: Standards and Quality in Education 1995/96*, London: HMSO.

—— (1998a) *Secondary Education 1993–97: A Review of Secondary Schools in England*, London: HMSO.

—— (1998b) *The Annual Report of Her Majesty's Chief Inspector of Schools: Standards and Quality in Education 1996/97*, London: HMSO.

—— (1998c) *Setting in Primary Schools*, London: HMSO.

—— (1999) *A Review of Primary Schools in England*, London: OFSTED.

—— (2000) *Annual Report of Her Majesty's Chief Inspector of Schools: Standards and Quality in Education 1998/99*, London: HMSO.

Ogborn, J. (1984) *Dynamic Modelling System*, Buckingham: Longmans Microcomputer Software.

O'Hear, P. and White, J. (1991) *A National Curriculum for All: Laying the Foundations for Success*, London: Institute for Public Policy Research.

Ormerod, M.B. and Duckworth, D. (1975) *Attitudes to Science: A Review of Research*, Slough: NFER.

Osborne, J. (1999) 'Science education: problems, issues and dilemmas', paper prepared for a Science and Technology Education seminar, King's College, University of London, 18 February.

Osborne, J. and Simon, S. (1996) 'Primary science: past and future dimensions', *Studies in Science Education* 27: 99 – 147.

Osborne, J., Wadsworth, P. and Black, P.J. (1992) *Processes of Life: Primary SPACE Research Report*, Liverpool: Liverpool University Press.

Osborne, J.F. (1996) ' Beyond constructivism', *Science Education* 80(1): 53–82.

Palmquist, B.C. and Finley, F.N. (1997) 'Pre-service teachers' views of the nature of science during a post-baccalaureate science teaching programme', *Journal of Research in Science Teaching* 34(6): 595–615.

Peacock, A. (ed.) (1991) *Science in Primary Schools: The Multicultural Dimension*, Basingstoke: Macmillan Education.

Perkins, D.N. (1995) *Outsmarting IQ: the emerging science of learnable intelligence*, New York: Free Press.

Perrenoud, P. (1998) 'From formative evaluation to a controlled regulation of learning processes: towards a wider conceptual field', *Assessment in Education* 5(1): 85–102.

Perrin, M. (1991) 'Summative evaluation and pupil motivation', in Weston, P. (ed.), *Assessment of Pupil Achievement: Motivation and School Success*, Amsterdam: Swets and Zeitlinger.

Phenix, P.H. (1964) *Realms of Meaning*, London: McGraw-Hill.

Prestt, B. (1976a) 'Science education: a reappraisal part 1', *School Science Review* 57(201): 628–34.

—— (1976b) 'Science education: a reappraisal part 2', *School Science Review* 58(203): 203–9.

Primary Science Process and Concept Exploration (1990–) *Research Reports*, CRIPSAT (Centre for Research in Primary Science and Technology), Liverpool: Liverpool University Press.

Pumfrey, S. (1991) 'History of science in the National Science curriculum', *The British Journal for the History of Science* 24(1): 61–78.

QCA (1998a) *Standards at Key Stage 3 Science: Report on the 1997 National Curriculum Assessments for 14-year-olds*, London: DfEE.

—— (1998b) *Standards at Key Stage 2 English, Mathematics and Science. Report on the 1997 National Curriculum Assessments for 11-year-olds*, London: DfEE.

—— (1998c) *Standards at Key Stage 2 English, Mathematics and Science. Report on the 1998 National Curriculum Assessments for 11-year-olds*, London: DfEE.

—— (1998d) *Science: A Scheme of Work for Key Stages 1 and 2*, London: DfEE.

—— (1999a) *The Review of the National Curriculum in England: The Secretary of State's Proposals*, London: DfEE.

—— (1999b) *Assessment and Reporting Arrangements: 2000 Key Stage 1 Years 1 and 2 and Reception*, London: DfEE.

—— (1999c) *Assessment and Reporting Arrangements 2000 Key Stage 2 Years 3 to 6*, London: DfEE.

—— (1999d) *National curriculum Key Stage 1–4, 1999: The Revised National Curriculum for 2000. What Has Changed?*, London: QCA.

—— (1999e) *Education 3–16: A Framework for Personal, Social and Health Education (PSHE) and Citizenship at Key Stages 1 to 4*, London: HMSO.

Rafferty, F. (1997) 'Real maths wins praise', *Times Educational Supplement*, 12 December 1997.

Ramsden, J. (1998) 'Mission impossible? Can anything be done about attitudes to science?', *International Journal of Science Education* 20(2): 125–37.

Ratcliffe, M. (1998) 'Discussing socio-scientific issues in science lessons – pupils' actions and the teacher's role', *School Science Review* 79(288): 55–9.

Reid, M.I., Clunies-Ross, L.R., Goacher, B. and Vile, C. (1981) *Mixed Ability Teaching: Problems and Possibilities*, Windsor: NFER–Nelson.

Reiss, M.J. (1993) *Science Education for a Pluralist Society*, Buckingham: Open University Press.

—— (1996) 'Food, smoking and sex: values in health education', in Halstead, J.M. and Taylor, M.J. (eds), *Values in Education and Education in Values*, London: Falmer.

—— (1998) 'Science for all', in Sherrington, R. (ed.), *ASE Guide to Primary Science Education*, Cheltenham: Stanley Thornes, and Hatfield: Association for Science Education.

—— (ed.) (1999) *Teaching Secondary Biology*, London: John Murray for the Association for Science Education.

—— (2000) 'Science in society or society in science', in Warwick, P. and Sparks Linfield, R. (eds), *Science 3–13: The Past, the Present and Possible Futures*, London: RoutledgeFalmer: 118–29.

Reiss, M.J. and Dale-Tunnicliffe, S. (1999) 'Conceptual development', *Journal of Biological Education* 34(1): 13–16.

Resnick, L.B. and Resnick, D.P. (1992) 'Assessing the thinking curriculum: new tools for educational reform', in Gifford, B. and O'Connor, M. (eds), *Changing Assessments: Alternative Views of Aptitude, Achievement and Instruction*, London: Kluwer Academic Publishers.

Revell, M. (ed.) (1995) *The Differentiation Book*, Northampton: Northamptonshire Inspection and Advisory Service.

Richmond, P.E. (1974) 'Approaches to integrated science teaching', *School Science Review* 55(192): 591–5.

Rieser, R. (ed.) (1995) *Invisible Children*, London: Save the Children, The Integration Alliance.

Rieser, R. and Mason, M. (1992) *Disability Equality in the Classroom: A Human Rights Issue*, London: Disability Equality in Education.

Roafe, C. (1998) 'Interagency Work in the Management of Inclusive Education', in Clough, P. (ed.), *Managing Inclusive Education: From Policy to Practice*, London: Paul Chapman Publishing.

Roberts, R. and Gott, R. (1999) 'Procedural understanding: its place in the biology curriculum', *School Science Review* 81(294): 19–25.

Robinson, P. and White, P. (1997) *Participation in Post-Compulsory Education*, Twickenham: Centre for Education and Employment Research, School of Education, Brunell University.

Roden, J. (1999) 'Young children are natural scientists', in David, T. (ed.), *Young Children Learning*, London: Paul Chapman Publishing Ltd.

Rodriguez, A.J. (1998) 'What is (should be) the researcher's role in terms of agency? A question for the 21st century', *Journal of Research in Science Teaching* 35: 963–5.

Rogoff, B. (1990) *Apprenticeship in Thinking: Cognitive Development in a Social Context*, New York: Oxford University Press.

—— (1999) 'Cognitive development through social interaction', in Murphy, P. (ed.), *Learners, Learning and Assessment*, London: Paul Chapman Publishing.

Rose, C. and Goll, L. (1992) *Accelerate Your Learning Action Handbook*, London: Accelerated Learning Systems.

Rosenthal, R. and Jacobson, L. (1968) *Pygmalion in the Classroom*, New York: Holt, Rinehart and Winston.

Roth, W.-M. (1995) *Authentic School Science: Knowledge and Learning in Open-Inquiry Science Laboratories*, Dordrecht: Kluwer.

Roth, W.-M. and Alexander, T. (1997) 'The interaction of students' scientific and religious discourses: two case studies', *International Journal of Science Education* 19: 125–46.

Royal Society (1999a) *Science and the Revision of the National Curriculum*, Statement, January.

—— (1999b) *New Frontiers in Science Exhibition*, London: The Royal Society (the Annual Royal Society Summer Science Exhibition, 16–17 June).

RSC (1996) *Career Choices in Chemistry at 11, 13, 15 and 17: Education Issues No. 17*, London: Royal Society of Chemistry.

Ruddock, J., Chaplain, R. and Wallace, G. (1996) *School Improvement. What Can Pupils Tell Us?*, London: David Fulton.

Ruiz-Primo, M.A. and Shavelson, R. (1995) 'Rhetoric and Reality in Science Performance Assessment: an Update', paper presented at American Educational Research Association, San Francisco.

Sandford Smith, D. (1999) 'ASE and Special Needs', *Education in Science* 183: 14–15.

SCAA (1994) *Evaluation of the Implementation of the National Curriculum for Science Key Stages 1, 2 and 3*, London: HMSO.

—— (1996) *Promoting Continuity Between Key Stage 2 and Key Stage 3*, London: SCAA.

Scaife, J. and Wellington, J. (1993) *Information in Science and Technology Education*, Milton Keynes: Open University Press.

Schagen, S. and Kerr, D (1999) *Bridging the Gap? The National Curriculum and Progression from Primary to Secondary School*, Slough: NFER.

Schools Council (1972) *With Objectives in Mind*, London: Macdonald.

SCI Centre (1998) *Citizenship and Science*, Leicester: Centre for Citizenship Studies in Education, University of Leicester.

Scottish Education Department (1987) *Curriculum and Assessment in Scotland: a Policy for the 1990s*, Edinburgh: SED.

Sears, J. (1993) 'GCSE balanced science: A-level uptake and student attitudes', *Physics Education* 28(6): 366–70.

—— (1994) *Research into A-level Science Uptake*, Hatfield: ASE.

—— (1995) 'The introduction of balanced science and pupil attitudes', *British Journal of. Curriculum and Assessment* 5(2): 26–9.

—— (ed.) (2000 in press) *Non-judgmental Differentiation: Video Training Pack*, Hatfield: ASE.

Shayer, M. and Adey, P. (1981) *Towards a Science of Science Teaching*, London: Heinemann Educational.

Shortland, M. and Warwick, A. (eds.) (1989) *Teaching the History of Science*, Oxford: Blackwell.

Shrigley, R.L. (1990) 'Attitude and behaviour are correlates', *Journal of Research in Science Teaching* 27(2): 97–113.

Shulman, L.S. (1986) 'Those who understand: knowledge growth in teaching', *Educational Researcher* 15: 4–14.

Simpson, M. (1993) 'Diagnostic assessment and its contribution to pupils' learning' in Edwards, D., Scanlon, E. and West, D. (eds) *Teaching, Learning and Assessment in Science Education*, London: OUP/Paul Chapman Publishing.

Sjøberg, S. (1999) *The SAS Study: Science and Scientists Cross-cultural Evidence and Perspectives on Pupil's Interests, Experiences and Perceptions*, Oslo: Science Education, ILS, University of Oslo.

Slavin, R.E. (1987) 'Ability grouping and achievement in elementary schools: a best evidence synthesis', *Review of Educational Research* 57(3): 293–336.

—— (1990) 'Achievement effects of ability grouping in secondary schools: a best evidence synthesis', *Review of Educational Research* 60(3): 471–99.

Slavin, R.E. and Karweit, N.L. (1985) 'Effects of whole class, ability grouped, and individualized instruction on mathematics achievement', *American Educational Research Journal* 22(3): 351–67.

Smith, A. (1998) *Accelerated Learning in Practice*, London: Network Educational Press Ltd.

Smith, R. (1991) 'The poverty of medical evidence', *British Medical Journal* 303: 798–9.

Smithers, A. (1997) 'Students' science choices, beyond 2000: science education for the future', paper presented at the Nuffield Seminar, January.

Smithers, A. and Robinson, P. (1991) *Beyond Compulsory Schooling: A Numerical Picture*, London: The Council for Industry and Higher Education.

Solomon, J. (1991) *Exploring the Nature of Science*, Glasgow: Blackie and Sons.

—— (1992) *Getting to Know about Energy – in School and Society*, London: Falmer Press.

Song, J. and Black, P.J. (1991) 'The effects of task contexts on pupils' performance in science process skills', *International Journal of Science Education* 13(1): 49–58.

—— (1992) 'The effects of concept requirements of task contexts pupils' performance in control of variables', *International Journal of Science Education* 14(1): 83–93.

Sorsby, B.D. (1999a) 'The child's world and the scientist's world; can argumentation bridge the culture gap?', *Proceedings of the Fifth International History, Philosophy and Science Teaching Conference*, University of Pavia (http://opus.cilea.it/cgi-bin/fisicasite/webdriver?MIval=qp_paviam&pg=PV).

—— (1999b) 'Primary children arguing in science', *Proceedings of the Fourth Summer Conference for Teacher Education in Primary Science*, University of Durham.

—— (1999c) 'The nature of science in pupils' education and teacher training curricula', *Proceedings of the Fifth International History, Philosophy and Science Teaching Conference*, University of Pavia (http://opus.cilea.it/cgi-bin/fisicasite/webdriver?MIval=qp_paviam&pg=PV).

Spours, K. (1995) *Learning for the Future: The Strengths and Weaknesses of GNVQs: Principles of design Working Paper 3*, London: Institute of Education, and Warwick: Centre for Education and Industry.

SSCR (1987) *Better Science*, London: Heinemann/ASE.

Stevenson, D. (1998) *Information and Communications Technology in UK Schools: An Independent Inquiry*, London: The Independent ICT in School Commission 1996/7.

Stillman, A. and Maychell, K. (1984) *School to School. LEA and Teacher Involvement in Educational Continuity*, Windsor: NFER–Nelson.

Stobart, G. and Gipps, C. (1997) *Assessment: A Teacher's Guide to the Issues*, London: Hodder and Stoughton.

Stobart, G., White, J., Elwood, J., Hayden, M. and Mason, K. (1992) *Differential Performance at 16+: English and Mathematics*, London: Schools Examination and Assessment Council.

Stout, J. and Tymms, P. (1999) *Science and the Literacy Hour*, Hatfied: ASE.

Strand, S. (1999) 'Ethnic group, sex and economic disadvantage: associations with pupils' educational progress from Baseline to the end of Key Stage 1', *British Educational Research Journal* 25: 179–202.

Strang, J. (1989) *Measurement in School Science. Assessment Matters No. 2*, Edinburgh: (EMU) SEAC.

Sukhnandan, L. and Lee, B. (1998) *Streaming, Setting and Grouping by Ability: A Review of Research*, Slough: NFER.

Sutherland, A., Johnston, L. and Gardner, J. (1996) *The Transition Between Key Stages 2 and Key Stage 3. A Report for the Northern Ireland Council for Curriculum, Examinations and Assessment*, Belfast: NICCEA.

Sutton, C. (1992) *Words, Science and Learning*, Buckingham: Open University.

Swain, J. (1991a) *Consortium for Assessment and Testing in Schools (CATS) Science KS3 Pilot 1991: Report and Appendices*, London: CATS, King's College.

—— (1991b) 'The nature and assessment of scientific explorations in the classroom', *School Science Review* 72(260): 65–77.

Taylor Fitz-Gibbon, C. (1996) *Monitoring Education: Indicators, Quality and Effectiveness*, London: Cassell.

Taylor, R.M. (1990) 'The National Curriculum: A Study to Compare Levels of Attainment with Data from the APU Science Surveys', *School Science Review* 72(258): 31–7.

Taylor, R.M. and Swatton, P. (1989) *Graph Work in School Science. Assessment Matters No. 1*, Edinburgh: (EMU) SEAC.

The Children's Act (1989) London: HMSO.

The Institute of Biology (1998) 'Biologists look forward to a more scientifically literate world. National Curriculum Review', *School Science Review* 80(291): 25–8.

The Royal Society (1999) *Science and the Revision of the National Curriculum*, Statement, January.

Thomas, G. (1997) 'Inclusive schools for an inclusive society', *British Journal of Special Education* 24(3): 103–7.

Thomas, S. and Mortimore, P. (1994) *Report on Value Added Analysis of 1993 GCSE Examination Results in Lancashire*, Lancashire Quality Development Division.

Thompson, R.B. (1994) 'Gender differences in communicative style: possible consequences for their learning process', in Foot, H., Howe, C., Anderson, A., Tolmie, A. and Warden, A. (eds), *Group Tutoring*, Southampton: Computational Mechanics Publications.

Thomson, R. (1993) *Religion, Ethnicity and Sex Education: Exploring the Issues*, a resource for teachers and others working with young people produced on behalf of the Sex Education Forum, London: National Children's Bureau.

Thorpe, S. (1991) *Race, Equality and Science Teaching: An INSET manual for teachers and educators*, Hatfield: ASE.

Thorpe, S., Deshpande, P. and Edwards, C. (eds) (1994) *Race, Equality and Science Teaching*, Hatfield: ASE.

Tones, K. and Tilford, S. (1994) *Health Education: Effectiveness, Efficiency and Equity*, London: Chapman and Hall.

Tulving, E. (1972) 'Episodic and semantic memory', in Tulving, E. and Donaldson, W. (eds), *Organisation and Memory*, New York: Academic Press.

—— (1983) *Elements of Episodic Memory*, Oxford: Clarendon Press.

Tunstall, P. and Gipps, C. (1996) 'Teacher feedback to young children in formative assessment: a typology', *British Educational Research Journal* 22(4): 389–404.

Turner, S.A. (1995) 'Teaching strategies in science: games and simulations' in J. Frost (ed.), *Teaching Science*, London: Woburn Press.

—— (1997) 'Children's understanding of food and health in primary classrooms', *International Journal of Science Education* 19(5): 491–508.

—— (1998) 'Cross-curricular issues and the science curriculum', in W. Di Marco and A.D. Turner (eds), *Learning to Teach in the Secondary School: A Companion to School Experience – Science*, London: Routledge.

Turner, S.A., Levinson, R., Desli, D., Douglas, A., Kirton, A. and Koulouris, P. (1999) *Teaching about Social and Ethical Issues related to Biomedical Research*, Interim Report prepared for The Wellcome Trust, November.

Turner, S.A., Öberg, K. and Unnerstad, G. (1999) 'Biology and health education', *European Journal of Teacher Education* 22(1): 89–100.

Turner, S.A., Zimvrakaki, H. and Athanasiou, K. (1997) 'Investigating children's ideas about fat consumption and health: a comparative study', *Health Education Journal* 56(4): 329–39.

Tytler, R. and Swatton, P. (1992) 'Critique of AT1 based on case studies of students' investigations', *School Science Review* 74(266): 21–35.

Tytler, R., Duggan, S. and Gott, R. (1999a) 'Dimensions of evidence, the public understanding of science and science education', submitted to *International Journal of Science Education*, October.

—— (1999b) 'Publics and sciences: understanding an environmental dispute', submitted to *Public Understanding of Science*, January 2000.

UNESCO (1994) *The Salamanca Statement and Framework for Action on Special Needs Education*, Paris: UNESCO.

United Nations (1989) *Convention on the Rights of the Child*, New York: United Nations.

Versey, J., Fairbrother, R., Parkin, T., Bourne, J., Dye, A. and Watkinson, A. (1993) *Managing Differentiated Learning and Assessment in the National Curriculum (Science)*, Hatfield: ASE.

Vygotsky, L. (1978) *Mind in Society: The Development of Higher Psychological Processes*, Cambridge, MA: Harvard University Press.

Wallace, F. (1994) *Balanced Science Survey*, Hatfield: ASE.

Waring, M. (1979) *Social Pressures and Curriculum Innovation: A Study of the Nuffield Foundation Science Teaching Project*, London: Methuen.

Watson, J.R. (1994) 'Students' engagement in practical problem-solving: a case-study', *International Journal of Science Education* 16(1): 27–43.

Watson, J.R., Black, P.J., Fairbrother, R.W., Jones, A. and Simon, S. (1990) *A Task Framework*, London: King's College London.

Watson, J.R., Swain, J.R.L. and McRobbie, C. (1999) 'The interaction between teaching styles and pupil autonomy in practical science investigations: a case-study', in Leach, J. and Paulsen, A. (eds), *Practical Work in Science Education: Recent Research Studies*, Roskilde: Roskilde University Press.

Watson, R., Goldsworthy, A. and Wood-Robinson, V. (1998) 'Getting AKSIS to Investigations', *Education in Science* 79(177): 20–1.

—— (1999a) *One Hundred and Twenty Hours of Practical Science Investigations: a Report of Teachers' Work with Pupils Aged 7 to 14*, Proceedings of May 1998 Conference: Practical Work in Copenhagen, Royal Danish School of Educational Studies.

—— (1999b) 'What is not fair with investigations', *School Science Review* 80(292): 101–6.

Watson, R., Wood-Robinson, V. and Goldsworthy, A. (in press) *Investigations: Targeted Learning – Using Classroom Assessment for Learning*. Hatfield: Association for Science Education.

Watson, R. (2000) 'The role of practical work', in Monk, M. and Osborne, J. (eds), *Good Practice in Science Teaching*, Buckingham: Open University Press.

Watson, R. and Wood-Robinson, V. (1998) 'Learning to Investigate', in Ratcliffe, M. (ed.), *The ASE Guide to Secondary Science Education*, Cheltenham: Stanley Thornes.

Watters, J. and Ginns, I. (1994) 'Self-efficacy and science anxiety among pre-service primary teachers: origins and remedies', *Research in Science Education* 24: 334–57.

Watts, M. and McGrath, C. (1998) 'SATISfactions: approaches to relevance in science education', *School Science Review* 79(288): 61–5.

Wedell, W. (1995) 'Making inclusive education ordinary', *British Journal of Special Education* 22(3): 100–04.

Wellcome Trust (1994) *HIV and AIDS – A Resource Pack for Use with 11 to 14 year olds*, London: The Wellcome Trust.

—— (1999) 'From genome to health', *Wellcome News* 20 (Q3).

West, R.A. (1981) 'A case against the core', *School Science Review* 63(222): 226–36.

Weston, P., Taylor, M., Lewis, G. and MacDonald, A. (1996) *Differentiation and Learning: Research Summary*, National Foundation for Educational Research, http://www.nfer.ac.uk/summary/diffsum.htm, 24 July.

White, J. (1969) 'The curriculum mongers: education in reverse', *New Society*, 6 March: 359–61.

White, R. and Gunstone, R. (1992) *Probing Understanding*, London: Falmer.

White, R.T. (1991) 'Episodes, and the purpose and conduct of practical work', in Woolnough, B. (ed.), *Practical Science*, Buckingham: Open University Press.

Whitelegg, E. and Parry, M. (1999) 'Real-life contexts for learning physics: meanings, issues and practice', *Physical Education* 34(2): 68–72.

Williams, T., Wetton, N. and Moon, A. (1989) *A Picture of Health*, London: Health Education Authority.

Williams, T., Roberts, J. and Hyde, J. (1990) *Exploring Health Education: Materials for Teacher Education*, London: Macmillan for HEA.

Willingham, W.W. and Cole, N.S. (1997) *Gender and Fair Assessment*, London: Lawrence Erlbaum Associates.

Wood-Robinson, V., Watson, J.R. and Goldsworthy, A. (1999) 'Practice and perceptions at Key Stage 2', in publication of 4th Durham Conference for Teaching in Primary Science, *The Challenge of Change*, Durham: University of Durham.

Woolgar, S. (1988) *Science: The Very Idea*, Chichester: Ellis Horwood.

Woolnough, B.E. (1991) *The Making of Engineers and Scientists*, Oxford: Oxford University Department of Education Studies.

—— (1994) *Effective Science Teaching*, Buckingham: Open University Press.

World Health Organisation (1993) *Health for All Targets: The Health Policy for Europe*, European Health for All Series, No.4, Geneva: WHO.

Wragg, E.C. (1992) 'Primary education', in Black, P. (ed.), *Education: Putting the Record Straight*, Stafford: Network Education Press.

Young, M. and Glanfield, A. (1998) 'Science in post-compulsory education: towards a framework for a curriculum of the future', *Studies in Science Education* 32: 1–20.

Index